Emotions in the Ottoman Empire

History of Emotions

Series Editor:

Peter N. Stearns, University Professor in the Department of History at George Mason University, USA and Susan J. Matt, Presidential Distinguished Professor of History at Weber State University, USA.

Editorial Board:
Rob Boddice, Senior Research Fellow, Academy of Finland Centre of Excellence in the History of Experiences, Tampere University, Finland
Charles Zika, University of Melbourne & Chief Investigator for the Australian Research Council's Centre for the History of Emotions, Australia
Pia Campeggiani, University of Bologna, Italy
Angelika Messner, Kiel University, Germany
Javier Moscoso, Centro de Ciencias Humanas y Sociales, Madrid, Spain

The History of Emotions offers a new and vital approach to the study of the past. The field is predicated on the idea that human feelings change over time and they are the product of culture as well as of biology. Bloomsbury's History of Emotions series seeks to publish state-of-the-art scholarship on the history of human feelings and emotional experience from antiquity to the present day, and across all seven continents. With a commitment to a greater thematic, geographical and chronological breadth, and a deep commitment to interdisciplinary approaches, it will offer new and innovative titles which convey the rich diversity of emotional cultures.

Published:
Fear in the German Speaking World, 1600–2000, edited by Thomas Kehoe and Michael Pickering
Feelings and Work in Modern History, edited by Agnes Arnold-Forster and Alison Moulds
Feeling Dis-Ease in Modern History, edited by Rob Boddice and Bettina Hitzer
Emotional Histories in the Fight to End Prostitution, by Michele Renee Greer
Emotions and Migration in Argentina at the Turn of the 20th Century, by María Bjerg

Forthcoming:
The Business of Emotion in Modern History, edited by Andrew Popp and Mandy Cooper
The Renaissance of Feeling, by Kirk Essary

Emotions in the Ottoman Empire

Politics, Society, and Family in the Early Modern Era

Nil Tekgül

BLOOMSBURY ACADEMIC
LONDON • NEW YORK • OXFORD • NEW DELHI • SYDNEY

BLOOMSBURY ACADEMIC
Bloomsbury Publishing Plc
50 Bedford Square, London, WC1B 3DP, UK
1385 Broadway, New York, NY 10018, USA
29 Earlsfort Terrace, Dublin 2, Ireland

BLOOMSBURY, BLOOMSBURY ACADEMIC and the Diana logo are
trademarks of Bloomsbury Publishing Plc

First published in Great Britain 2023
Paperback edition published 2024

Copyright © Nil Tekgül, 2023

Nil Tekgül has asserted her right under the Copyright,
Designs and Patents Act, 1988, to be identified as Author of this work.

For legal purposes the Acknowledgments on pp. viii–xi constitute an
extension of this copyright page.

Cover image © A nineteenth-century Turkish lady dressed in traditional clothing,
with her face veiled in a yashmak. Whitemay/Getty.

All rights reserved. No part of this publication may be reproduced or transmitted
in any form or by any means, electronic or mechanical, including photocopying,
recording, or any information storage or retrieval system, without prior
permission in writing from the publishers.

Bloomsbury Publishing Plc does not have any control over, or responsibility for,
any third-party websites referred to or in this book. All internet addresses given in this
book were correct at the time of going to press. The author and publisher regret any
inconvenience caused if addresses have changed or sites have ceased to exist,
but can accept no responsibility for any such changes.

A catalogue record for this book is available from the British Library.

A catalog record for this book is available from the Library of Congress.

ISBN: HB: 978-1-3501-8054-3
       PB: 978-1-3503-2391-9
       ePDF: 978-1-3501-8055-0
       eBook: 978-1-3501-8056-7

Series: History of Emotions

Typeset by Integra Software Services Pvt. Ltd.

To find out more about our authors and books visit www.bloomsbury.com
and sign up for our newsletters.

Contents

A Note on Transliteration and Translation   vii
Acknowledgments   viii

Introduction: Emotions and the Concept of Protection   1
   Ottoman Politics of Difference   3
   Emotions in Historical Studies   5
   Emotions in Ottoman Studies   11
   Methods and Sources   14

1   Emotion Knowledge   23
   Kınalızade's *Ahlak-ı Ala'i*   24
   Faculties of Vegetative, Animal, and Human Soul   27
   Emotions in *Ahlak-i Ala'i*   33
   Emotions and the Domain of Medical Knowledge   36
   Absence of Emotions in Ottoman Self-Narratives   38
   Concluding Remarks   41

2   Ottoman Politics of Emotion   43
   Protection with Compassion   46
   Uniting with the Hearts of the Subjects (*telif-i kulüb* and *istimalet*)   56
   The Path of Love (*mahabbet*)   63
   Concluding Remarks   67

3   Emotions in Intracommunal Relations: *Rıza* and *Şükran*   69
   Sub-communities in Ottoman Society   70
   Neighborhoods and Guilds as "Domains of Gratitude"   73
   Sensations and Drawing the Boundaries of Communities:
      Kendü halinde olmak   79
   Expulsions from Domains of Gratitude   83
   Emotions as Practices   87
   Concluding Remarks   92

4	Regulating Communities by an Emotion: Shame	95
	Shame in Different Cultures	97
	Shame in Ottoman Sources	100
	Gendered Emotion of Shame: *Ar*	104
	Shaming Others in Ottoman Society	106
	Concluding Remarks	109
5	Emotions in the Ottoman Family	111
	Emotionology of the Ottoman Family: House of Companionship and Love (*Hane-i Ülfet ve Mahabbet*)	112
	Expressions of Emotions in Engagement	119
	Expressions of Emotions in Divorce	124
	Concluding Remarks	129
6	Changing Meanings of Protection and Transformation of Emotions	131
	Modernization Efforts in the 19th Century	132
	From *Mahabbet* to Love of Fatherland	136
	Change in the Domain of Medical Knowledge	138
	Transformation of Emotions in Societal and Familial Relations	140
	Concluding Remarks	142
Conclusion		145
Bibliography		152
Index		163

A Note on Transliteration and Translation

For Ottoman Turkish words I have been guided by the *International Journal of Middle East Studies* (*IJMES*) transliteration system, and have used the Turkish alphabet and conventional modern Turkish orthography. The following characters are pronounced as indicated:

c = "j" as in joke
ç = "ch" as in children
ş = "sh" as in ship
ı = undotted "i," sounds like the "e" of women
ğ = soft g, lengthening the sound of the preceding vowel
ö = sounds like the "u" of fur
ü = like French u

Arabic and Turkish terms usually appear in the singular form and are italicized and explained on the first appearance. Whenever the plural form of such terms is required, a Romanized "s" is added to them.

All translations from Ottoman Turkish are the author's own, unless indicated otherwise.

Names of places commonly known to readers of English have been written in their usual forms.

Acknowledgments

This book is a revised and improved version of my PhD dissertation completed under the supervision of Prof. Özer Ergenç at İhsan Doğramacı Bilkent University in 2016. I owe thanks to Bilkent University for all the academic facilities that it provided, without which it would not have been possible to conduct and publish my research. I would like to express my sincere thanks to all those people who contributed and made this unforgettable experience of mine possible.

First and foremost, I would like to express my deepest gratitude (*şükran*) to my advisor Prof. Özer Ergenç for his continuous support and everlasting patience with my questions. His immense knowledge of Ottoman history and his guidance always enlightened my way throughout my time of research. It would have been impossible to study as elusive a concept as "emotions" without his continuous encouragement. Throughout the process he was not only my advisor but also my mentor, and I always considered myself lucky to feel his deep support. Thank you Hocam for making my journey not only fulfilling but also enjoyable. I am also proud to consider myself a part of an "academic lineage" starting from Mehmet Fuat Köprülü and continuing to Halil İnalcık and Özer Ergenç, who was the first doctorate student of Halil İnalcık. I am and will always be proud to be one of his students.

I would like to extend my deepest thanks to Peter Stearns and Susan Matt. My journey of writing a book started with their call, published on *H-Emotions*, for international treatments of the history of emotions. They are prominent historians in the field, and I learned a great deal from their valuable insights and comments on earlier drafts of the manuscript. This book would not have been possible without them. Thank you.

I also thank Margrit Pernau, a prominent historian in the field of "history of emotions," whom I met while I was at Harvard University. It was her work, in several publications, that enlightened my thinking on the emotions, and made it possible to improve my dissertation by moving from expressions to experience of emotions and senses. It was also she who made me realize the amazing legacy of Persian culture in Ottoman intellectual life.

I would also like to thank Cemal Kafadar, for not only kindly accepting to be on my dissertation committee but also for being my faculty sponsor while

I was at the Harvard University Center for Middle Eastern Studies (CMES) as a post-doctoral visiting scholar. I was lucky to attend the Ottoman history courses that he was offering. His theatrical style of teaching, his immense knowledge of history (always coupled with his modesty), and the wide range of topics and questions that he's interested in definitely shaped my understanding of history and my own style of teaching history. I do not know how he did it, but I always wanted to head for the library once his lecture was over and start a new research on the little wonders and marvels of the ordinary Ottoman people to better understand a complex phenomenon. Thank you.

My thanks and appreciation are also due to CMES for offering me an ideal environment where I had a chance to be a part of an intellectual community that wholeheartedly welcomes academics from all over the world having a passion for seeking knowledge. I have very fond memories of the year I spent at Harvard University. I am also thankful to my colleagues and friends Tarık Tansu Yiğit, Bedriye Poyraz, Neşe Gürallar, Belgin Turan Özkaya and Jun Akiba for sharing and encouraging my passion in emotions in history and their thoughtful comments on my lecture given at CMES. I miss many of our discussions, and our conversations in Tate Bakery and Shay's Pub, and thank them all for making my post-doctoral studies unforgettable.

I also owe thanks to Mehmet Kalpaklı, Ali Yaycıoğlu and Tülay Artan, who accepted to be a member of my dissertation committee and also for making thoughtful and valuable remarks to improve my understanding of emotions in history.

Many thanks are due to my colleague and friend Christiane Czygan, who has expertise in Ottoman poetry and the historical expressions of emotions in poems and personal letters, for reading earlier drafts of the manuscript and for her valuable comments.

There's also someone special whom I would like to thank who passed away long ago. My grandmother, Ferhunde Betin, born in 1907 in Van, a city in the eastern Anatolia, was a member of late Ottoman society in her childhood. She studied in an elementary school in Beyoğlu, İstanbul and shared her memories with me, including how she and her classmates used to shout "long live Sultan" while standing on the Ottoman sultan's way to the Friday prayer. With the promulgation of the Turkish Republic, however, she had always been a proud citizen of the Turkish Republic until she passed away in 1998. After graduating from Kandilli and Erenköy Kız Lisesi (a high school for girls) she worked as an elementary school teacher who taught in several cities, towns and villages in Çorum, İzmir and İstanbul. She always felt that she was serving her fatherland in the best possible way by teaching students who would design the future of the republic. I always loved to listen to her life story and felt as if I always accompanied her. Her stories, however, based on memories of a distant past, did not resemble the history courses that I had been taking in my high school, for which I did not have much interest. Sadly, I thought "history" was what we had been learning at high school. It was only in my graduate studies that I realized indeed that "history" was, or at least should be, what she used to narrate. I should admit that my passion for history owes a great deal to her. I hope she's in peace in heaven now. Thank you "Fırıldak"—that's what we used to call her. I believe her life, indeed like everyone else's, deserves to be written, which will hopefully constitute one of my future projects that I eagerly look forward to.

Words feel insufficient to express my deepest sense of gratitude towards my friends who are not historians but willingly and patiently read earlier drafts of this book and shared their valuable comments and suggestions. I would like to extend my huge and warm thanks to Birgül Ak, Lale Ak, Canan Alp, Sevgi Güvenç, Ayşe Özsoy Koru, Neslihan Özdemir and Lisa Haner Çelik. They were always there whenever I needed them, helping me to relieve my anxieties and making me laugh and think. Their interest in the subject and their thoughtful questions and comments regarding the continuities of our past in today's world contributed much to my understanding of emotions. I'm thankful for their sincere support. Life would be boring without them. My special thanks to Lale and Ayşe for sharing inspiring podcasts on psychology and philosophy at times when I felt desperate. Many thanks to my friend Erten Harwood, who kindly accepted to be my editorial assistant. I also thank Felicia, Rachel and Harte from Cambridge Editors for their support and sincere service.

I also owe special thanks to my dear brother Can Erkey, who has always been my hero and will definitely continue to be so in the future. He always encouraged me in my graduate studies, making me laugh even at times of my worst anxiety. Thank you.

I would like to thank Yusuf Oğuzoğlu, who was always kind enough to provide many of the archival material that I used in my research, and also for his several calls for academic conferences held in Bursa. His everlasting interest in organizing an academic event and sharing knowledge on Ottoman history for the good of public have always inspired me.

I would also like to thank Harvard University Widener Library, particularly Cheryl LaGuardia, the research librarian, who was always there when I needed help. Many thanks also to András Riedlmayer from Harvard University Fine Arts Library for his help and for kindly sharing a Bosnian manuscript on emotions with me. Thanks also to Harvard University CMES and Harvard University Middle East Beyond Borders (MEBB, an initiative of graduate students) for inviting me to give a lecture. The several comments and questions of the participants shaped the content of this book.

I am also grateful to Bloomsbury editors Maddie Holder and Megan Harris for their support and patience, and to anonymous reviewers for their valuable suggestions. Each one of their comments helped me to improve the manuscript.

Last but not least, I would like to thank my dear husband Serdar and my beloved son Hakan, who have always been supportive, thoughtful and appreciative in making my dream come true. There were times when I felt distressed, particularly during the early phases of the Covid-19 pandemic, which resembled a nightmare in all of our lives. But I was at the same time happy since we were all together once again, after five years of separation, and always felt thankful for being safe and healthy. I realized once more that we, as a family, together with our lovely golden retriever Bobo who joined our family during the pandemic, could face up the difficulties together. Thanks to Bobo, too, for being a good friend of mine. I cannot imagine a life without them, and it is exactly why I dedicate this book to them.

Introduction

Emotions and the Concept of Protection

In the mid-sixteenth century, the Ottoman Empire stretched from the Persian steppes to the Danube River basin, from the northern Black Sea to northern Africa, and was one of the empires that ruled the world. Indeed, it was not any different from other early modern empires: they were all expansionist; they all used intermediaries such as generals, governors, or tax collectors to take charge of territories they incorporated; and they were interested in more than just economic exploitation.[1] Empires differed, however, in their repertoires of power and how they employed the politics of difference. Jane Burbank and Frederick Cooper, in their book *Empires in World History*, focused on a set of empires as remarkably durable polities, and analyzed the different strategies empires chose as they incorporated diverse peoples into their polity. The Ottoman Empire appears at the center of their story, as an empire that managed to blend Turkic, Byzantine, Arab, Mongol, and Persian traditions into durable, flexible, and transformative power.[2] The longevity of the Ottoman Empire, which endured for over 600 years, has been investigated by several scholars, but the secret to its durability remains a puzzling question for historians.

Although it is not possible to fully capture the complexities of this distant past, I would like to start with an illustrative scene to answer this challenging and puzzling question. In this historical scene, the residents of a small town or city in Anatolia in the 1550s, an early part of the early modern era, learn that an imperial decree is to be read out loud in a few hours. We might notice that people are gathering slowly, either outside the house of the town's judge, used also as the judicial court, or perhaps in the courtyard of the town's mosque,

---

[1] Jane Burbank and Frederick Cooper, *Empires in World History: Power and the Politics of Difference* (Princeton: Princeton University Press, 2011), 6.
[2] Ibid., 18.

to listen. The imperial decree (*ferman*) will be read by Mustafa Çavuş, the sultan's *mübaşir* (agent), representing the sultan's executive power. We would see both Muslims and non-Muslims entering the courtyard, since a mosque, a place of worship for Muslims, was also a natural place for social gatherings for the residents. Here is a Jew, a tavern owner, shutting the door of his place of business hastily and hurrying down the road to hear the news from the Ottoman sultan. The senior master of the tailors' guild and one of the most respected members of the community, in his forties, is among the first to arrive to listen to Mustafa Çavuş. There's somebody from a nearby village, who happens to be in town to sell his produce, either agricultural or pastoral, and having heard that an imperial decree will be read, heads for the courtyard of the mosque. A couple of women join the crowd, having heard about the special event, but are careful to stay in the back of the crowd. Perhaps an old man would also be on the scene, not very wealthy (judging from his clothes), having just had wheat soup from a nearby public kitchen (*imaret*), maybe worrying whether the decree from the sultan will demand a new tax burden to finance a new war.

Mustafa Çavuş will soon dismount from his horse and look at the residents of the small town in his superior manner. He will extract the decree from the small bag attached to his midriff and start reading it aloud. It is still early evening, and there is a light, refreshing breeze over the mosque, adding a feeling of calm to the serenity that follows prayer. There might be a few literate men around, but most of the audience does not know how to read or write. Mustafa Çavuş will make sure to adopt a superior tone so that everyone will understand not only that he brings the words of the sultan's decree, but also the importance of his role as a mediator of the sultan's message. We may easily assume that none of the town residents have ever seen their sultan before. Furthermore, not all have the vocabulary to understand every word of the decree, which is full of embellishments and metaphorical expressions praising the sultan and the Sublime Porte.

We would hear the state agent's voice, sometimes strident and sometimes gentle, echoing off the walls of the mosque. All the subjects listen to him with the utmost attention, as he represents their protector's power, and will soon begin to pass on what they have understood to those who could not attend. In doing so, they will add their own interpretations and opinions that reflect their perceptions of the world, using concepts available in their own language.

The residents of this small town, as subjects of the empire, regardless of their faith, ethnicity, occupation, settlement practices, gender and wealth, were "protected" subjects of their sultan; hence, the Ottomans always referred to their lands as *memalik-i mahruse*, meaning "protected domains."³ Was it deference, respect, or admiration that the townspeople would feel towards their leader, the sultan, who is the shadow of God on earth and their "protector," while listening to Mustafa Çavuş? Would these feelings show on their faces? Was it love or gratitude that they felt for their protector, whom they had never met and were unlikely ever to meet? Was it the performance of the state agent himself that evoked such feelings through his chosen tone of voice? Was it in fact fear that they felt, but expressed instead as respect, or was it a combination of subtle emotions that they did not know how to describe, if ever asked? Would any other subject, listening to the same decree in the city of Sofia in the Balkans, let's say, or in Syria, feel the same love, respect, and gratitude? How would they express their emotions? Would they all be sincere in doing so? How did they conceptualize and theorize emotions in their philosophical framework? Were the emotions that they may have felt the same as what we would now label as respect, love, fear, or gratitude?

Exploring emotions of the early modern Ottoman society, without refuting the existing research on the social or political history of the empire, I propose, adds to our understanding of power relations, how hierarchies were structured, how communities themselves could bypass secondary identities, how and why little violence occurred, how legally or socially subordinate groups conceptualized their inferior status, how identities were formed, and how one defined oneself. This book attempts to answer the question what it *meant* and how it *felt* in the early modern era to protect (*siyanet, himayet, hiraset, muhafaza*) and be protected. I claim that emotions were the key to assigning meaning to the culturally specific and historically contingent concept of protection.

Ottoman Politics of Difference

What has most attracted historians' attention to the Ottoman Empire's politics of difference has been how the empire ruled non-Muslims and earned their loyalty until the nineteenth century, without any policy of persecution and little violence—a strategy that was key to its longevity. Non-Muslim subjects of the

---

[3] Although vague in its physical boundaries, the geographical region of Anatolia and Rumelia was called "the Lands of Rum" with changing cultural associations over time. For an excellent analysis of the changing political and cultural meanings of "the Lands of Rum" during the medieval, early modern, and modern periods, see Cemal Kafadar, "A Rome of One's Own: Reflections on Cultural Geography and Identity in the Lands of Rum," *Muqarnas* 24, no. 1 (2007): 7–25, https://doi.org/10.1163/22118993_02401003.

empire fell under the legal status of *zimmi*, pre-established under the framework of Islamic law, according to which they were to be protected, regardless of their inferior legal status. In her excellent analysis, Eleni Gara traces how historians, beginning from the 1930s until now, conceptualized interreligious relations.[4] Apparently, the complexity of the issue gave rise to diverse and conflicting interpretations. At the beginning of the twentieth century, nationalist historiographies of successor states of both Southeastern Europe and Arab countries conceptualized the Ottoman reign as a time of enslavement, oppression, and 600 years of mutual hostility under the "Turkish yoke" paradigm.[5] Others tried to explain the infrequency of violence as a top-down effect in which either Islam's characteristic tolerance, or the empire's successful implementation of the *millet* system, was the key to the peaceful co-existence of subjects of different faiths. Karen Barkey, for example, claimed in her book *Empire of Difference* that little intercommunal violence took place because "the state typically dispensed justice fairly, treating *zimmi* as separate, unequal, and protected."[6] However, people of different faiths did not, according to sources, live parallel, distinct, or separate lives. On the contrary, several empirical studies based on Ottoman judicial court records provided evidence for extensive interreligious interaction both at the individual and communal level. Starting in the 1980s, there was a shift in historians' approach, whereby scholars began to conceptualize these interreligious relations in terms of co-existence and tolerance, redefining them to fit their own conceptualization of Ottoman practices.[7]

Yet, how the empire ruled and configured Muslim and non-Muslim relations constitutes only a part of what we may refer to as "difference." It also corresponds to differences in settlement practices, traditions, occupations, language and dialect, status, wealth, and gender. Subjects' legal status was determined according to sharia by whether they were a Muslim or non-Muslim, a slave or a free person, or a man or a woman. These various categories were unequal in legal status. However, according to *kanun*, a different body of law based on the sultan's will but always expected to be in compliance with Islamic law, what mattered most was whether one was a tax-paying subject or a member of the military class, *askeri*, who were exempt from tax. Differences in legal and social

---

[4] Eleni Gara, "Conceptualizing Inter-religious Relations in the Ottoman Empire: The Early Modern Centuries," *Acta Poloniae Historica* 116 (2017): 57–93. http://dx.doi.org/10.12775/Aph.2017.116.03.
[5] Ibid., 61.
[6] Karen Barkey, *Empire of Difference: The Ottomans in Comparative Perspective* (Cambridge: Cambridge University Press, 2008), 120.
[7] Gara, "Conceptualizing Inter-religious Relations," 74–75.

status were a fact of life. How the Ottoman Empire incorporated diverse peoples into this polity, and more importantly, how society itself managed to govern intracommunal relations, still demands an answer.

Now, as Gara has rightly suggested, is the time to revisit these established paradigms and look for a new approach. I claim in this book that the contested concept of "protection," related to how and who to protect, was culturally specific and historically contingent, and stands at the center of all debates about how the Ottoman Empire and society itself employed the politics of difference. My central thesis is that it was emotions which provided the meaning of the concept of "protection."

Answering the question of what it *felt* like to be protected can explain how Ottoman subjects conceptualized the unequal power relations between the subjects and the sultan, between men and women, and how the communities conceptualized intracommunal relations in a world of given differences in social and legal status, wealth, faith, ethnicity, and settlement practices. Moreover, investigating how emotions functioned as the meaning-making mechanism of the concept of "protection" may also provide an answer to the puzzling question of the longevity and durability of the Ottoman Empire.

Emotions in Historical Studies

Historians have been under the influence of the "classical view" of emotions, also known as "universalist" or "presentist," for a long time, which brings forth the idea that they may not be historicized. According to this view, emotions are innate and universal, which means people of every age, culture, and part of the world experience emotions the same way we do. I believe one of the reasons why emotions have always been tangential to the historical enterprise is the bias in both academic and lay discussions that views emotions as irrational, unreasonable, subjective, uncontrollable, involuntary, wild, and primitive forces.[8] They are thought to be a brute reflex, at odds with rationality, which we should control with our rational minds.

---

[8] Catherine Lutz, "Emotion, Thought, and Estrangement: Emotion as a Cultural Category," *Cultural Anthropology* 1, no. 3 (1986): 287–309. Lutz explores the unspoken assumptions embedded in the concept of emotion and argues that emotion is either assumed to be opposed to the positively evaluated process of thought, or to a negatively evaluated estrangement from the world. In other words, when we label someone "unemotional," we either mean that they are calm, rational, and deliberate, or they are uninvolved and alienated. Emotion is either assumed to be opposed to the positively evaluated process of thought, or to a negatively evaluated estrangement from the world. This contrast of emotion to rationality and thought has been the dominant and common use of the concept.

However, there is abundant scientific evidence, offered by psychologist and neuroscientist Lisa Feldman Barrett together with many of her colleagues, that this view cannot possibly be true. In Barrett's theory of constructed emotions, which has contributed to our understanding of emotions with experiment-based research, emotions emerge as a "combination of the physical properties of your body, a flexible brain that wires itself to whatever environment it develops in, and your culture and upbringing, which provide that environment."[9] Barrett acknowledges not only the biological core systems in our brain and body, but also the importance of our culture and past experiences in the process of constructing emotions.[10] "We are indeed in the midst of a revolution in our understanding of emotion, the mind and the brain, or more specifically, what it means to be human," Barrett asserts.

Having read the lines above, you may rightly find the idea of turning to neuroscience problematic for historical analyses, since psychologists or neuroscientists, unlike historians, make universalizing claims, and their models or propositions change rather frequently. However, it is worthwhile to be aware of their insights and even the universal claims of how our brains, minds, and emotions work, since they contribute to our understanding of how people felt over the course of history.[11] Emotion is such an elusive concept that its analysis certainly demands a multidisciplinary approach. The findings of the life sciences and social sciences confirm and complement one another, even if their focus and methods are quite different.

---

[9] Lisa Feldman Barrett, *How Emotions Are Made: The Secret Life of the Brain* (New York: Houghton Mifflin Harcourt, 2017), xii.

[10] Ibid., 33. According to Barrett, our brains' core systems combine in various ways to construct our perceptions, memories, thoughts, feelings, and other mental states, and there is no difference in the processes that make our feelings and thoughts. Secondly (p. 27), our brains are fed outside information by our senses as they try to figure out how to best navigate chaos. We are continuously faced with ambiguity; noisy information from the eyes, ears, nose, and other sensory organs. Our brains use past experience to construct a hypothesis as a scientist does and continually make predictions, a process called simulation. Our brains then compare the simulation to what our senses perceive. Simulation lets our brains impose meaning, selecting what is relevant and ignoring the rest. Likewise, simulation is our brain's guess about what is happening in the world. Scientific evidence appears to show that what we see, hear, touch, taste, and smell are largely simulations of the world. In other words, our brains make meaning of sensations and prescribe action from sensory input and past experience. Thirdly (pp. 30–31), our brains use concepts to simulate the outside world and make physical sensations from the outside world meaningful. If we didn't have concepts that represent our past experiences, all our sensory inputs would just be noise. Indeed, what is universal for all humans is the ability to form concepts, and it is our culture that hands us a particular system of concepts, values, and practices. Just as we build concepts for objects, such as an apple, we also build concepts for a complex idea like impressionism. This is how we communicate with others.

[11] For historians' different opinions on neuroscientific aproaches and whether they can or should be utilized in historical analyses pls. See Nicole Eustace et al., "AHR Conversation: The Historical Study of Emotions," *American Historical Review* December 117, no. 5 (2012): 1487–531.

It was Peter Stearns and Carol Stearns who first published a groundbreaking article in 1985 that could be regarded as a manifesto for scholars of the history of emotions. In this article, they coin the term "emotionology," to which I will be referring in detail in the following chapters.[12] To explore the change of emotions over time, they attempt to find the "emotional standards" of societies by examining popular advice manuals, which offered evidence of changing emotional standards over time.

Barbara Rosenwein, on the other hand, coins the term "emotional communities."[13] She proposes that scholars should seek to "uncover systems of feeling that they value, and seek the evaluations that they make about others' emotions, the nature of the affective bonds between people that they recognize, and the modes of emotional expression that they expect, encourage, tolerate, and deplore."

In the early phases of scholarly research on the history of emotions, several scholars convincingly showed with empirical evidence that emotional norms, prescriptions, linguistic expressions, ways of conceptualizing emotions, and the meanings attributed to them changed across time and space. They did so, however, without much attention to the experience of emotions. William Reddy, an American historian and anthropologist, was one of the first historians to incorporate neuroscientific research into his methodology, and aimed to fill the

---

[12] Peter N. Stearns and Carol Z. Stearns, "Emotionology: Clarifying the History of Emotions and Emotional Standards," *American Historical Review* 90, no. 4 (1985): 813–36. Emotionology is defined as "the attitude or standards that a society, or a definable group within a society, maintains toward basic emotions and their appropriate expression and ways that institutions reflect and encourage these attitudes in human conduct."

[13] Barbara Rosenwein, "Worrying About Emotions in History," *American Historical Review* 107, no. 3 (2002): 842. She defines "emotional communities" as "social communities—families, neighborhoods, parliaments, guilds, monasteries, parish church membership—which define and assess the same feelings as valuable and harmful to them." Also see Eustace et al., "AHR Conversation," 1516, where she argues that "an emotional community is a group in which people have a common stake, interests, values, and goals which has particular shared emotional phrases and expressions." Regarding the change of emotional norms in time, she argues that in every period there is more than one emotional community, although the ones in power tend to monopolize the sources that historians see. In a talk given at TORCH (The Oxford Research Centre in the Humanities) on May 11, 2015, Rosenwein was asked by Ute Frevert whether emotions founded the emotional community, or instead came out of group processes that were defined otherwise, such as belonging to a certain religious or any other value system. In other words, Frevert asked if emotions had a foundational value or if they were a consequence of being in a community or group structure that then breeds certain emotions. Rosenwein indicated that she did not mean for an emotional community to be reified, she just suggested the concept as a heuristic device, as a tool for historians who want to be thinking of emotions, and at the same time are troubled by having to make sense of so many sources on emotions and emotion words. Whether they were communities founded because members valued the same emotions or emotions were a consequence of communities that are defined otherwise, she stated, her main concern was the relations established between community members.

gap between the expression and the experience of emotions, coining the term "emotive."[14] Additionally Reddy coins the terms "emotional regimes" to refer to the codes of expression and repression created and enforced by societies and governments; "emotional refuges" as those spaces—physical and social—that offer opportunities for emotional expressions not sanctioned by the dominant regime; and "emotional liberty" as the freedom to change goals in response to bewildering, ambivalent thought activations.[15] An emotional regime is the total of prescribed emotions with their related rituals and other symbolic practices. For example, swearing on the flag in the army would be considered an emotive of a modern national emotional regime.

It was Monique Scheer, a cultural anthropologist, who proposed conceptualizing emotions as practices emerging from bodily dispositions conditioned by culturally and historically specific social contexts. Her most important contribution to the field was her assertion that the body is not a static, timeless, and universal foundation that produces ahistorical emotional arousal, but is itself socially situated, adaptive, trained, plastic, and thus historical, reminiscent of the concept of "plasticity" in neuroscientific research.[16] Emotions, she argues, can be viewed as "acts executed by a mindful body, as cultural practices."[17] Thinking of emotions as a kind of practice, she argued, helps historians reconcile the dichotomy between the expression/expectation and experience of emotions, and the history of emotions is not only a history of changing emotional norms, but a change in feelings as well.[18] Scheer suggests that historians look into "doings and sayings" as a road to emotional practices. Research has focused on how the practices of courtship, for example, are embedded in cultural norms and economic interests. But, Scheer argues, they also serve to cultivate a certain kind of feeling between

---

[14] William Reddy, *The Navigation of Feeling: A Framework for the History of Emotions* (Cambridge: Cambridge University Press, 2001). Borrowing from John Austin's speech act theory (in which constatives are descriptive statements of the world, such as "this fir branch is green"; and performatives are descriptive statements that change a state in the world, such as "I hereby marry thee"), Reddy coins the term "emotive": For example, the sentence "I am happy" is an emotive, because it not only describes the condition of the world using emotion but also seeks to influence this condition. He points out that emotions are the most complicated zone of conflict and negotiation between individuals and society. Even though we cannot fully understand others' feelings, we are constantly trying to do so, and he coins the term "emotive" to describe the process by which emotions are managed and shaped, not only by society and its expectations, but also by individuals themselves as they seek to express how they feel. He emphasizes the performative power of emotions as "goal-relevant activations of thought material."

[15] Susan Matt, "Current Emotion Research in History: or, Doing History from the Inside Out," *Emotion Review* 3, no. 1 (2011): 117–24.

[16] Monique Scheer, "Are Emotions a Kind of Practice (and Is That What Makes Them Have a History)? A Bourdieuian Approach to Understanding Emotion," *History and Theory* 51, no. 2 (2012): 193.

[17] Ibid., 205.

[18] Ibid., 220.

potential marriage partners, which can range from dutiful obedience to honor, to passion, admiration, familiarity, or respect. Courtship, for Scheer, is thus not just a behavior but has performative effects on the constitution of feelings and the gendered self.[19]

Inspired by Scheer, Margrit Pernau and Imke Rajamani later offered a theoretical model to capture the experience of emotions.[20] Since conceptual history's exclusive focus on language fails to capture the meanings that can be derived from emotional expressions in other media such as painting, music, architecture, film, or even food, their theoretical model expands the conceptual history beyond language by exploring three processes that they call "emotional translations."[21] Moreover, the History of Concepts Group (HCG), which is incorporated as a non-profit entity in Finland, affiliated with the Center for Intellectual History at Helsinki University, aims to bring conceptual history and the history of emotions into a dialogue from which both will profit.

Spearheaded by historians such as Peter Stearns, Barbara Rosenwein, and William Reddy, and several others including Ute Frevert, Margrit Pernau, Jan Plamper, and Rob Boddice, just to cite a few, the field of the history of emotions has led to the development of new insights into human motivations and thus enriched our understanding of the past.[22] The field offers a new way to understand the past by exploring the effects and dimensions of emotions

---

[19] Ibid.

[20] Margrit Pernau and Imke Rajamani, "Emotional Translations: Conceptual History Beyond Language," *History and Theory* 55 (February 2016): 46–65. They argue that sensory experience itself is already socially framed and it is built on incorporated memories of previous experiences and their interpretations. Moreover, concepts cannot be reduced to written texts, as the meaning of concepts is also shaped by multimedia sources.

[21] Ibid. In their model, they introduce emotional translations at three points. For the first point, they argue that material reality can be linked to interpretation only through the intermediary of the body and the senses. Secondly, the interpretation does not proceed only through language-based concepts, but also through visual, auditory, tactile, and olfactory signs, which together form a multimedial semantic net. Thirdly, for interpretation to shape material reality through practices, the body has to be brought in again. They thus suggest that conceptual history needs to take into account the historically changing figurations of the body and the senses and the relations the actors establish between the senses, and that concepts can and need to be investigated through a multimedia semantic net.

[22] Although it is not possible to cite all the works, for some of the major studies that may serve as reference texts see Barbara Rosenwein and Riccardo Cristiani, *What Is the History of Emotions?* (Cambridge: Polity Press, 2018); Rob Boddice, *The History of Emotions* (Manchester: Manchester University Press, 2018); idem, *A History of Feelings* (London: Reaktion Books, 2019); Jan Plamper, *The History of Emotions: An Introduction* (Oxford: Oxford University Press, 2015); William Reddy, *The Navigation of Feeling: A Framework for the History of Emotions* (Cambridge: Cambridge University Press, 2001); idem, *The Making of Romantic Love: Longing and Sexuality in Europe, South Asia and Japan, 900–1200 CE* (Chicago: University of Chicago Press, 2012); Jonas Liliequist, ed., *A History of Emotions, 1200–1800* (London: Pickering & Chatto, 2012); Barbara Rosenwein, *Emotional Communities in the Early Middle Ages* (Ithaca: Cornell University Press, 2006); Stearns and Stearns, "Emotionology."

on behavior, culture, institutions, rituals, and others. It also demands a fresh look at our familiar sources, which begin to look quite different as we account for emotion.

Drawing on a wide range of sources from different genres, and utilizing the terms coined by the emotion historians mentioned above, historians started to ask new questions and provided empirical evidence to some of the puzzling questions in history. In the European context, for example, Katie Barclay explored *caritas* (a form of love) and posits it as an "emotional ethic" designed to provide a particular type of community relations in early modern Europe, to which I will be referring in detail in Chapter 3.[23] Her empirical findings also contribute to the debates on the rise of the individual in the eighteenth century.[24] Attending to emotions in history also provides insights into gender studies. For example, in *Authority, Gender, and Emotions in Late Medieval and Early Modern England*, edited by Susan Broomhall, authors explore how gender and emotions shaped the ways in which different individuals could assert or maintain authority, or indeed disrupt or provide alternatives to conventional practices of authority.[25] Today, the field has expanded so dramatically that some historians, such as Plamper, have even suggested that history has taken an "emotional turn."[26] Whether or not it's an "emotional turn," there's a growing interest in emotions not only among historians but also across the humanities and natural sciences.

There are, however, very few comparative studies in the field of the history of emotions. One of the few researches that takes a comparative approach is *The Making of Romantic Love*, by William Reddy. Reddy compares Western conception of romantic love with different practices of sexual partnerships in the regional kingdoms of Bengal and Orissa in South Asia from the ninth through twelfth centuries and Heian Japan in the tenth and eleventh centuries. He argues that the dichotomization of sexual desire and love is unique to Western societies, where it was socially constructed after the twelfth-century Gregorian reforms as a dissent from the sexual teachings of the Christian churches.[27] Another book,

---

[23] Katie Barclay, *Caritas: Neighbourly Love and the Early Modern Self* (Oxford: Oxford University Press, 2021).
[24] Ibid.
[25] Susan Broomhall, ed., *Authority, Gender, and Emotions in Late Medieval and Early Modern England* (Hampshire: Palgrave Macmillan, 2015).
[26] Jan Plamper, "The History of Emotions: An Interview with William Reddy, Barbara Rosenwein, and Peter Stearns," *History and Theory* 49, no. 2 (2010): 237–65.
[27] Reddy, *The Making of Romantic Love*.

Civilizing Emotions: Concepts in Nineteenth-Century Asia and Europe, edited by Margrit Pernau, Helge Jordheim et al., explores the interface between emotions and civilization, understood as "the process through which civility is brought forth, from a historical and global perspective," with a focus on the period 1870 to 1920.[28] The authors investigate the concept of civility and its semantic networks and how emotions relate to changing and contested concepts of civility. They explore four regions and thirteen languages; starting with Europe, moving eastwards to the Middle East, then to India and finally East Asia. Several authors argue that, in the period under consideration, emotions lay at the core of the concept of civilization, with the expectation that emotions needed to be carefully civilized through education.[29]

Yet what is evident about the scholarship produced so far is that it is overwhelmingly European.[30] Although new historical research is now available on the emotions of various societies around the world, including research on Mexico, China, Russia, and Indo-Muslim societies, the relative scarcity of non-European research makes comparisons across societies difficult. One of the goals of this book is to, however partially, fill this geographical gap. It is also my goal to engage in dialogue with emotion studies worldwide by showing how the theoretical and methodological approaches offered so far can be utilized (or not) given the constraints imposed by Ottoman primary sources.

Emotions in Ottoman Studies

Emotions have not been an especially prominent subject of study for historians of the Ottoman Empire. Barbara Rosenwein's view on the relations of the discipline of history to the emotions is borne out forcefully in Ottoman history studies.

> *Although history began as the servant of political developments, and despite a generation's work of social and cultural history, the discipline has never quite lost its attraction to hard, rational things, and emotions have seemed tangential (if not fundamentally opposed) to the historical enterprise.*[31]

---

[28] Margrit Pernau et al., *Civilizing Emotions: Concepts in Nineteenth-Century Asia and Europe* (Oxford: Oxford University Press, 2015).

[29] Ibid., 3.

[30] For a comprehensive review of recent studies on the field, see Merry Wiesner-Hanks, "Overlaps and Intersections in New Scholarship on Empires, Beliefs, and Emotions," *Cromohs (Cyber Review of Modern Historiography)* 20 (2015–16): 1–24.

[31] Rosenwein, "Worrying About Emotions," 821.

The field has only recently attracted the attention of scholars of Ottoman history.[32] It was Walter Andrews and Mehmet Kalpaklı who, in their pathbreaking study published in 2005, first analyzed the emotion of "love" using literary sources to better understand relations in Ottoman society.[33] The authors attempted to depict "love" not as an object of the private sphere, but as a part of a cultural script, claiming that "it's in language that we learn how and whom to love, what is normal and what is deviant, what the words and actions of love are," emphasizing the socially constructed feature of emotions.[34] Zeynep Yelçe, for example, has explored the norms of anger in pre-modern Ottoman courtly culture, particularly who gets to experience and display anger and when, why, toward whom, how, and to what extent, by using Ottoman sources.[35] She argues that royal wrath was a tool of intimidation reinforcing the authority of the sultan, and its expression served as a warning and threat against possible opposition. Görkem Özizmirli[36] and Robert Dankoff,[37] on the other hand, explore the narratives of fear and shame, respectively, in the travelogue of the

---

[32] Walter G. Andrews and Mehmet Kalpaklı, *The Age of Beloveds: Love and the Beloved in Early-Modern Ottoman and European Culture and Society* (Durham: Duke University Press, 2005); Walter Andrews and Ayşe Dalyan, "Poetry, Culture, Neuroscience, Emotions and the Case of Bonding, Separation, and Separation Anxiety in Sixteenth Century Ottoman Culture: A Theoretical Preface," *JOTSA* 7, no. 2 (2020): 147–74, https://doi.org/10.2979/jottturstuass.7.2.10; Fabian Steininger, "Morality, Emotions, and Political Community in the Late Ottoman Empire (1878–1908)" (unpublished PhD diss., Freien Universitat Berlin, Berlin, 2017); Hakan T. Karateke, H. Erdem Çıpa and Helga Anetshofer, eds, *Disliking Others: Loathing, Hostility, and Distrust in Premodern Ottoman Lands* (Boston: Academic Studies Press, 2018); Şeyma Afacan, "Of the Soul and Emotions: Conceptualizing 'the Ottoman Individual' Through Psychology" (unpublished PhD diss., University of Oxford, 2016); Ido Ben-Ami, "Wonder in Early Modern Ottoman Society: A Case Study in the History of Emotions," *History Compass* no. 17 (2019): 1–12, http://doi.org.10.1111/hic3.12578; Mirco Sardelic, "John of Plano Carpini vs Simon of Saint-Quentin: 13th Century Emotions in the Eurosian Steppe," *Golden Horde Review* 5, no. 3 (2017): 494–508; Pınar Şenışık, "Politics of Emotions in the Late Ottoman Empire: Our Beloved Crete," *Journal of Balkan and Near Eastern Studies* (2021): 1–22, http://doi.org.10.10 80/19448953.2021.2006003; Zeynep N. Yelçe, "Royal Wrath: Curbing the Anger of the Sultan," in *Discourses of Anger in the Early Modern Period*, ed. Karl Enenkel and Anita Traninger (Leiden: Brill, 2015): 439–57; Walter Andrews, "Ottoman Love: Preface to a Theory of Emotional Ecology," in *A History of Emotions, 1200–1800*, ed. Jonas Liliequist (London: Pickering & Chatto, 2012), 21–48; Robert Dankoff, "Ayıp Değil! (No Disgrace!)," *Journal of Turkish Literature* 5 (2008): 77–90; Görkem Özizmirli, "Fear in Evliya Çelebi's Seyahatname: Politics and Historiography in a Seventeenth Century Ottoman Travelogue" (MA diss., Koç University, 2014); Christiane Czygan, "Power and Poetry: Kanuni Sultan Suleyman's Third Divan," in *Contemporary Turkey at a Glance II: Turkey Transformed? Power, History, Culture*, ed. Meltem Ersoy and Esra Ozyurek (Weisbaden: Springer VS, 2017), 101–13; Christiane Czygan, "Depicting Imperial Love: Songs and Letters Between Sultan Süleyman (Muhibbi) and Hürrem," in *Kanûnî Sultan Süleyman ve Dönemi. Yeni Kaynaklar, Yeni Yaklaşımlar*, ed. Muhammed Fatih Çalışır, Suraiya Roschan Faroqhi and Mehmet Şakir Yılmaz (İstanbul: İbn Haldun Yayınları, 2020), 247–65.

[33] Andrews and Kalpaklı, *The Age of Beloveds*.
[34] Ibid., 38.
[35] Yelçe, "Royal Wrath," 442.
[36] Özizmirli, "Fear in Evliya Çelebi's Seyahatname."
[37] Dankoff, "Ayıp Değil!"

seventeenth-century Ottoman traveler Evliya Çelebi. Ido Ben-Ami regards the early modern Ottoman elite society of Istanbul as an emotional community and demonstrates how powerful individuals of this social group relied on a medieval Islamic theory about cosmographic "wonder" and encouraged its members to embrace it. Andrews demonstrates "how the idea of love can be used to describe one possibly central feature of an Ottoman emotional ecology."[38] Examining literary genres such as poetry and exploring the cultural symbols inherent to them, he claimed that "a particular notion of love was indeed central to the ways in which Ottoman society understood and scripted the emotional content of a broad range of primary relations: for example, parent–child, lover–beloved, friend–friend, patron–client, student–teacher, employer–employee, master–servant, spiritual adept–disciple, courtier–ruler, believer–God, etc."[39] Likewise, Christiane Cyzgan analyzes the emotion of love in both the collection of poems known as *Third Divan* written by Sultan Süleyman the Lawgiver (r. 1520–66) as well as letters written to him by his wife Hürrem/Roxelana.[40] All of these works date from the early modern period, and what is common in them is that they all used narrative sources such as chronicles, travelogues, and poetry, and analyzed specific emotions such as fear, love, anger, and shame.

For the modern period, Şeyma Afacan focuses in her PhD dissertation on the psychological writings of four Ottoman intellectuals to examine the transformations of key psychological concepts—such as the soul, will, and emotions—in the late nineteenth century, with respect to the gradual dominance of scientific thinking and Ottoman modernization. Afacan argues that the psychological literature on the soul and emotions testifies to acute concern about how to integrate individuals into the progressive discourses of the late Ottoman Empire.[41] Fabian Steininger, in his PhD thesis, analyzes the link between morality, emotions and political communities in the Hamidian era of the late Ottoman Empire (1878–1908) and focuses geographically on İstanbul and the imperial center. Analyzing three interrelated debates on manners, the economy and the city space, he argues that during the Hamidian era, morality was a crucial factor informing a limited, strongly hierarchical and stratified political community. Emotions in the debates figured either as motivational forces or rewards for

---

[38] Andrews, "Ottoman Love."
[39] Ibid., 21.
[40] Czygan, "Depicting Imperial Love."
[41] Afacan, "Of the Soul and Emotions." I am thankful to her for sharing her unpublished dissertation with me.

acting out desired behavior.⁴² Pınar Şenışık, on the other hand, analyzes the narratives of Muslims from Crete to the various provinces of the Ottoman Empire in the late nineteenth and early twentieth centuries. She investigates the place of the politics of emotions in public demonstrations and deals with the question of how emotion shaped public opinion and helped to construct patriotic ideals as well as contributing to the formation of a national future.⁴³

While all of these studies are valuable contributions to the field, there remains a consistent need for a more holistic approach that acknowledges emotions as a new perspective and lens through which to view Ottoman history while utilizing different genres such as chronicles, judicial court records, advice manuals and archival sources. Moreover, further research is needed to compare different periods of Ottoman history and thereby discern how Ottoman society's understanding of emotions and their influence on social, cultural, and political practices changed over time. This book, by focusing on the early modern period, also aims to serve as a reference for future studies on either the medieval or modern period of Ottoman history.

Methods and Sources

Seeking to answer the question of what it *meant* and how it *felt* to be protected in the early modern period implicitly assumes that what they may have felt is not what we may now feel, and that emotions are subject to change or transformation, or sometimes are even lost over time. This constitutes the premise of this book.⁴⁴ In other words, drawing on the assumption that emotions change across space and time, consistent with recent findings by not only cultural psychologists and neuroscientists, but also historians, I argue that historicizing emotions can shed light on long-contested historical questions in Ottoman history, one of which is how the Ottoman rulership incorporated diverse peoples into their polity and their communities. How did the state conceptualize its responsibilities as a protector of its subjects, and how did the subjects conceptualize their rights

---

[42] Steininger, "Morality, Emotions, and Political Community."
[43] Şenışık, "Politics of Emotions in the Late Ottoman Empire."
[44] Ute Frevert, *Emotions in History: Lost and Found* (Budapest: Central European University Press, 2011). Frevert for example argues that honor represents a lost emotion or a disposition whose emotional power has more or less vanished, and that emotions do change over time, with some disappearing and others changing in context, and the process of change is dynamic in the sense that the experience of emotions, too, continuously enacts and reacts to cultural, social, economic, and political challenges.

to protection in a world of unequal power relations? Similarly, what role did emotional knowledge and emotional norms play in providing meaning to the concept of protection in political, social, and familial relations? How did the communities themselves relate emotions to the concepts of protection, co-existence, and solidarity? How did emotions relate to morality?

Borrowing from anthropology, I will utilize the long-known and debated approaches known as emic and etic, which are two distinct, but I believe, complementary perspectives.[45] On the one hand, by taking an emic approach, which usually is called an "inside perspective" and used to describe a particular culture on its own terms, I will explore what the early modern Ottomans thought of emotions, how they theorized them, the meanings that they ascribed to these emotions, how they expressed their emotions, and how emotions functioned in political, social, and familial interactions in relation to concepts of protection. On the other hand, I will also take the etic approach, known as the "outside perspective," which in anthropological studies usually links cultural practices to external factors such as economic or ecological conditions that may not be salient to cultural insiders. In my research, these external factors would include our current knowledge on how our brains, minds, and bodies work, in other words, what we now know of emotions based on bodies of scientific research, including psychological, neuroscientific, and historical studies.

I examine this question from the perspective of three domains: the political, as subjects of the Ottoman Empire; the social, as members of spatial or occupational sub-communities; and finally, the familial, as husbands and wives in a world that assumed unequal status.

Although I use a wide range of sources, including imperial decrees, chronicles, petitions, travelogues, self-narratives and *fetva* collections, my main sources consist of two different genres. One of them is *The Book of Ethics* (*Ahlak-i Ala'i*), written by a sixteenth-century Ottoman intellectual Kınalızade (1510–1572). Ethics books provide ample information regarding the idealized form of relations expected between both the state and its subjects and husbands and wives. They are also a part of Islamic advice literature (*siyasetname-nasihatname*), which is similar to the genre of "mirror for princes" in the Western tradition. *Ahlak-i Ala'i* was one of the "bestsellers" of the Ottoman book market from the sixteenth to the eighteenth

---

[45] I am grateful to Cemal Kafadar for his valuable comments and letting me know of these two approaches. For understanding the etic and the emic approaches, I referred to Michael W. Morris, Kwok Leung, Daniel Ames and Brian Lickel, "Views from Inside and Outside: Integrating Emic and Etic Insights About Culture and Justice Judgment," *Academy of Management Review* 24, no. 4 (1999): 781–96.

centuries, according to Ottoman historian Baki Tezcan. The Süleymaniye Library in Istanbul has twenty-two manuscript copies of this book; a single scribe, Derviş Mehmet Ahlaki, is known to have copied it forty times in the late sixteenth century.[46] The popularity of *Ahlak-i Ala'i* is evident, and it thus seems to be a good representative of the philosophical knowledge until the nineteenth century.

The second genre is Ottoman judicial court case records. The earliest of these records date back to the fifteenth century for the Anatolian towns of Bursa and Kayseri and continued to be recorded across the Ottoman dominium until the fall of the empire. These case records in registers have been especially valuable resources for social historians of the Ottoman Empire, mainly because everyone—men, women, slaves, Muslims, non-Muslims, notables, and commoners—had the right to appeal to judicial courts. Thus, all have left their marks in history for us to examine. These court records contain accounts of a variety of activities that took place across the empire, from the capital city to districts and villages in remote places of the empire. Moreover, they provide ample evidence about subjects' daily lives and communal relations. The seventeenth- and eighteenth-century judicial case records from the Anatolia region that I utilized are not unique in any sense, but rather represent fairly typical examples of the records that Ottoman judges meticulously recorded in their registers. However, once we acknowledge that emotions change across time and space, and thus should be historicized, these documents offer a new way to understand the past by exploring the effect and dimensions of emotions on behavior, culture, institutions, rituals, and other factors, representing a fresh look at familiar sources of Ottoman history.

There have been methodological debates regarding judicial court records' limitations/potentials. In this regard, the article by Agmon and Shahar remains the most comprehensive study on the recent methodology of *sicil* (court case records) studies.[47] According to them, in the mid-1990s a methodological discontent emerged on *sicil* studies.[48] Then Dror Ze'evi published an influential

---

[46] Baki Tezcan, "Ethics as a Domain to Discuss the Political: Kınalızâde Ali Efendi's Ahlâk-ı Alâî," in *Ircica International Congress on Learning and Education in the Ottoman World (Istanbul, 12–15 April 1999)*, ed. Ali Çaksu (Istanbul: Ircica, 2001), 110. For Tezcan, the popularity of *Ahlak-i Ala'i* is because it laid down the theoretical foundations for the compartmentalization of social order used by the succeeding Ottoman writers of advice literature. It could also have been popular because it provided a more holistic view of politics, starting from the ethics of an individual, followed by and intertwined with the governance of a household and the governance of a city, state, or a realm as a form of political organization.

[47] Iris Agmon and Ido Shahar, "Theme Issue: Shifting Perspectives in the Study of Sharia Courts: Methodologies and Paradigms," *Islamic Law and Society* 15 (2008): 1–19.

[48] Ibid., 12.

article in which he discussed and criticized the use of *sicil*s.⁴⁹ Ze'evi observed that in many *sicil*-based social histories, *shari'a* court records are treated as a transparent record of reality, "a source that reflects society and culture as through a simple looking glass or a mirror," which he argues is a fallacy, since "no source may be regarded as a mirror."⁵⁰ Another part of the debate regarding *sicil* studies is about the uttered words and their inscription. Ze'evi also doubts "the extent to which the inscribed record reflects its purported creators—the people present in the court—said, even when they seem to have been quoted directly." He argues that there are many "barriers to the floating free-spoken words" from the time they were uttered till the time they were recorded. For example, "most court cases in Arab lands were mediated by interpreters who translated the claims and counter claims into Turkish." Or sometimes the words uttered in colloquial language were translated into a more literary register or into court jargon, all of which Ze'evi considers to represent barriers.⁵¹ Ze'evi is right, court records have several barriers. Yet, this is inevitable for all historical sources; none of them provide unmediated access to the worlds of historical actors. It is not even unique for Islamic judicial court records. For example, Barclay explores the concept of *caritas* in the early modern Scottish setting and utilized eighteenth-century Scottish legal sources, and while they may be different in style and function from Islamic court records, they too were traditionally thought to stand in the way of authentic voice or experience, a barrier to subjectivity.⁵² Moreover, motivations were lacking in Scottish legal sources, in the same way as they are in Islamic judicial records. The legal function of legal sources is essential for their interpretation, Barclay argues, but adds that "law is not separate from the society and culture in which it operates, and law is designed to produce a particular form of society, to promote certain types of community relations and discourage others."⁵³ Ze'evi proposed that the first concern of historians should be the *sicil* as a text, looking into the linguistic and literary aspects of the source. In other words, historians should "take *sicil* as a cultural product and therefore an end in itself," and I will be following his suggestion.

The court records have a unique form and structure, and words spoken in the court had to be transformed in such a way as to fit into the template of that

---

[49] Dror Ze'evi, "The Use of Court Records as a Source of Middle Eastern Social History: A Reappraisal," *Islamic Law and Society* 5 (1998): 35–56.
[50] Ibid., 40.
[51] Ibid., 50.
[52] Barclay, *Caritas*, 22.
[53] Ibid., 23.

structure. The most important part of the cases for this study are the claim of the plaintiff where the words of the plaintiff are quoted, describing what happened and why he is appealing to court, and the reply of the defendant. Regarding each court record as a template filled out either by the judge himself or the scribe, I argue that although the uttered words are transformed into either literary or court jargon, the essence of the above parts of the template was neither lost nor distorted. Indeed, for some cases it seems quite probable that the judge or the *katip* (scribe) recorded the utterance of the legal actors without any editorialization; particularly those involving the expression of emotions, and such cases have been priceless for my research.[54] I therefore propose that frequently used, seemingly formulaic terms and concepts in *sicils* should be further investigated by taking lexicological, cultural, legal, and contextual approaches, since they provide ample evidence on several historical questions, and particularly on how emotions interfere with their political and social relations.

It is apparent that there is no "one" way of studying emotions in history, and not all the approaches always agree with one another. Moreover, not all of them are suitable as tools for Ottoman history, given the constraints of Ottoman sources. Yet, from the literature produced so far, only some of which is referenced above, some of the terms coined by prominent historians of the field provide excellent tools for historians exploring emotions and how they relate to our historical questions. Rosenwein, for example, suggested that historians use her conceptual coinage of "emotional communities" as a heuristic device, as a tool for historians who want to be thinking of emotions, and at the same time are troubled having to make sense of so many sources on emotions and emotion words. Following Rosenwein in this regard, this book builds on some of the concepts coined by emotion theorists, discussing their connection to Ottoman sources in the following chapters and developing them further within the context of Ottoman early modern society.

Since how one feels depends on emotion knowledge and emotion norms, in my attempt to understand what it *meant* and how it *felt* to protect and be protected in the early modern Ottoman society, I explore in the first chapter the emotion knowledge of the Ottoman society. I define "emotion knowledge" as the

---

[54] Judith Tucker, *In the House of Law: Gender and Islamic Law in Ottoman Syria and Palestine* (Berkeley: University of California Press, 2000). Tucker explores women's roles in seventeenth- and eighteenth-century Syria and Palestine using the court records of the Islamic courts of Damascus, Nablus, and Jerusalem, and focuses on cases regarding family law. She also finds that cases involving familial relations were much more contentious in tone than those involving business and property exchange.

ways in which the Ottomans theorized and conceptualized emotions. It is one of the important determinants of what people felt. In other words, how one feels depends on whether one perceives emotions as obstacles to rational thinking, or closely connected to morality, or as instinctual and inborn brute reflexes, or that there is no difference between feeling, thinking and remembering, which are all processed in the same way in our brains, representing efforts of our brains to predict the outside world. For this purpose, by taking an emic approach, I utilized a sixteenth-century book of ethics, *Ahlak-i Ala'i*, written by sixteenth-century Ottoman scholar Kınalızade Ali Çelebi (d. 1571), giving special attention to the first volume, entitled "The Science of Ethics." Exploring how the Ottomans theorize emotions provides valuable insights for historians, particularly in finding new ways to search for emotions in historical texts. I claim in this chapter that emotions should be sought not only in linguistic expressions of historical actors in the texts, but even more so in their relations, actions, and practices, and I recurrently refer to emotion knowledge of Ottoman society in the following chapters to evidence my claims. In the second part of this chapter, I suggest that exploring the emotion knowledge of Ottoman society also offers a plausible answer to the still puzzling question of why very few self-narratives from the early modern Ottoman era have been discovered and why expressions of emotions in the ones that have survived are almost non-existent.

What people felt was also determined and constrained by emotional norms. Thus, the next four chapters first trace the emotional norms in the political language of the state, then in intracommunal relations, and finally in familial ties, which relate to their understanding of the concept of protection. Apart from tracing the prescriptions and the descriptions of emotions in the political, social, and familial levels, I also traced emotions as practices, which was also compatible with the early modern Ottoman philosophical framework of emotions that I explore in the first chapter.

The second chapter delves into the political sphere and scrutinizes the power relations between the sultan and his subjects. I analyze the relations between the state and its subjects and look for terms, concepts, and metaphors for emotions in the textual sources. Sources reveal that the concept of protection played a significant role in determining the political ideology of the state. Tracing and contextualizing the emotional concepts of compassion (*merhamet*) and love (*mahabbet*), I argue in this chapter that protection as a concept was realized through these two emotion terms, which stand as political emotions. They were not only expressions in the political rhetoric, but duly practiced as well and significant for identifying hierarchical political relations. Moreover, the relationship between the sultan and his subjects, wherein the sultan protected with compassion, is further conceptualized in Ottoman documents by the metaphoric expression "winning the hearts of the subjects," literally expressed as "uniting with the hearts" (*te'lif-i kulûb*) of the subjects. Metaphors bring language and imagery together and may be integrated into historical semantics. Verbal images and the figurative language of winning the hearts of the subjects in the metaphoric expression provides a visual medium and complements it, making the concept of protection plausible.

The third chapter questions how communities themselves conceptualized protection in intracommunal relationships, with a specific focus on neighborhoods as spatial sub-communities and guilds as occupational sub-communities. Again, their understanding of protection was a key factor in drawing the borders of their communities. It was the emotions of *rıza* and *şükran* (roughly, being pleased and feeling grateful) that characterized the communal concept of protection that made co-existence possible. I coin the term "domains of gratitude" for neighborhood and guild communities, mirroring Rosenwein's "emotional communities." I also focus on emotions of gratitude as a medium of communication. Moreover, I claim that sources reveal not only expressions of emotions. Once we see emotions as bodily practices, as acts executed by a mindful body, emotions can be traced as practices that serve to cultivate feelings of solidarity. It was emotions again that made concepts such as co-existence and identity plausible and transformed them into actions and behaviors.

The fourth chapter scrutinizes the emotion of shame. At least twelve different words were used to express the emotion of shame, each differing in intensity or meaning. While the simultaneous use of Arabic, Persian, and Turkish emotion words may be regarded as the source of this rich vocabulary, it also demonstrates the diversity of the experience of shame in Ottoman society. Based on my linguistic and contextual analysis of shame-words, I argue that the cultivation of shame functioned as a tool to motivate obedience to social and emotional norms regulating social ties and helped sustain communities themselves. The state in the early modern period did not yet have either the intention or the capacity to control social and emotional norms, and shame functioned as a fundamental factor in the sustainability of the intracommunal relations.

The fifth chapter explores the power balance in familial relations, which was asymmetric: the husband was the head of the family, all-powerful and legally and socially superior. The wife, on the other hand, was legally subordinate and inferior and was to be protected by either her husband or a male relative. However, scrutinizing what it felt like to be protected as a wife shows a different picture of how wives interiorized and could transcend this unequal relationship. I analyzed the emotionology of families from *Ahlak-i Ala'i* and judicial court records related to engagement and divorce cases to find descriptions of emotions related to the concept of protection. I argue that the emotions of *mahabbet, rıza,* and *musafat*, which characterize the specific meaning of protection in familial contexts, also serve as evidence for affective ties in familial relations.

The sixth chapter scrutinizes change and discusses how the modernization efforts of the nineteenth century impacted the Ottoman understanding of protection and how it also led to a change in the emotions of *merhamet, mahabbet, rıza ve şükran,* and *musafat*, albeit gradually. While some of the emotions were transformed, others disappeared. Equally important was the change in medical knowledge. With the advent of psychology as a modern field of science, emotions were no longer conceived as either virtues or vices characterizing relationships. Rather, emotions were positioned as internal processes waiting to be revealed by self-reflection. Then is also when emotions started to be viewed in opposition to rationality. In this chapter, I show how the meaning of protection, and thus the feelings associated with it, either changed, were lost, or were transformed in all three domains. While this process was gradual, the emerging understanding of emotions as irrational led to the steady enactment of laws and regulations that were believed to be devoid of emotions, and thus expected to protect the subjects of the empire from any arbitrary use of power.

Now let's return to the illustrative scene of a diverse crowd of subjects listening to the words of their protector. In the following chapters, I will illuminate how emotions provided the meaning of the contested and changing concept of protection for those living in this small town in Anatolia for the members of spatial communities of neighborhoods and occupational communities of guilds, and for husbands and wives with my final remarks on how the change in the meaning of protection in time transformed their feelings associated with it.

1

Emotion Knowledge

How one feels depends on emotion knowledge and emotion norms. I define emotion knowledge as how one theorizes and conceptualizes emotions. It is apparent that throughout history, philosophers, intellectuals, religious authorities, then scientists have always been attentive to emotions, and developed different theories explaining how to situate emotions, and how to conceptualize them. For example, a group of scholars investigated emotional knowledge of societies within the European context, for the period between 1700–2000 and showed how people's understanding of emotions and their use of vocabulary regarding emotions changed through time.[1] As Angelika Messner rightly suggests, emotional knowledge demands to be viewed as "being situated in contexts of different knowledge domains such as aesthetic knowledge, philosophical knowledge, and medical knowledge."[2] To investigate emotion knowledge of early modern society, I will focus in this chapter on a book of ethics, *Ahlak-i Ala'i*, written by the famous sixteenth-century Ottoman scholar Kınalızade Ali Çelebi (d. 1571),[3] which has often been utilized by Ottoman historians as a means of understanding the economic and political mindset of sixteenth-century Ottoman society.[4]

---

[1] Ute Frevert et al., eds, *Emotional Lexicons: Continuity and Change in the Vocabulary of Feeling 1700–2000* (Oxford: Oxford University Press, 2014).

[2] Angelika C. Messner, "Aspects of Emotion in Late Imperial China: Editor's Introduction to the Thematic Section," *Asiatische Studien Études Asiatiques* 66, no. 4 (2012): 897.

[3] For works on *Ahlak-i Ala'i*, see Baki Tezcan, "The Definition of Sultanic Legitimacy in the Sixteenth Century Ottoman Empire: The *Ahlâk-ı Alâ'î* of Kınalızâde Alî Çelebi (1510–1572)" (unpublished MA diss., Princeton University, 1996); Ayşe Sıdıka Okyay, "Kınalızade Ali Efendi ve Ahlak-i Ala'i" (unpublished PhD diss., Marmara University, 1998); Fahri Unan, *İdeal Cemiyet İdeal Devlet İdeal Hükümdar* (Ankara: Lotus, 2004); Mustafa Koç, ed., *Ahlak-i Ala'i* (Istanbul: Klasik, 2007); Hüseyin Öztürk, *Kınalızde Ali Çelebi'de Aile Ahlakı* (Ankara: Aile Araştırma Kurumu Başkanlığı, 1991). I am thankful to Baki Tezcan for sharing his unpublished thesis with me.

[4] See for example Fatih Ermiş, *A History of Ottoman Economic Thought Developments Before the Nineteenth Century* (New York: Routledge, 2014). Ermiş utilizes *Ahlak-i Ala'i* to depict the main parameters of Ottoman economic thinking before the modernization of the empire. Tezcan's thesis on "the definition of sultanic legitimacy," on the other hand, aims to understand the dynamics of mid-sixteenth-century Ottoman politics through his analysis of *Ahlak-i Ala'i*. Since Kınalızade incorporated the Irano-Islamic concept of rulership into the context of Ottoman politics, he rightly suggests situating Kınalızade's work within the larger framework of Islamic history.

Exploring emotion knowledge of a society provides insightful remarks for historians, particularly for those tracing emotions in historical texts. After a brief introduction of *Ahlak-i Ala'i* as a genre of advice manual, I utilize its first volume, titled "The Science of Ethics," to explore where Kınalızade situates emotions, in order to understand how early modern Ottomans perceived emotions. He makes several categorizations regarding faculties of the animal and human soul, as we will see below and finally situates them in morality, as emotion-vices or emotion-virtues. Drawing on evidence from *Ahlak-i Ala'i*'s first volume, I suggest, when tracing emotions, that linguistic representations of emotions should not be the only indicators of emotion. Whether we label them as emotions, emotion concepts, or emotion-virtues and emotion-vices, in this philosophical framework emotions were conceptualized as inseparable from both morality and its practices.

Then I explore the medical knowledge of Ottoman society based on Galenic humoral theory and show how it was compatible with their philosophical knowledge, both built on the idea of "moderation" (*adl*). These two well-matched frameworks partly explain the continuity of emotion knowledge for such a long time, until the nineteenth century. As we will see below, emotions were perceived either as emotion-virtues or -vices, and more importantly, realized through actions, practices and in their relations starting from the familial, to the societal and finally to the political sphere. Thus, feeling, knowing, or discriminating between good and evil were only realized if acted upon. Such an understanding of emotions also allows one to trace emotions as social practices, and I will thus frequently be referring to this concept in the following chapters as much as my sources allow. Emotions were not understood as belonging to the inner space of humans and requiring self-reflection to be expressed, but rather as something always expressed through their relationships and practices. Basing my claims on the Ottoman emotion knowledge, in the last section of this chapter, I suggest a plausible answer to one of the still puzzling questions in Ottoman history, which is the relative absence of emotional expressions in Ottoman self-narratives.

Kınalızade's *Ahlak-i Ala'i*

Shahab Ahmed argues that Muslims historically tended to discuss political theory, the subject of how Muslims should govern their collective affairs in a polity, mostly under the conceptual umbrella of *ahlak*, which is the plural of *hulk* (disposition), a term also used for morals.[5] Thus, as a work situated in the genre of *ahlak* literature, Kınalızade's work was mainly concerned with the achievement and sustainability of political order in what he calls a virtuous city. The seminal work in this genre was the book of Nasreddin Tusi (1201–74), the *Ahlak-i Nasıri*, which served as a model for all subsequent *ahlak* texts.[6] Tusi was commissioned to translate Ibn Miskawayh's (ca. 932–1030) *Tezhibü'l Ahlak* (Refinement of ethics) from Arabic; but his work eventually turned into much more than a translation.[7] The first part of *Ahlak-i Nasıri* was a summary organized differently from that of Miskawayh's *Tezhib*, to which Tusi added two new parts; one on the household and family management, and another on politics.[8] One of the most important influences on *ahlak* texts was Aristotle's *Nicomachean Ethics*, which was known to the Muslim world through translations and adaptations since the tenth century, starting with the first adaptation by Ibn Miskawayh's *Tezhibü'l Ahlak*.[9] Over the course of the half millennium following Tusi's death, his work was routinely paraphrased and elaborated upon in discussions of rulers' relations to law-making.[10] After Tusi, the tradition continued with Celaleddin Devvani's (1422–1506) *Ahlak-i Celali* and later with Kınalızade's *Ahlak-i Ala'i*.[11]

Like his predecessors, Kınalızade was influenced by philosophers such as Aristotle, Plato, and Galenus, and extensively referred to Farabi and the Sufi philosopher Al-Ghazali (d. 1111), making use of several literary sources, such as the famous Persian poet Sadi's *Gülistan and Bustan* and the poems of Rumi and Hafız. He also frequently used verses from the Quran in justifying his arguments. His philosophical knowledge was also closely intertwined with his

---

[5] Shahab Ahmed, *What Is Islam? The Importance of Being Islamic* (Princeton: Princeton University Press, 2015), 462. For *ahlak* texts, also see Muzaffar Alam, *The Languages of Political Islam: India, 1200–1800* (Chicago: University of Chicago Press, 2004). Alam argues (p. 11) that *ahlak* texts represent the best example of the appropriation into the medieval Muslim intellectual world of non-Islamic ideas and they provide a philosophical, non-sectarian, and humane solution to emergent problems. However, *ahlak* texts were one trend among many others in Islamicate political thought, and thus other sources, including moral treatises, historiographical works, copybooks of protocol and official correspondence, administration manuals, literary works, treatises on theology and kalam, collections of legal opinions (*fetva*) and encyclopedic works also discuss political theories; Marinos Sariyannis, ed., *Ottoman Political Thought up to the Tanzimat: A Concise History* (Rethymno, Crete: Institute for Mediterranean Studies, 2015), 12.

[6] *The Nasirean Ethics by Nasir ad-Din Tusi*, trans. G. M. Wickens (London: George Allen & Unwin, 1964).

[7] Alam, *The Languages of Political Islam*, 47.

[8] Ibid.

[9] Margrit Pernau, "Male Anger and Female Malice: Emotions in Indo-Muslim Advice Literature," *History Compass* 10, no. 2 (2012): 121.

[10] Ahmed, *What Is Islam?*, 462.

[11] For a detailed analysis of Miskawayh, Tusi, Devvani, and Aristotle's influence on Kınalızade's *Ahlak-i Ala'i*, see Tezcan, "The Definition of Sultanic Legitimacy."

religious knowledge. It is also apparent that he synthesized the ancient traditions and works of his predecessors in his own understanding of man and society. However, my aim is not to compare Kınalızade to his predecessors, whose legacy is apparent. Instead, I will analyze his conceptualization of emotions and the complexity of human behavior. Since there is still no direct English translation of *Ahlak-i Ala'i*, I frequently make use of *The Nasirean Ethics by Nasir ad-Din Tusi*, translated from the Persian by G. M. Wickens, in cases when Kınalizade cites Tusi's work verbatim. When I prefer a different translation of a concept, I give Wickens' translation in a footnote.

In the introduction to his book, Kınalızade first defines wisdom (*hikmet*),[12] which may as well be translated as philosophy, as "knowing the external existents in whatever condition they are within the capacity of the humanity and human ability."[13] He then adds, however, that this definition is incomplete and does not include practice. Referring to Tusi, he gives a more refined definition of wisdom, and indeed specifies it as "absolute wisdom": "knowing things as they are and fulfilling functions as one should."[14] His definition of absolute wisdom, we may infer, encompasses *both* knowing *and* doing.

He then categorizes absolute wisdom in terms of the existents that it examines.

"Since the external existents fall into two categories—those in whose existence human will does not have any role, and those in whose existence human will has a role, theoretical wisdom (*hikmet-i nazariye*)[15] deals with the first group of existents, which is further divided into three: the science of divinity (*ilm-i ilahi*), the science of mathematics (*ilm-i riyazi*), and the natural sciences (*ilm-i tabi'*)."[16]

"Practical wisdom (*hikmet-i ameliye*)[17] on the other hand, examines the second group of existents."[18] Practical wisdom, Kınalızade claims, should not be considered a body of knowledge per se, since it involves refinement of behavior and perfection of practices, just as the tree of knowledge should not be separated from the fruits of practice.[19]

---

[12] The word *hikmet* can be translated as "philosophy," "knowledge," or "wisdom." Wickens, in translating the work of Tusi and Tezcan in his translation and interpretation of *Ahlak-i Ala'i*, translated the word *hikmet* as "philosophy," but I prefer to use "wisdom" instead.

[13] "Hikmet mevcudat-i hariciyye nefü'l emrde ne hâlde ise ol hâl üzerine bilmektir, velâkin tâkat-ı beşeriyye vefâ ettikçe, ve kudret-i insânîde mümkin olduğu mikdâr." Koç, ed., *Ahlak-i Ala'i*, 41.

[14] "Hikmet eşyayı layık ne ise eyle bilmek ve ef'ali layık nice ise eyle kılmaktır." Koç, ed., *Ahlak-i Ala'i*, 42; Tezcan, "The Definition of Sultanic Legitimacy," 66.

[15] Wickens' translation is "speculative philosophy."

[16] Tezcan, "The Definition of Sultanic Legitimacy," 66.

[17] Wickens' translation is "practical philosophy."

[18] Tezcan, "The Definition of Sultanic Legitimacy," 66.

[19] "hikmet-i ameliyye fâyide-i müterettibe ve gâyet-i müterakkıbesi mücerred ilm değil, belki tahsîn-i efâl ve tekmîl-i a'mâldir. şöyle ki şecere-i ilm semere-i amele makrûn olmaya …," Koç, ed., *Ahlak-i Ala'i*, 42.

The subject of his work is practical wisdom, and what we now would assess as emotions are situated in human behavior and practices. In this framework, practical wisdom, he indicates, is the science of human actions that aims to direct the human soul toward beneficial actions, which are the root of true happiness,[20] while avoiding harmful actions that lead to flawed behavior and evil.[21]

He divides practical philosophy into three parts, which he addresses in three volumes: the science of ethics (*ilm-i ahlak*), the science of household governance (*ilm-i tedbirü'l- menzil*), and the science of city governance (*ilm-i tedbirül'l-medine*).[22] While the second volume addresses relations among the household members and the third relations between the rulers and the ruled, the first volume focuses exclusively on the individual and one's own behavior rather than communal behavior.[23] Perfection and completion, for Kınalızade, required government of self, household relations, and political relations, which are viewed as intertwined and interdependent.[24] In this chapter, however, I will only focus on the first volume of his work, on the government of the self.

Faculties of Vegetative, Animal, and Human Soul

Kınalızade first categorizes three types of soul: the vegetative, the animal, and the human soul. All three souls have several faculties, which together constitute the source and the reason of several actions (*ef'al*).[25] He then describes the faculties (*kuvvet*) of each of the souls. *Kuvvet* has several meanings, one of which is "faculty." But it also has meanings including "sense," "power," and "ability related to being moved." *Kuvvet* (pl. *kuvva*) is usually translated as "faculty," and I follow that tradition.

The vegetative soul (*nefs-i nebati*) has four faculties: the nutritive faculty (*kuvvet-i gadiye*), augmentative faculty (*kuvvet-i namiye*), reproductive faculty

---

[20] "Nefs-i insaniyeye mûcib-i kemâl-i sa'âdet-i hakîkiyyedir," Koç, ed., *Ahlak-i Ala'i*, 42.
[21] "zât-ı âdemîye mûris-i noksân u şekâvet-i uhreviyyedir," Koç, ed., *Ahlak-i Ala'i*, 42.
[22] Tezcan translates *ilm-i tedbiri'l-menzil* as "the science of household management" and *ilm-i tedbiri'l-medine* as "the science of city management." Tezcan, "The Definition of Sultanic Legitimacy," 65.
[23] "Evvel kısm ol ef âl ü a'mâldir ki âdemîden şahs-ı vâhid olduğu cihet-ten sâdır olup gayr-ı şahs mülâhaza olunmadığı zâhir olur. Bu makûleden bahs eden hikmet-i ameliyyeye 'ilm-i ahlâk' derler... Meselâ âdemî hadd-i nefsinde ten-i tenhâ vü bî-mesken ü me'vâ dahi olsa halîm ve sehî ve afif olup gazûb ve bahîl ve hafif olmamak gerek, ilâ gayri zâlik," Koç, ed., *Ahlak-i Ala'i*, 44–45.
[24] For the interdependence of the personal, social, and political in *ahlak* texts, see Margrit Pernau, "Love and Compassion for the Community: Emotions and Practices among North Indian Muslims, c. 1870–1930," *The Indian Economic and Social History Review* 54, no. 1 (2017): 21–42; eadem, "From Morality to Psychology: Emotion Concepts in Urdu, 1870–1920," *Contributions to the History of Concepts* 11, no. 1 (2016): 38–57.
[25] Koç, ed., *Ahlak-i Ala'i*, 64.

(*kuvvet-i müvellide*), and faculty of generation of one's like in the species (*kuvvet-i musavvire*). While the reproductive faculty enables the production of a seed from some of its parts, the faculty of generation of one's like enables formation of a new plant from a seed planted in a proper or favorable land. The first two powers are necessary for individual survival, while the last two are required for the propagation of new life.[26]

The animal soul (*nefs-i hayvani*) has two basic faculties: the faculty of perception (*kuvvet-i müdrike*)[27] and the faculty of movement (*kuvvet-i muharrike*).[28]

The faculty of perception in turn encompasses two sets of capacities. The five external senses (*havass-ı zahire*) include touching (*kuvvet-i lamise*), smelling (*kuvvet-i şamme*), tasting (*kuvvet-i za'ika*), hearing (*kuvvet-i sami'a*), and seeing (*kuvvet-i basıra*). The five internal senses (*havass-ı batıne*) include common sense (*hiss-i müşterek*), the faculty of remembering (*hayal*), the faculty of speculation (*kuvvet-i vahime*), the faculty of recollection (*kuvvet-i hafıza*), and the faculty of imagination (*kuvvet-i mutasarrıfa*).[29]

Kınalızade further defines these internal senses as follows: Common sense is the soul's perception of the representations perceived by the external senses, which, following philosophical tradition, he likens to a pool into which the water of five rivers flows together.[30] The faculty of remembering is the guardian of common sense, since it preserves the representations perceived by the external senses if they dissolve or disappear.[31] The faculty of speculation is the power to perceive concepts such as friendship or hostility, which are not themselves senses but originate from sensations triggered by friends or foes. Without this, a sheep would not be able to perceive the hostility of a wolf and flee, nor would it be able to feel affection towards a lamb and nurture it. The faculty of recollection is the power to remember and retain the concepts perceived by the speculative power.

---

[26] "Gadiye ile nâmiye, şahsın bekası için lâzımdır, zîrâ gâdiye ve nâmiye olmasa şahs bâkî olup kemâl-i matlûba erişmek mümkin olmaz. Ammâ müvellide ve musavvire bekâ-yı şahs için lâzım değil, bekâ-yı nev' için lâzımdır, zîrâ müvellide ve musavvire olmasa şahs fânî olmaz, lâkin şahsın halefi kalmaz, innîn olan âdemî gibi. Halef kalmamak inkırâz-ı nev'e mü'eddî olur." Koç *Ahlak-i Ala'i*, 64. In Tusi, the vegetative faculty has three divisions. Wickens, *The Nasirean Ethics*, 42.

[27] In Tusi it is called "*kuvvet-i idrak-i ali*," translated by Wickens as "faculty of organic perception." Koç, ed., *Ahlak-i Ala'i*, 66.

[28] In Tusi it is called "*kuvvet-i tahrik-i iradi*," translated by Wickens as "faculty of voluntary motion." Koç, ed., *Ahlak-i Ala'i*, 68.

[29] In Tusi, external senses are *hiss-i müşterek*, *hayal*, *fikr*, *vehm*, and *zikr*. Wickens translates these as common sense, fantasy, reflection, estimation and recollection, respectively.

[30] Koç, ed., *Ahlak-i Ala'i*, 64; Okyay, "Kınalızade Ali Efendi ve Ahlak-i Ala'i," 106.

[31] Wickens, *The Nasirean Ethics*, 42; Koç, ed., *Ahlak-i Ala'i*, 67; Okyay, "Kınalızade Ali Efendi ve Ahlak-i Ala'i," 107.

Finally, the faculty of imagination is the power that connects, associates, and differentiates representations of objects one perceives and related concepts. It is this power that enables one to imagine a mountain made of rubies, or a cypress tree from silver, he wrote.[32] In this model, the faculty of perception is common to both animals and humans, which include internal and external senses, and they both perceive the world through their senses.

The second faculty of the animal soul, the faculty of movement (*kuvvet-i muharrike*), is the power that moves the animal soul and can be broken into two types: the appetitive faculty (*kuvvet-i şeheviyye*),[33] which is the soul's power to attract things appropriate to it;[34] and the faculty of repulsion (*kuvvet-i gazabiyye*),[35] which enables it to avoid or distract itself from things that are abominable or inappropriate.[36]

Kınalızade adds that the appetitive and repulsive faculties are in need of the faculty of perception, and that there is a relationship between the two. The animal soul first perceives with its senses, which is the reason for willpower, and it is the willpower that induces the muscles and the nerves, making movement of the body possible.[37] The faculty of movement, too, is common both to animals and humans.

Kınalızade continuously emphasizes that the human soul itself encompasses both the vegetative and animal soul. For him, what differentiates humans from animals is rationality (*nefs-i natıka*), which is possessed by humans only, and it is this that makes the human soul the noblest among the three souls.

Since the subject of the science of ethics is the human soul, he presents the human soul as rational (*nefs-i natıka*) and discusses its properties as a means towards the perfection and completion of human behavior.[38] This soul is the

---

[32] Wickens, *The Nasirean Ethics*, 42; Koç, ed., *Ahlak-i Ala'i*, 67–68; Okyay, "Kınalızade Ali Efendi ve Ahlak-i Ala'i," 107.

[33] The same term is used in Tusi; and in Wickens, *The Nasirean Ethics*, it is translated as "concupiscible faculty," which corresponds to a sexual desire, but I prefer to use a more neutral term: "appetitive faculty."

[34] Koç, ed., *Ahlak-i Ala'i*, 68: "Ve ol bir kuvvettir ki bu kuvvet sebebi ile nefs kendiye matlûb u mülâyim olan nesneyi cezb ü tahsil eyler."

[35] The same term is used in Tusi; and in Wickens, *The Nasirean Ethics*, it is translated as "irascible faculty." I prefer to use "repulsive faculty" as a more neutral term instead.

[36] Koç, ed., *Ahlak-i Ala'i*, 68: "Ve ol bir kuvvettir ki bu kuvvet sebebi ile nefs kendiye menfur u nâ-mülâyim olan nesneyi def ü teb'îd eyler."

[37] Koç, ed., *Ahlak-i Ala'i*, 68: "Ve kuvvet-i muharrike elbette kuvvet-i müdrikeye muhtâcdır ve andan müstemiddir, zîrâ nefsin mülâyimin mülâyemetine şu'ûru ve idrâki olmak gerek ki anın cezb ü tahsiline meyi ü inbi'âsı olup ol meyi irâdete sebeb ola. İrâdet dahi tahrîk-i a'sâb u adalâta sebeb olup fi'l' vücûda gele."

[38] He also adds that the human soul in religious jargon is synonymous with spirit (*ruh*).

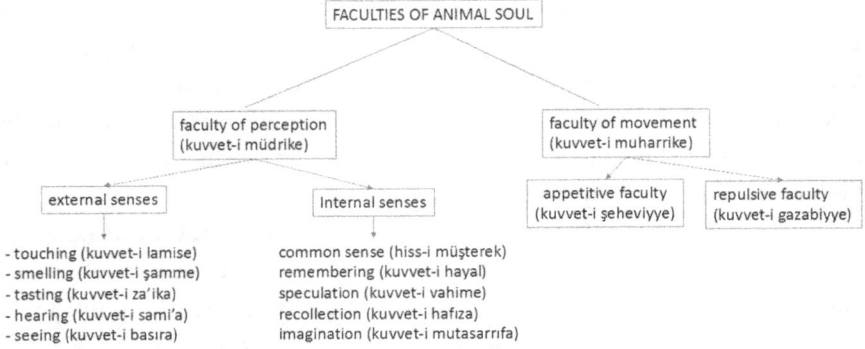

source and the cause of intellect (ta'akkul-i külliyat), reason (nutk), laughing (dıhk), and such.[39]

Kınalızade indicates that in his book, the subject of which is the practical faculty, he focuses only on the faculties of the human soul that emerge as a consequence of opinion (ihtiyâr), willpower (irâdet), thought (fikr), and reflection (reviyyet) and whose attainment, he argues, fosters perfection and happiness.[40]

His model of the human soul includes four faculties. Besides the two faculties shared by animals and humans, which are the faculty of perception (kuvvet-i müdrike) and faculty of movement (kuvvet-i muharrike),[41] he posits two distinctly human faculties, which are the faculty of rationality (kuvvet-i âlime), and the faculty of action (kuvvet-i âmile).

The faculty of rationality (kuvvet-i âlime) is also called nutk. Although nutk literally means "speech," Kınalızade understands nutk to involve both the faculty to perceive the intelligible, the capacity for thinking and reflection, and the

---

[39] Koç, ed., Ahlak-i Ala'i, 63: "nev'-i insâna mahsûs u mukârin ve nev'-i insân sâyir envâ'-ı hayvânâttan bu nefs ile mümtâz u mübâyindir. Ve insân havâssı ki gayr-i envâ-ı hayvânât ve ecnâs-ı nebâtatta yoktur, ta'akkul-i külliyyât ve nutk u dıhk gibi, cümlesinin mebde' ü illeti bu nefstir."

[40] Koç, ed., Ahlak-i Ala'i, 70. "ma'lûm olsun ki bu kuvâ-yı mezkûrenin içinden ba'zı vardır ki âsârı anlardan şu'ûr u reviyyet ve ihtiyârla ve irâdede sâdır olur. Ve insânın kemâl ü tekmili ve merâtib-i sa'âdâtı kesb ü tahsili bu makule kuvvetler ile olur ... pes bizim bu kitâbda -ki hikmet-i ameliyye için müellefttir- zîrâ murâdımız kesb-i kemâl ve neyl-I sa'âdât-ı hakikîye sebeb olan nesnelerden bahs etmektir."

[41] Koç, ed., Ahlak-i Ala'i, 70. "ol kuvvetler ki âsârı ihtiyâr u irâdet ve fikr ü reviyyet ile olur, dört kuvvettir. ikisi kuvvet-i hayvâniyyeden kuvvet-i müdrike ve kuvvet-i muharrike; ikisi kuvâ-yı insânîden kuvvet-i âlime ve kuvvet-i âmiledir." The root of the word 'âmil is 'amel, which means act, action, practice, performance, and 'âmil is the one who performs such acts.

ability to discriminate between good and evil behavior (*temyiz*).[42] Thus, the faculty of rationality is divided into two. The first part is the faculty to know through theoretical wisdom (a subcategory of absolute wisdom), which is thus called theoretical intelligence (*akl-ı ilmî*). (Kınalızade also uses the term theoretical faculty (*kuvvet-i nazari*) interchangeably.) The purpose of this faculty is to perceive the realities of existing beings and generate intelligible understandings of reality.[43] It is this faculty that enables humans to attain intelligent perception.[44] In simpler terms, it is "knowing the know-ables." The second faculty of rationality is practical wisdom, which Kınalızade refers to interchangeably as practical intelligence (*akl-i ameli*) and the practical faculty (*kuvvet-i ameli*). The purpose of practical intelligence is to discriminate between good and evil behavior, thus understanding the actions that lead to perfection and happiness and those that lead to evil.[45] This is the faculty that excites the body.[46] In other words, it is "knowing the do-ables."

While the first distinct human faculty is rationality in the human soul, the second faculty is the faculty of action (*kuvvet-i âmile*) which is further divided into the appetitive faculty (*kuvvet-i şeheviyye*) and the repulsive faculty (*kuvvet-i gazabiyye*), as it is in the animal soul. Unlike the faculty of rationality, it is more concerned with movement, action and practice. It is "doing the do-ables." Kınalızade asserts that the appetitive faculty is physically housed in the liver. The faculty of repulsion, on the other hand, is housed in the heart and is the source

---

[42] Koç, ed., *Ahlak-i Ala'i*, 80: "nutktan murâdımız nutk-ı zahir -ki telaffuz-ı hurûf ve tekellüm-i elfâzdır- değildir, ... murâdımız nutktan kuvvet-i idrâk-i ma'kûlât ve fikr ü reviyyete iktidâr ve ef âl ü ahlâk-ı mahmûde vü mezmûmeyi temyiz etmeğe temekkündür."

[43] Koç, ed., *Ahlak-i Ala'i*, 69: "kuvvet-i âlime dahi iki kısımdır. Birisi hikmet-i nazarî cihetinden âlim olan kuvvettir ve birisi hikmet-i amelî cihetinden âlim olan kuvvettir. Ammâ hikmet-i nazarî cihetinden âlim olan kuvvetin eseri vü ameli hakâyık-ı mevcûdât ve asnâf-ı ma'kûlâtı idrâk etmektir."

[44] Koç, ed., *Ahlak-i Ala'i*, 94: "Mukaddime-i kitâbda işâret geçmişti ki nefs-i insânînin iki kuvveti vardır: birisi 'kuvvet-i müdrike'dir ki nefs anın sebebi ile idrâkât-ı akliyeye kadir olur."

[45] Koç, ed., *Ahlak-i Ala'i*, 69: "Ve hikmet-i amelî cihetinden âlim olan kuvvetin eseri vü ameli ahlâk-ı hasene ve a'mâl-i sâlihayı ahlâk-ı zemîme ve a'mâl-i kabîhadan fark u temyîz edip niçe amel ki işlemesi sebeb-i kemâl ü sa'âdettir ve niçe ameldir ki işlemesi mûris-i noksân u şekavettir, anları idrâk eylemektir. Ve evvelkisine 'akl-ı ilmî' ve ikinciye 'akl-ı amelî' dahi derler."

[46] Koç, ed., *Ahlak-i Ala'i*, 94: "ikincisi 'kuvvet-i muharrike' dir ki nefsten anın sebebi ile tahrîkât-ı bedeniyye sâdır olur." Tusi did not divide the faculty of rationality into two. Although similar, he made a distinction in terms of the direction the faculty of rationality is steered: "the faculty of rationality is endowed with the ability to perceive without organ, and to distinguish between the things perceived. If it is directed to knowledge of the realities of existent beings and comprehension of the types of intelligibles, this faculty is called the speculative intelligence (akl-i nazari), if directed to the control of objects, distinction between good and evil actions, and the discovery of arts for the ordering of life's affairs, this faculty is called practical intelligence (akl-ı ameli)." Wickens, *The Nasirean Ethics*, 42.

of life and the animal soul.⁴⁷ In humans, it is responsible for the ability to repel or avoid frightening or harmful objects or situations, as well as for arrogance and the desire to dominate and control.

According to Kınalızade, the faculty of perception (*kuvvet-i müdrike*) and the faculty of movement (*kuvvet-i muharrike*) in the animal soul may resemble the faculty of rationality (*kuvvet-i alime*) and the faculty of action (*kuvvet-i ameli*) in the human soul—however, he argues, they are distinct. While the animal soul has the faculties of remembering (*kuvvet-i hayal*) and speculation (*kuvvet-i vahime*), it lacks intelligence (*ta'akkul*). In the human soul, however, intelligence enables humans to decide whether or not to react and take appropriate actions. Kınalızade also emphasizes that it is not always the faculty of rationality that compels humans to take action. Most people, rather than using their power of rationality to make decisions and act, use their faculties of remembering and speculation, which refer to internal senses in the animal soul.⁴⁸

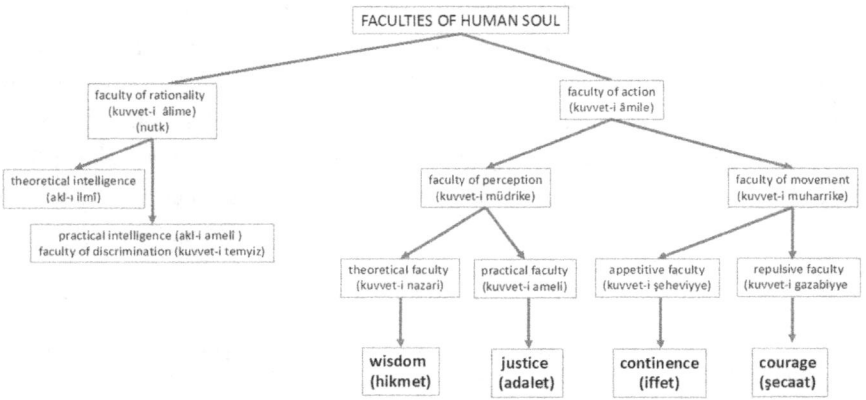

The theoretical, practical, appetitive, and repulsive faculties, as the fundamental faculties of the human soul, are the topic of his work, he asserts, which are all categorized under the faculty of action. In other words, the first volume of his work is particularly concerned with "doing the do-ables," and directing human behavior to constitute the basis for ethics. "Knowing the know-ables" and

---

47 Koç, ed., *Ahlak-i Ala'i*, 70: "Kuvvet-i şeheviyye cezb-i menâfi' ve tahsîl-i melâz-ı şehiyye, me'âkil ü meşârib ü menâkih gibi, ana müte'alliktir. Ve bu uzvun menba'ı ciğerdir ki tagdiye andan olup cemi'-i a'zâya bedel mâ yetehallel andan sirâyet eder. Ve kuvvet-i gazabiyye de f-i mazârr u mahûfât ve ikdâm-ı ahtâr ve taleb-i tasallut u tecebbür ve izhâr-ı nahvet ü tekebbüre müte'alliktir. Ve bu kuvvetin ma'deni yürektir ki menba'-ı hayât ve menşe'-i rûh-ı hayvânîdir."

48 Koç, ed., *Ahlak-i Ala'i*, 70; see also Okyay, "Kınalızade Ali Efendi ve Ahlak-i Ala'i," 109.

"knowing the do-ables" are not enough for perfection. Only "doing the do-ables" can enable one to reach perfection and thus happiness.

From these four faculties emerge four cardinal virtues, which represent the balance of each faculty: wisdom (*hikmet*), originating from the balance of the theoretical faculty (*kuvvet-i nazari*); justice (*adâlet*), originating from the balance of the practical faculty (*kuvvet-i amelî*); continence (*iffet*), originating from the balance of the appetitive faculty; and courage (*şecâat*), originating from the balance of the repulsive faculty.[49]

Emotions in *Ahlak-i Ala'i*

Kınalızade further elaborates the four cardinal virtues and their corresponding qualities:

The virtue of wisdom (*hikmet*) encompasses intelligence (*zekâ*), quick understanding (*sür'at-i fehm*), clarity of mind (*safâ-yı zihn*), ease of learning (*sühûlet-i taallüm*), excellence of intellect (*hüsn-i taakkul*), memorization (*tahaffuz*), and recall (*tezekkür*).[50]

The virtue of courage (*şecaat*) encompasses a mature soul (*kibr-i nefs*), bravery (*necdet*), zealousness (*ulüvv-i himmet*), patience (*sebât*), mildness (*hilm*), calmness (*sükûn*), vigor (*şehâmet*), perseverance (*tahammül*), humility (*tevâzu*), a sense of honor (*hamiyet*), and tenderheartedness (*rikkat*).[51]

The virtue of continence (*iffet*) encompasses shame (*hayâ*); meekness (*rıfk*); right guidance (*hüsn-i hedy*); a peaceable nature (*müsâlemet*); keeping the soul still while the appetite is in motion (*da'at*); fortitude (*sabr*); contentment (*kanâat*); dignified calm (*vakar*); modesty (*vera*); order (*intizâm*); acquiring wealth fairly and spending for the good, without acquiring wealth by unethical means (Wickens translates this as "freedom")[52] (*hürriyet*); and generosity

---

[49] Koç, ed., *Ahlak-i Ala'i*, 95: "faziletin şu'beleri: Pes kuvvet-i nazarî mühezzeb olup i'tidâl üzerine ef'âl sâdır olursa ol hulk 'hikme'tir. Ve eğer kuvvet-i amelî mühezzeb olup i'tidâl üzerine ef'âle sebeb olursa ol hulk 'adâlet'tir. Eğer kuvvet-i muharrike-i şehevânî mühezzeb ü mü'eddeb olup andan ef'âl-i mu'tedile sâdır olursa ol hulk 'iffet'tir. Eğer kuvvet-i gazabî mühezzeb ü mü'eddeb olup ef'âl-i mu'tedileye sebeb ü menşe' olursa ol hulk 'şecâ'at'tir. Pes usûl-i fezâyıl bu dört hulktur, a'nî hikmet ve adâlet ve iffet ve şecâattir."
[50] Koç, ed., *Ahlak-i Ala'i*, 99–100.
[51] Ibid., 100–102.
[52] I do not think that the term *hürriyet*, which means "liberty" in contemporary Turkish, denotes the same thing as Wickens' translated term. The term hürriyet has several meanings, and Ibn Miskeviyeh used the term to refer to a faculty that enables one to earn a living by appropriate means and to spend one's money on appropriate things, and which restrains one from generating wealth by inappropriate means. It is better to interpret the meaning of hürriyet as Ibn Miskeviyeh did. See Mustafa Çağrı, "Hürriyet," in *TDV Encyclopedia of Islam* (İstanbul: Türkiye Diyanet Vakfı, 1998).

(Wickens translates this as "liberality") (*sehavet*). Under *sehavet*, he defines eight more virtues: generosity (*kerem*), altruism (*isar*), forgiveness (*afv*), manliness (*mürüvvet*), hospitality (*nübl*), assisting friends and others in need and helping them share sustenance and property (Wickens translates this as "charity") (*muvasat*), munificence (*semahat*), and lenience (*müsamahat*).[53]

The virtue of justice (*adalet*) encompasses sincerity (*sadâkat*), amity (*ülfet*), fidelity (*vefâ*), concern (*şefkat*), care for kin (*sıla-i rahim*), requittal (*mükâfât*), friendship (*hüsn-i şirket*), fairness (*hüsn-i kazâ*), affection (*teveddüd*), acceptance (*teslîm*), reliance (*tevekkül*), and devotion (*ibâdet*).[54]

Each of the four fundamental virtues has two corresponding vices, one representing an excess of the virtue and the other its absence: Excessive wisdom results in deviousness (*cerbeze*), while its absence results in foolishness (*beladet*); excessive courage results in foolhardiness (*tehevvür*), while its absence results in cowardice (*cübün*); excessive continence results in immorality (*fücur*) and greed (*şereh*), while its absence results in sloth (*humud*).[55] There is no excess or deficiency of justice, there exists only the opposite of justice, which is oppression (*cevr*).[56] In the rest of the volume, Kınalızade defines the illnesses of the soul in terms of these vices, and explains their causes, symptoms, and treatment.

For example, the illnesses resulting from immoderation in the repulsive faculty are anger (*gazab*), cowardice (*cübn*), and fear (*havf*).[57] The causes of anger in turn are conceit (*ucb*), pride (*iftihar*), contentiousness and quarrelsomeness (*mira'*), jesting (*mizah*), arrogance (*tekebbür*), scorn (*istihza*), treachery (*gadr*), unfairness (*zaym*), and the quest for valuables (*münafeset*).[58] The illnesses resulting from immoderation in the appetitive faculty include excessive appetite (*ifrat-ı şehvet*), love of idleness (*betalet*), grief (*hüzn*), and envy (*hased*).[59] It is worth mentioning that Kınalızade's discussion of the treatments of vices, which

---

[53] Ibid., 102–5.
[54] Ibid., 105–7.
[55] Ibid., 95.
[56] Ibid., 95.
[57] Ibid., 174.
[58] I use Wickens' (129) translations of these concepts. *Ahlak-i Ala'i*, 177–8: "Esbâb-ı gazab on nev'dir. Evvel ucb, ikinci iftihar, üçüncü mirâ, dör-düncü lecâc, beşincisi mizâh, altıncısı tekebbür, yedincisi istihzâ, sekizinci gadr, dokuzuncu zaym, onuncu mûnâfesettir. Ucb, kişi kendisini beğenmek ve evsâf u ahvâlini iyi i'tikâd etmektir. İftihâr, öğünmek ve kendide kemâl anlayıp mesrûr olmaktır. Mirâ, cüz'i nesnelerde ceng ü cidâl etmektir. Lecâc, önegülük etmektir. Mizâh, lâğ etmektir. Tekebbür, ululanmaktır. Istihzâ, âher kimesneyi masharaya almaktır. Gadr, bir kimesneye vefâ etmek vâcib olduğu yerde cefâ vü ezâ etmektir. Zaym, bir kimesneyi za'îf ü hakir add edip zulm etmektir. Münâfeset, emvâl ü esbâbdan ba'zı nesneyi âherden kıskanmaktır."
[59] Koç, ed., *Ahlak-i Ala'i*, 206: "gâyet-i mazarrı dörttür: Biri ifrât-ı şehvet; İkincisi betâlet, üçüncüsü hüzn, dördüncüsü haseddir." I have used Wickens' translation, 142.

he regarded as illnesses, is much longer than those of Tusi and Devvani.[60] While this may be interpreted as demonstrating Kınalızade's desire to further clarify what his predecessors had written, it could also be interpreted as his belief that the society of his time called for the redefinition and re-examination of the vices.

Although emotions do not constitute a separate and a distinct category in *Ahlak-i Ala'i*, and the rationality of human beings is emphasized, how emotions were situated in the domain of philosophical knowledge and where emotions were positioned in the context of human behavior seems to be far more complicated. According to emotion knowledge of the Ottoman society for the early modern period, as reflected in *Ahlak-i Ala'i*, then, emotions—or more precisely, what we would now call emotion concepts—do not appear as a distinct category, but are rather categorized as either emotion-virtues or emotion-vices. What we would now label as emotion concepts such as bravery, mildness, calm, a sense of honor, and tenderheartedness appear under the category of courage; shame, meekness, fortitude, and dignified calm under the category of continence; sincerity, amity, fidelity, concern, care of kin, affection, and acceptance under the category of justice; and anger, cowardice, fear, pride, arrogance, scorn, grief, and envy appear as deviations from the balance of the related faculties.

In this model, virtues, including emotions, are defined in terms of equilibrium and balance (*adl*) in the faculties of the human soul. For example, excessive anger must be suppressed, but insufficient capacity to anger was considered cowardice, an illness. Thus, the difference between an emotional virtue and an emotional vice was not a matter of type, but degree. Kınalızade likens the concepts of medium, moderation and the equilibrium to the center of a circle. While the center of a circle represents a virtue, each position on the circumference represents a vice, either as excessive on the one side, or the deficiency on the other side. If one were to draw a line across the diameter of the circle, the central median point would represent the relevant virtue, but the vices would be on a continuum, as innumerable vices, situated at various points along the straight line.[61] This shows that the concept of balance and moderation was central to Kınalızade's understanding of the world and how humans situated themselves in the world.

For Kınalızade, dispositions are actions that do not require thinking; are easily practiced without much effort; are put into action without much exertion, as if

---

[60] Okyay, "Kınalızade Ali Efendi ve Ahlak-i Ala'i," 165–6.
[61] Okyay, "Kınalızade Ali Efendi ve Ahlak-i Ala'i," 137; Koç, ed., *Ahlak-i Ala'i*, 112; Tezcan, "The Definition of Sultanic Legitimacy," 74.

habitually; and endure for a long time. For instance, laughing and being ashamed are not dispositions for Kınalızade but rather are categorized as states (*hal*), since they are not enduring. Bravery or generosity, on the other hand, are enduring, but considered dispositions only if practiced easily without much effort.[62] For him, every human has his own distinct characteristics and dispositions. The reasons for such a diversity in human beings are what they naturally inherit from their forefathers, the impact of their environment which includes air, water and other natural sources, and lastly the effect of dispositions maintained by the way of training or imitation.[63] As far as nature is concerned, Kınalızade suggests that humans are not born either evil or good, but rather that they all have a tendency towards both. It is, in other words, possible to change dispositions with guidance, discipline, and training, with the exception of those who are wooden-headed, dull and stupid. Otherwise, he concludes, the law of the Prophet or the laws of the rulers regarding politics and training would be useless. It is also how he justifies the benefits of and necessity for the science of ethics.[64] As we will see in Chapter 3, particularly while exploring communal relations, people always sought to understand whether a vicious behavior was habitual or not, and always tried to train and discipline members of their communities before appealing to courts. It also shows that, in his understanding, emotions as virtues could be trained and disciplined.

Emotions and the Domain of Medical Knowledge

The Ottomans' philosophical understanding was closely interconnected and indeed compatible with the domain of medical knowledge, which in Kınalızade's time was based on the Galenic humoral theory, in which a healthy body required a balance of bodily fluids called humors. Kınalızade frequently highlights the similarity between the sciences of ethics and of medicine. Ethics, he writes, is perceived as the science of medicine for the soul (*tıbb-ı ruhani*), and just as medicine preserves health and cures illness, ethics preserves good character and cures bad character.[65] Just as a medical doctor strives to preserve the health

---

[62] "Hulk ki bir melekedir ki anın sebebi ile nefsten e f âl sühûletle sâdır olur ve fikr ü reviyyete muhtâc olmaz. Ve bu ta'rîfin tefsiri oldur ki 'meleke' hey'et-i nefsâniyye-i râsihaya derler, zîrâ keyfiyyet-i nefsâniyye iki kısmdır: Biri hâl ve biri melekedir. Zîrâ serî'ü'z-zevâl ve gayr-ı râsih olursa, hacâlet ü dıhk gibi, ana 'hâl' derler; eğer batî'ü'z-zevâl ve râsih olursa, sehâ vü şecâ'at gibi, ana 'meleke' derler." Koç *Ahlak-i Ala'i*, 93, Okyay, "Kınalızade Ali Efendi ve Ahlak-i Ala'i," 69.
[63] Okyay, "Kınalızade Ali Efendi ve Ahlak-i Ala'i," 85: Koç, ed., *Ahlak-i Ala'i*, 74–75.
[64] Okyay, "Kınalızade Ali Efendi ve Ahlak-i Ala'i," 71–73: Koç, ed., *Ahlak-i Ala'i*, 50–53.
[65] Tezcan, "The Definition of Sultanic Legitimacy," 67.

of a patient and restore lost health, the main effort of an individual should be, according to Kınalızade, to preserve and maintain the virtues formed in their soul and restore lost or weakened virtue. Thus, he treats practical philosophy as medicine for the soul.

Greek medical texts, notably the works of Hippocrates and Galen, were translated into Arabic starting from the eighth and ninth centuries as part of the integration of Greek philosophy into Islamic thought under the Abbasids. They were further elaborated on by the works of ar Razi (864–925) and Ibn Sina (980–1037), through which they influenced not only Arabic but also European medicine, based on the same Greek heritage.[66] Under Galenic humoral theory, the human body was proposed to contain four humors (phlegm, blood, yellow bile, and black bile), and each represented one of the four natural elements (earth, fire, wind, and water). Health represented an equilibrium or balance of the humors in the body, while illness in their understanding resulted from an imbalance.

Medical knowledge shaped not only the understanding of bodies and health, but also of justice and ultimately the world: Healthy states in all these domains required balance and equilibrium. Vasileios Syros, in his investigation of the use of ancient Greek theories of the four humors/elements of the human body by seminal political theorists, historians, and figures of intellectual and political life in early modern Florentine, Persian, and Ottoman traditions from the thirteenth to the seventeenth centuries, argued that "Galenic medicine was used by Italian and Islamic writers as a common frame of reference in their quest for the means of upholding a cohesive and well-regulated society and the synergy among the segments of the body politic was a key condition for the integrity and well-being of human society, just as the bodily humors work together and contribute to the harmonious function of the human organism."[67]

Their understanding of their bodies, its faculties, with four cardinal virtues representing the balance of four faculties, was closely related to four basic humors, which in turn were represented by the four basic natural elements of air, water, earth and fire. Their self was closely connected to the society in which they lived, to the world and the universe, all of which depended on harmony, balance and moderation. This compatibility between the domains of philosophical and medical knowledge based on the concepts of moderation and harmony may be

---

[66] Margrit Pernau, "The Indian Body and Unani Medicine: Body History as Entangled History," *Paragrana* 18, no. 1 (2009): 108.

[67] Vasileios Syros, "Galenic Medicine and Social Stability in Early Modern Florence and the Islamic Empires," *Journal of Early Modern History* 17 (2013): 161–213.

regarded as one of the reasons for the persistency of Ottoman philosophical knowledge until the nineteenth century. It was only in the nineteenth century, as we will see in Chapter 6, when a change in their perception of emotions got started, when the medical knowledge started to change.

Absence of Emotions in Ottoman Self-Narratives

Exploring emotion knowledge of Ottoman society is also important in understanding the still puzzling question of why very few self-narratives from the early modern Ottoman era have been discovered so far. It is apparent that the custom of writing self-narratives was not much cultivated, even among the elites. One possible explanation is that only few of the self-narratives survived, but it does not seem very likely. Some scholars, on the other hand, explained the rarity of self-narratives in terms of the paradigm of modernity, representing a period of transformation from communal self to that of an individualized self, but this seems too reductionist as a view to hold.

In a recent roundtable, published in *International Journal of Middle East Studies*, Ottoman historians discussed the state of the art of Ottoman ego-documents, or self-narratives (the two terms usually being employed interchangeably), which refer to materials such as diaries, memoirs, autobiographies, personal letters, and travelogues.[68] Karahasanoğlu, for example, rightly argued that the rarity of ego-documents from early modern times may be related to practical reasons as well, such as the limited availability of paper and limited circulation, rather than the idea of oneself being an unworthy subject to write about.[69] While Jacob Burckhardt (1818–97) attributed the increase in self-narratives in Europe to the rise of individualism in the fifteenth century, Binbaş in the same roundtable discussion suggested that in Islamic societies the path to individualism was not that clear.[70] Moreover, while a few such narratives have survived, expressions of emotions

---

[68] See the following papers, all from *International Journal of Middle East Studies* 53, no. 2 (2021): Selim Karahasanoğlu, "Ottoman Ego-Documents: State of the Art," 301–8; İlker Evrim Binbaş, "Autobiographies and Weak Ties: Sa'in al-Din Turka's Self-Narratives," 309–13; A. Tunç Şen, "The Emotional Universe of Insecure Scholars in the Early Modern Hierarch of Learning," 315–21; R. Aslıhan Aksoy Sheridan, "Nostalgia of a Frustrated Ottoman Subject: Reading Osman Agha of Timişoara's Memoirs as Self Narrative," 323–30; Semra Çörekçi, "The Dream Diary of an Ottoman Governor: Kulakzade Mahmud Pasha's Düşnama," 331–5.
[69] Karahasanoğlu, "Ottoman Ego-Documents," 307.
[70] Binbaş, "Autobiographies and Weak Ties."

in them are almost non-existent, and the absence or rarity of emotions is still puzzling for Ottoman historians, thus calling for clarification.

The diary of Seyyid Hasan, a dervish from seventeenth-century Istanbul, is one of the few surviving self-narratives that offers clues about variation in the expression of emotions. During the first months of his diary, his friends and family members were dying in a plague epidemic, and while he was away visiting his relatives outside the city, he learned that his wife had also been infected with the fatal disease.[71] He immediately returned home, but his wife passed away within a few hours of his arrival. On the night of her death, he wrote in his diary that at home that evening, a traditional *helva* (originally halva in Arabic), a type of dessert, was prepared, and he commented on how delicious it tasted.[72] While this seems to run counter to our contemporary understanding of how to express respect and sorrow at the loss of a loved one, he also wrote that he couldn't sleep that night and went to his dead wife's bedside and cried until morning. However, this remains the only passage in the diary where he records a display of sorrow. Having returned from the funeral, he immediately added in his diary a note that he had cheese and watermelon after the ceremony.[73] Cemal Kafadar in his influential and extensive analysis of Seyyid Hasan's diary argues that "the early modern Islamicists believed that individuals existed in broader groups and that the boundary between the self and society was a dynamic one, it shifted and was redrawn in different times and contexts."[74] For Kafadar, the difference between self and others was rather porous.

In the diary of Sadreddinzade Telhisi Mustafa Efendi, written in the early eighteenth century, no expression of sorrow appeared when his son passed away.[75] Karahasanoğlu ascribes this to the possibility that his son died at a very early age, and that the father and son did not have enough time to develop a close emotional bond. Although his record of the death of his grandson was more detailed, giving the cause of death as smallpox, there still was no mention of any expression of emotions in his verses.

The self-narrative of an Ottoman *medrese* instructor Muhammed b. Evrenos, with the penname Zaifi (d. 1557), seems to be an exceptional one. A. Tunç Şen,

---

[71] Cemal Kafadar, "Self and Other: The Diary of a Dervish in Seventeenth-Century Istanbul and First Person Narratives in Classical Ottoman Literature," *Studia Islamica* 69 (1989): 143.
[72] Ibid., 144.
[73] Ibid.
[74] Binbaş, "Autobiographies and Weak Ties," 313.
[75] Selim Karahasanoğlu, *Kadı ve Günlüğü Sadreddinzade Telhisi Mustafa Efendi Günlüğü (1711–1735) Üstüne Bir İnceleme* (Istanbul: Türkiye İş Bankası Kültür Yayınları, 2013), 8.

in his analysis, searched for emotions expressed in the diary and argued that Zaifi did not fail to note what he had "felt," and that the overarching themes in the records were a sense of distress about his career and envy and jealousy about his peers in the strictly hierarchical path of learning.[76] Acknowledging the field of history of emotions, however, he criticizes crafting of grand narratives with epochs specifying specific feelings or vocabularies of particular groups or communities. He proposes instead to look at how specific individuals self-expressed their emotions.

Individuals' failure to write about what they felt certainly should not be considered as evidence of the absence of emotions. I would rather suggest that the relative absence of linguistic expressions of emotions in self-narratives was related to two things. One of them was emotional norms of the period under consideration. Plamper, for example, searched for evidence of fear in the Russian army. The absence of talk about fear among Russian soldiers in the early nineteenth century, he argued, did not mean that they were fearless; rather, talk of fear was non-normative for the soldiers up until the beginning of the twentieth century, and showed that how one expresses feelings depends on emotion norms of the period.[77] Similarly, it was non-normative for the early modern Ottomans to write about what they felt. The second was the prevailing understanding of emotions framed under their philosophical knowledge. Writers of the time did not think of their feelings as something happening inside that needed to be navigated, labeled, and expressed in their self-narratives as part of a process of self-reflection. As we have seen in the previous sections of this chapter, emotions were understood to be realized only if acted upon, evidencing themselves in bodily practices, social practices, actions and in their relations with the outside world. Nicole Eustace, for example, encountered a historical example from eighteenth-century Virginia in which a wealthy slaveholder had recorded the loss of his son in his diary with no mention of grief. While some historians interpreted this text as demonstrating an early modern family's lack of love for their children, one historian, basing his claim on the slaveholder's report of disabling stomach complaints at the time of his loss, inferred that he had expressed his emotional pain as a physical suffering.[78] Eustace's research also suggests that feelings may be expressed or displayed by bodily practices.

---

[76] Şen, "The Emotional Universe of Insecure Scholars."
[77] Jan Plamper, "Emotional Turn? Feelings in Russian History and Culture (Special Section)," *Slavic Review* 68, no. 2 (2009): 229–37.
[78] Eustace, "AHR Conversation," 1503.

Concluding Remarks

In this chapter I have explored Kınalızade's influential work *Ahlak-i Ala'i* to understand the emotion knowledge of early modern Ottoman society. Emotions emerge from the particular faculties of human soul in this model and there are a couple of things that stand out that are valuable for the focus of this book. Firstly, his book is about practical wisdom, of which emotions are a part, showing themselves in practices, actions, and behaviors. Emotions consist in their bodily practices, and knowing the "know-ables" and "do-ables" is insufficient for perfection and happiness. His main concern is doing the "do-ables," which also justifies why in his model emotions appear as emotion-vices and -virtues. If not acted upon, emotions are not realized. Secondly, since virtues and vices vary between individuals across space and time according to Kınalızade, it may also be inferred that emotion concepts also change across time and place. Thirdly, the training, discipline, and practice of virtuous actions were critical for transforming actions into habits. The correction of dispositions and the acquisition of virtues, some of which would be labeled emotions, was thus a matter of discipline, and if practiced meticulously, could be habitual. Fourthly, we may infer that the idea of balance was crucial in the understanding of the physical body as well as morality and politics. Physical health required a balance of humors in the body, while psychological health required a balance of human faculties defined as virtues. The same understanding in the domains of both philosophical and medical knowledge also explains the continuity of emotion knowledge for a long time, which started to change with the change in scientific and medical knowledge in the nineteenth century. Finally, unlike the popular understanding of emotions as a part of our inner space, in this framework, emotions always remain in their worldly relations—social, familial, and political—which allows historians to trace emotions in historical texts as social practices, which also explains the relative absence of emotion in early modern Ottoman self-narratives. Moreover, having understood emotion knowledge of early modern Ottomans, as we will see in the following chapters, allows us to trace not only linguistic expressions of emotions associated with protection, but also to trace them as social practices, in political, social, and familial relations.

2

Ottoman Politics of Emotion[1]

In this chapter, I will explore the political relations between the subjects and the rulers in Ottoman society in my quest to understand what it *meant* and how it *felt* to protect and be protected. Since how one feels depends on emotional knowledge, which I covered in Chapter 1, and also depends on and is constrained by emotion norms, in this chapter I first explore the "emotionology" of the Ottoman state and society, which is a term coined by Peter Stearns and Carol Stearns, as "the attitude or standards that a society, or a definable group within a society, maintains toward basic emotions and their appropriate expression and ways that institutions reflect and encourage these attitudes in human conduct."[2] Modern historians have usually focused on governmental structure of the empire and the policies implemented in the early modern period, and have failed to realize the emotive aspects of the rulership. Yet, once we acknowledge that emotions should be historicized, and trace the "emotionology" of political relations, it provides a new lens to approach rulership in the Ottoman Empire. I start with an imperial decree, which is not unique in any sense and thus has a high representational value, and explore emotions in the political language. I then carry out a lexicological and contextual analysis of the emotion words that appear in the decree, following an emic approach. Compassion as an emotion appears frequently in archival sources used as a tool for politics. Yet, we have seen in the first chapter that, according to their emotion knowledge, emotions are conceptualized and theorized as performatives, manifesting themselves in their moral behaviors. Thus, in addition to tracing for emotional norms and linguistic expressions of emotion words and concepts in the historical texts, representing "sayings," it is also necessary to analyze emotions as practices, and performatives, representing "doings" in their political relations, compatible with

---

[1] This chapter constitutes an improved version of my article titled 'Early Modern Ottoman Politics of Emotion: What Has Love Got to Do With It? published in *Turkish Historical Review* 10 (2019): 132–154.
[2] Stearns and Stearns, "Emotionology."

the philosophical framework of their emotion knowledge. Emotions evidence themselves in the behaviors, practices, and political undertakings.[3] Therefore, I also explore in this chapter how and when compassion, as a norm, was practiced in the political relations between rulers and the ruled. Then, utilizing the third volume of Kınalızade's *Ahlak-i Ala'i*, I explore another emotion, *mahabbet* (love), which also stands as an emotional norm. In the final section, I analyze frequently used metaphoric expressions in the political language, such as *telif-i kulüb* and *istimalet*, which literally mean "uniting with the hearts of the subjects," and how they were employed in the political strategies of the early modern Ottoman Empire.

On May 5, 1637, the Ottoman Sultan Murad IV (r. 1623–40) issued an imperial decree addressing all judges and military officials throughout his empire. In this decree, the sultan declared that he had been informed that his subjects were being oppressed (*zulm*). Their rights were being transgressed (*taaddi*) and they were thus being aggrieved (*teezzi*) by his delegated agent, grand vizier Mehmet Paşa, who was illegally levying extra taxes.[4]

The sultan could have learned of his subjects' complaints either directly from officials consulting with him or from petitions sent by the subjects themselves to the Imperial Council (*divan-ı hümayun*), which functioned broadly as a court of appeal. In theory, the subjects, both men and women, and even peasants in remote areas of the empire, whether Muslim, Christian or Jewish, had the right to bring their complaints to the attention of the central authorities, and all Islamic leaders were responsible for maintaining open communication between the ruler and the ruled. Several registers of decrees had been written in response to such complaints, serving as evidence that the Ottomans upheld the principle of petitioning rights not only in theory but also in practice.

The sultan's decree began with a phrase declaring that it was the sultan's will that justice (*adalet*) prevail, and that state affairs should be executed in compliance with the established order that was needed to "prosper (*terfih*) the hearts" of the subjects and the government officials. Indeed justice, as a concept of crucial importance for understanding the political structure of Middle

---

[3] For the terms "doings" and "sayings," coined by Monique Scheer, see her article "Are Emotions a Kind of Practice," 220.

[4] Halil İnalcık, "Adaletnameler," in *Osmanlı'da Devlet, Hukuk, Adalet*, ed. Muhittin Salih Eren (Istanbul: Eren, 2005): 142–4. The decree is published in Arabic script, and is to be found in the Register of Important Affairs (*mühimme defteri*) no. 37, p. 74, document no. 186.

Eastern states, has been the subject of many studies.⁵ Justice has been defined as "the prevention and elimination of oppressive acts (*zulm*) by those who exercise power in the name of the ruler."⁶ It was not simply a principle of equality and imperial judgment, but also a principle of social action.⁷

The sultan in his decree announced the appointment of Bayram Paşa to replace Mehmet Paşa as his grand vizier to prevent any future oppression of his subjects. He also issued orders to stop the illegal levying of extra taxes. Moreover, in the concluding section of the decree, the sultan warned both the newly appointed grand vizier and other officers that they would be severely punished and vehemently chastised as an admonition (*ibret*) and an example (*nasihat*) to others who might seek to violate the law.

Before taking a closer look at the concepts embedded in this decree with a focus on language and the use of words, to explore what the subjects had *felt* upon hearing or learning about this order from their protector, it would be beneficial to discuss how their protector's words and messages would be transmitted to a vast, heterogenous population of subjects living under very different circumstances. The population of the Ottoman state comprised various religious, ethnic, spatial, occupational, or otherwise subsidiary identities. Although it was not common for any sultan/king in pre-modern times to give speeches to their subjects, there are records of many imperial orders in the Ottoman archives regarding important affairs of the empire, presented as the Ottoman sultan's personal directives and addressed to all Ottoman subjects. The decisions taken on political issues in the Imperial Council were recorded in the registers of important affairs and formalized as if they were the personal orders from the sultan. Based on these records, imperial decrees (*ferman*) and warrants from the sultan (*berat*) were issued, with wording and language that suggests the sultan had listened to all the discussions of the Imperial Council and personally settled or redressed the

---

⁵ For example see İnalcık, "Adaletnameler," 75–191; Fahri Unan, *İdeal Cemiyet İdeal Devlet İdeal Hükümdar* (Ankara: Lotus Yayınevi, 2004); Mehmet Öz, "Klasik Dönem Osmanlı Siyasi Düşüncesi: Tarihi Temeller ve Ana İlkeler," *İslami Araştırmalar* 12, no. 1 (1999): 27–39; Boğaç Ergene, "On Ottoman Justice: Interpretations in Conflict (1600–1800)," *Islamic Law and Society* 8, no. 1 (2001): 52–87; Linda Darling, *A History of Social Justice and Political Power in the Middle East: The Circle of Justice from Mesopotamia to Globalization* (New York: Routledge, 2013).

⁶ Halil İnalcık, "State and Ideology under Sultan Süleyman I," in *The Middle East and the Balkans under the Ottoman Empire*, ed. İlhan Başgöz (Bloomington: Indiana University Press, 1993): 71. İnalcık claims that the prevention and elimination of oppressive acts was achieved by the Ottoman *divan-ı hümayun* (Imperial Council) functioning as the supreme court with a constant check and spying on the governors, punishments under the *siyasa* laws, the periodic promulgation of *adaletname*s (rescripts of justice) and by the *arz-ı mahzar* (petition) right of the subjects against the abuses of power of the public agents.

⁷ Ibid.

issue. Moreover, the Ottoman Empire did not enjoy advanced communication technologies, and communication was mostly oral because of low literacy rates. Yet, Ottoman subjects were nevertheless well informed on general issues and problems pertaining to the empire. The wording of the decrees, including that cited above, frequently consisted of strict orders that the decree be read aloud in a public space or marketplace and that its content be further explained to ensure all subjects understood it, so that nobody could claim that they had not heard or known about the order. A copy of the order was to be recorded in the judicial court registers, for anyone who requested a copy later. Svetlana Ivanova, for example, explores how the subjects living in the European provinces were informed of the Ottoman Empire's political events using the standard royal decrees of the seventeenth and eighteenth centuries. She demonstrates convincingly that the circulation of decrees established an information channel linking the capital to the tax-paying communities in the provinces, thereby spreading news about important state-political events, and the transmission of socio-political information was well established throughout the empire.[8]

Protection with Compassion

The aforementioned decree could be read as just one of many political maneuvers that the Ottoman sultan employed to prevent oppression and ensure justice in his realm. But I would like to shed light on how this decree can contribute to our understanding of the political relations between rulers and subjects, particularly of the concept of protection, if we acknowledge that emotions should be historicized.

The protection (*himaye, muhafaza, siyanet, hiraset*) of subjects, regardless of their secondary identities, stands as a recurrent and central theme of imperial decrees. Protection is a "concept," which I previously referenced in the introduction. According to neuroscientist Lisa Feldman Barrett, our brains use concepts to mentally reconstruct the outside world and make meaning of physical sensations from it; and while forming concepts is universal, each culture provides its own system of concepts, values, and practices. This also resembles Pernau's definition of knowledge: "the contested interpretation of

---

[8] Svetlana Ivanova, "The Ottoman Decrees 'Up' in Istanbul and What the Rumelia Subject Perceived at the 'Bottom' (Seventeenth–Eighteenth Centuries)," in *Political Initiatives "From the Bottom Up" in the Ottoman Empire*, ed. Antonis Anastasopoulos (Rethymno: Crete University Press, 2012): 345–78.

the world by its actors, which encompasses knowledge about how the society is organized, which categories matter for the identification and self-identification, and how these categories [that] overlap or are mutually exclusive shape social and political practices."[9]

When the subjects listened to or heard from their fellows about the imperial decree, for example, this sensory input became meaningful only through the concepts it invoked. Without being heard, the material reality represented by the sultan's decree could not be interpreted. Hence, material reality can be linked to interpretation only through the body and senses. Of course, a concept can be any single word, but here, we are more interested in concepts in which a multitude of meanings are tied together and in which contestation is key to them.[10] Not every word is a concept, but only those that are used with the intention to interpret the world and create meaning. Concepts do change their meaning over time, and indeed this is the way humans communicate with one another.

I claim that protection may well be regarded as a contested concept/knowledge since protection of whom, from what, in which circumstances, with which constraints is historically contingent. For example, our current expectations of the protection to be provided by a nation-state are quite different from what any subject of an Ottoman Empire in the mid-seventeenth century would expect from their sultan, who served as a protector acting as the shadow of God on earth. Indeed, the superior–subordinate relationship between the Ottoman ruler and his subjects has usually been described using the metaphor of a shepherd acting as the protector of his flock, consistent with ancient Indo-Persian theories of governance. However, the model seems inadequate to explain the willing obedience of subjects to their ruler. However, once we analyze emotions associated with protection, it provides a fuller picture of this unequal relationship.

Returning to the sultan's decree, the sultan, having learned that his subjects were being oppressed and their rights transgressed, made the following statement: "My subjects are entrusted to my safekeeping by the Almighty Creator (*reaya ki, vedayi-i Halik-i Kibriya*)" and in their understanding of rulership, that is exactly why the subjects should be protected.[11] The word *reaya* denotes all subjects of the empire, regardless of their religion, ethnicity, occupation, or any

---

[9] Margrit Pernau, "Feeling Communities: Introduction," *The Indian Economic and Social History Review* 54, no. 1 (2017): 7.
[10] Pernau and Rajamani, "Emotional Translations," 62.
[11] İnalcık, "Adaletnameler," 143. In other rescripts of justice, the phrase is also written as "reaya ki, vedayi-i Halikü'l berayadır...," meaning "my subjects are entrusted to my safekeeping by the Creator of all mankind."

other standing, and more specifically, all tax-paying subjects. Moreover, it was not only the ruler who was obliged to protect the subjects. Officials working under him, his agents, who represented his executive and judicial powers, were likewise expected to protect the sultan's subjects in the same way.

The main determinant of the reciprocal relationship between the Ottoman ruler and his subjects was the concept of protection, which encouraged people to think in a specific way that was commonly understood and accepted. In other words, in their understanding of the rights and responsibilities of the state and society, the mutual relationship between rulers and their subjects demanded that rulers protect their subjects if they were to be considered just and legitimate rulers. Conversely, subjects trusted that they had a right to such protection. For example, the words *fukara* (pl. of *fakir*) and *zuefa* (pl. of *zaif*) literally mean "the poor" and "the weak," respectively, in contemporary Turkish. However, in Ottoman political language, these terms do not denote material poverty or physical weakness, but rather, defenselessness, and therefore, dependence on the protection of a ruler and his agents.[12]

The same decree then goes on as follows: "you [as my delegated agents] should manifest abundant clemency and tenderness and profuse generosity and compassion to [my] subjects."[13] Thus, the legitimacy of a ruler depended not only on the obligation to protect, but to do so with compassion, a notion recalling Stearn's "emotionology," the norms regarding emotions. As we will see, these culturally based emotional norms proved to play a critical role in the political actions of the Ottoman state.

Sources indicate that protection in the political language of the early modern Ottoman state was always accompanied by the emotional code of compassion, *merhamet*. Indeed, in early modern Ottoman society, as in its many others of the time, the state was personified as the ruler's body, denoting a unification of the state with the sultan, who was expected to show compassion to his subjects, in sharp contrast to modern societies and their notion of the nation as an abstract entity.[14]

---

[12] Marlene Kurz, "Gracious Sultan, Grateful Subjects: Spreading Ottoman Imperial 'Ideology' Throughout the Empire," *Studia Islamica* 107 (2012): 102. Similarly, the word *gureba* (pl. of *garib*), which literally means (i) strangers, people away from home, and (ii) the poor and the destitute, also denotes those who are in need of protection.

[13] İnalcık, "Adaletnameler," 143: "reaya ki, vedayi-i halik-i kibriyadır, haklarında mezid refet ve şefkat ve vufur-ı mekremet ve merhametim zuhura getürdüb."

[14] For a different opinion on the separation of state from the ruler see Rifa'at 'Ali Abou-El-Haj, *Formation of the Modern State: The Ottoman Empire, Sixteenth to Eighteenth Centuries* (Syracuse, NY: Syracuse University Press, 2005), 65–66. Abou-El-Haj argues that "as early as the later sixteenth and seventeenth centuries ... documents testify to a narrowing specialization of functions within the

The word *merhamet* is a complex and broad concept, linked in meaning with other words that cluster around it and enrich its conceptual meaning. It is also distinctive in allowing us to understand the relationship between the Ottoman state and its subjects. *Merhamet* was sometimes used synonymously with words such as tenderness (*şefkat*), benevolence (*atıfet*), grace (*inayet*), clemency (*re'fet*), munificence (*mürüvvet*), beneficence (*mekremet*), and generosity (*fütüvvet*).

Compassion is an emotion word very frequently employed in the holy book of the Quran. While *fear* is the most frequently mentioned emotion word (337 times with all the derivatives from the three roots (root w-q-y, 165 times; root kh-w-f, 124 times; root kh-sh-y, forty-eight times)), *mercy/compassion* is the second (327 times (root r-h-m)).[15] Although fear was an important emotion, it was balanced by compassion, happiness, and love; and positive words generally outnumbered negative ones.[16] Although counting the number of emotion words is not a fully accurate method of identifying expressions of emotion, it certainly gives an idea of the general emotional content. According to Karen Bauer, who researched emotions in the Quran, in the opening of the Quran, the *Fatiha*, "humans are not assured of God's love and mercy: they must earn His approval through their actions. God will respond with the appropriate emotions based on a person's behavior."[17] Accordingly, "people are divided into groups: Those towards whom He bestows His mercy/compassion, those at whom He is angry, and those who are astray." According to Bauer, "the *Fatiha* tells the audience that God is intrinsically merciful, but that He can become angry."[18] Islam and the Quran encourage believers to cultivate specific emotions, which stands as an example of a powerful structure regulating emotional norms.

We frequently encounter phrases in imperial decrees ordering addressees "to care for the well-being of subjects purely on account of compassion and tenderness"[19] or "to treat subjects with tenderness and those who are needy

---

Ottoman central administration ... that specialization of function preceded the tanzimat by several centuries." Although there were signs of separation between the state and the ruler, with increased specialization in bureaucracy by the mid-seventeenth century, I still think that it should be regarded as a transitional period. Up until the advent of modernity (the Tanzimat reforms), for example, all the imperial decrees, personal orders of the sultan, continued to be written as if they were the direct words of the ruler, and any correspondence with the state was addressed to the sultan only.

[15] Karen Bauer, "Emotion in the Quran: An Overview." *Journal of Quranic Studies* 19, no. 2 (2017): 3.
[16] Ibid.
[17] Ibid., 10.
[18] Ibid., 10–11.
[19] "reayaya mahz-ı merhamet ve şefkat içün ... "

of protection with compassion,"[20] attitudes that mirror God's mercy and compassion. In the same decree, Bayram Paşa, the new grand vizier, was praised by Sultan Murad IV and introduced as one who "most illustriously guides the path to world order," "prudently manages important public affairs with his brightly shining ideas," and "perfects the public affairs of mankind with his sound judgment," reflecting the style of any imperial decree full of embellishments. Immediately afterwards, however, the decree praises Bayram Paşa's innate compassion, calling his compassionate disposition "natural" and manifested through sincere convictions of his heart expressed as boundless compassion and clemency.[21] Evident in the titles of rulers and political elites, compassion was regarded as both an innate feeling and a bodily disposition, with an understanding that rulers were selected on the basis of having such a disposition. Yet, it was also believed to be an emotion that could and should be nurtured; hence, moralists always advised rulers to act compassionately toward their subjects, transforming the emotion of compassion into practice. Hence, feeling compassion, as an emotion-virtue, as we have seen in the first chapter, demands one to act compassionately.[22]

One of the important historians of the Ottoman palace in the eighteenth century was Raşid Efendi (d.1735), who wrote the history of the Ottoman Empire for the period 1660–1729. In his work, we find numerous similar appraisals (and titles) regarding rulers, their agents, and even the palace itself. For example, in the introduction to his chronicle *Raşid Tarihi*, he praises the appointment of Damat İbrahim Paşa, the grand vizier (1718–30) during the reign of Sultan Ahmed III (1703–30), by emphasizing his compassion and benevolence as well as his execution of the rules of tenderness and generosity.[23] Likewise, the Ottoman palace was referred to in the documents as a refuge of the universe[24] and a threshold of felicity,[25] which denoted not only a desire for

---

[20] İnalcık, "Adaletnameler," 174–5; "reayaya şefkat ve fukara ve zuefaya merhamet ile hareket eyleyub…." See, for example, the rescript of justice dated February 1537, which refers to the new imperial subjects of Baghdad after it has been conquered: "feth olunmuş vilayet olmağın, anda vakii olan reayaya mezid himmet ve atıfet ve kemal-i şefkat ve merhametten…" (since [Baghdad] is one of the districts that we have conquered, the subjects living there [in Baghdad] should be treated with utmost benevolence, tenderness, and compassion…).

[21] İnalcık, "Adaletnameler," 143; "Bayram Paşa'nın cibilliyet-i zat-ı merhamet-nihad ve esniyye-i murad-ı fuadi'l halisi'l-itikadında asar-ı merhamet ve ref'et mevzu' olub."

[22] Scheer, "Are Emotions a Kind of Practice," 220. Scheer claims that "emotions are practices themselves—an emotion is not something that happens to us, but something that we do."

[23] Abdülkadir Özcan et al., *Tarih-i Raşid ve Zeyli Raşid Mehmed Efendi ve Çelebizade İsmail Asım Efendi (1071–1141 /1660–1729)* (Istanbul: Klasik, 2013), 1:8–9; "ayin-i merhamet ü mürüvveti ihya ve kavanin-i şefkat ve fütüvveti icra."

[24] "atebe-i aliyye-i alem-penah."

[25] "südde-i seniyye-i saadet-destgah."

universal sovereignty but also a promise of happiness for the sultan's subjects. The chronicle likewise frequently cites the emotional well-being of those who had accepted Ottoman sovereignty and thus led happy and prosperous lives under the protection of the sultan, thanks to the emotional constraints imposed to achieve political order.[26] What is important is that such depictions do not specifically reflect Raşid Efendi's perception of the empire but rather, should be regarded as traditional concepts transmitted from generation to generation.

Imperial decrees also provide tools for historians to explore how the concept of protection and its accompanying emotional code of compassion were practiced in the political negotiations of historical actors and thus were more than mere rhetoric, but indeed an emotional practice. In such cases, we may follow the sequential link from the expression of compassion to acting compassionately in daily politics; hence, we frequently encounter the phrase "out of compassion for their condition" (*hallerine merhameten*) in archival sources.

In some cases, this phrase reflects a ruler's pity for the suffering or pain of one of his subjects. For example, in an imperial order dated 1778, a military officer[27] Seyyid Mehmed Sadık, whose leg was broken when he fell off a horse, was ordered to be brought to Istanbul for treatment.[28] But more importantly, we can find several cases in which the ruler, in response to his subjects' demand for compassion,[29] issued orders to either forgive subjects, change the terms of a previously determined punishment, or make the traditionally implemented practice more flexible.

---

[26] "şimdiye değin dergah-ı saadet-destgahımıza istikametle tarik-i ubudiyyetin sabit-kadem olanlar enva'ı riayet ve inayetimizle hoşhal ve saye-i saadetimizde müreffehü'l-bal olub…," Akdes Nimet Kurat, *Rusya Tarihi: Başlangıcından 1917'ye kadar* (Ankara: TTK, 2014), quoted from mühimme defteri no. XVI, document 3:3–4.

[27] "dergah-ı mu'allem cebecileri çorbacılarından ikinci cema'atin çorbacısı."

[28] Kadir Özbay, "177 Numaralı Mühimme Defterinin Transkripsiyon ve Tahlili (H.1192–1193/M.1777–1778)" (MA diss., Yüzüncü Yıl Üniversitesi, Van, 2008): 241; "Bundan akdem İsmail ser-askeri maiyyetine me'mur dergah-ı mu'alla'm cebecileri çorbacılarından ikinci cema'atin çorbacısı Seyyid Mehmed Sadık zide kadruhu hidmet-i lazımesinde kıyam ve bezl-i makdur üzre iken bi-gaza'illahi te'ala atdan düşüb bir bacağı şikest olub bir istinad-ı sınıkcı olmadığından üç mahdan berü zahmi müşted ve … ve mahall-i mezkurda kalır ise telef-i nefs olacağını zabitan-ı ocak tarafından inha olunmakdan naşi mumaileyhin hal-i perişanına merhameten Astane-i aliyye'me gelüb hanesinde bir hazik sınıkcı ve cerrah ile deva ve illetinden halas oldukda yine hidmet-i me'mure azimet etmek üzre Der aliyye'me gelmesine müsa'ade-i aliyyem erzan kılınmış Dergah-ı mu'alla'm kapucubaşılarından olub hala cebecibaşı olan Şa'ban Ağa dame mecduhu i'lam etmeğin vech-i meşruh üzre amel olunmak fermanım olmağın imdi sen ki vezir-i müşarün-ileyhsin muma ileyhin hal-i ızdırabına merhameten Astane-i aliyye'mde illetine ba'de'l-müdava ve's-sıhha mahall-i me'muresine gelmek üzre Der aliyye'me vüruduna izn ü ruhsat-ı şahanem erzan kılındığı ma'lumun oldukda ber minval-i muharrer muma ileyhin Der-saadet'üme irca'ına mümana'at olunma(ma)k babında…."

[29] "istida-yı merhamet."

An imperial decree dating from the late sixteenth century[30] provides evidence that the sultan, whose obligation to provide protection for his subjects was fulfilled by his compassion, could change the law. This did not denote, however, an arbitrary use of power, but a principled application of emotional codes.[31] According to this decree, previously both the sons and daughters of shop and cellar owners had the right to inheritance, which enabled orphans to use the rent of shops and cellars as their allowances. However, waqf administrators ordered that only the sons of the deceased would be entitled to inherit shops and cellars. The owners of those shops (*ahali-i dekakin*) and craftsmen (*erbab-ı hiref*) had sent agents acting on their behalf to officially request mercy (*atıfet*) from the sultan and asked him to change this rule to give daughters the right to inheritance, contending that daughters had become destitute and were treated with contempt (*zelil*) after their father's death. Based on their petition, the sultan, expressing his compassion for the condition of the orphaned daughters (*hallerine merhameten*), ordered that the rule be changed accordingly.

According to another imperial decree dating from the late eighteenth century, the sultan granted *timars* as a source of revenue to slaves of the Porte (*kapıkulu*); regulations strictly demanded that these slaves provide service to the sultan in his palace in times of peace and join the sultan's expeditions in times of war. The practice of settling and residing in the granted units of taxation and administration, however, became so widespread for the *kapıkulus* that it had

---

[30] Hacı Osman Yildirim et al., eds, *12 Numaralı Mühimme Defteri (978-979/1570-1572)* (Ankara: Devlet Arşivleri Genel Müdürlüğü, 1996): 171; "Yenişehir kadısına hüküm ki: Taht-ı kazanda olan erbab-ı hıref ve ahali-i dekakin Asitane-i Sa'adet-aşiyanum'a adem gönderüp; Bundan akdem kendü mallarıyla kargir dekakin ü mehazin bina itdürüp veyahud akça ile satun alup vefat eyledüklerinde oğullarına ve kızlarına intikal idüp eytama sebeb-i ma'aş olurdı. Ba'dehu; kızlara dükkan ü mahzen virilmeye diyü mütevellilere ahkam virilmekle hal-i hayatlarında ma-meleklerin dekakin ü mehazine virenler vefat eyledüklerinde yetimeleri şiddet-i ihtiyac ile muhtac ü zelil oldukların bildürüp; kızlarına virilmek babında istid'a-yı atıfet eylemeğin mezid-i merhametümden işbu sene: 978 Cemaziye'l-ulası'nun sekizinci gününden kızlarına dahi virilmek emridüp buyurdum ki: Hükm-i şerif-i vacibü'l-ittiba'um vardukda, emrüm üzre evkafa müte'allik dekakin ü mehazinün eger kargir binalarıdur ve eger gayridür; anun gibi müste'cirleri vefat eyledüklerinde oğullarına ve kızlarına icare-i mu'ayyene-i cariye ile virdürüp mütevellileri ol babda dahl ü ta'arruz itdürmeyüp müste'cirlerden fevtolup evladı kalmayanlarun dekakin ü mehazini ve sayir evkafa müte'allik yirleri mukteza-yı şer'-i şerif üzre vakıf tarafından mütevellilere zabt u kabz itdürüp şer'-i şerife muhalif hariceden kimesneyi dahl itdürmeyesin ve bu emr-i şerifümi sicill-i mahfuza kaydıtdükden sonra ellerinde ibka eyleyesin ki, dayima mazmun-ı hümayunı ile amel oluna, şöyle bilesin ...."

[31] Some Ottoman historians used the term "pragmatism" as an explanatory term for the Ottoman sovereignty. For changing meanings of pragmatism in Ottoman historiography see Murat Dağlı, "The Limits of Ottoman Pragmatism," *History and Theory* 52 (2013): 194–213. Dağlı argues that for most proponents of Ottoman pragmatism the concept pertains to politics (which for Dağlı refers to the strategies, practices, institutions, or discourses whose purpose is to construct and retain hegemony within a polity) rather than to the political (which refers to the configuration of the power relations that organize a society as a legitimate entity) and thus cannot be used as explanatory or comparative category.

become difficult for them to obey the then-current requirement to return to the palace once a war was over. Despite the fact that this practice contravened the law, the sultan, out of compassion for their condition, used the emotion code of compassion to grant an order permitting his slaves to serve in the palace for six months and to live in their settled homes for the remaining six months of the year.[32]

Likewise, another imperial decree dating from the early eighteenth century[33] ordered that the *timar* and *zeamet* holders, who were then in the service of the vizier Mustafa Paşa for the protection of the fort of Gence, be pardoned and allowed to return to their *vilayet*s (which literally means "province," but here it denotes the lands in which they lived in and from which they drew their income). *Timar* was a military-administrative system in which the sultan granted tax revenues from state-owned (*miri*) land to members of the military class (*askeri*) in return for military and administrative services. It resembles the *iqta* of the Seljukids and the *pronoia* of the Byzantines. Such bestowals of tax revenues were called *timar, zeamet*, or *hass* depending on the size of the revenue they generated, *timar* being the smallest in size, bestowed to common cavalrymen. Although *timar* holders were required to serve in expeditions, they made a political claim to be allowed to return to their homes based on their

---

[32] "… malum ola ki, Rumilinde ve Anadolu'da zeamet ve tımara mutasarrıf olan gedüklü Dergah-ı Ali müteferrikaları ve çavuşları ve Divan-ı Alişan ve Defter-i Hakani katipleri ve şakirdleri; an-asl seferlerde vezir-i azamlar ile sefer eşüb, ve hazarlarda Der-i devlet-medarda zabitleri marifetiyle daima hidmette mevcud bulunmak üzere mevzu' olub, hatta yedlerine verilen nişan-ı alişanda ale'd-devam Divan-ı Ali makam hidmetinde bulunalar deyü meşruh ve mestur iken bu kaidenin riayetinde adem-i ihtimamdan naşi zümre-i mezbureden bazıları taşralarda zeamet ve tımarları olduğu yerlerde ve sair istedikleri mahallerde tavattun ve temekkün itmeleriyle esna-i hazarda kanun-ı kadime riayet etmeyüb, … ancak mezburların her biri taşralarda alaka hasıl etmeleriyle hallerine merhameten evlerinde ve yerlerinde külliyet ile mehcur olmayıb, kanun-ı kadim dahi bil'l-külliye terk olunmayıb fi'l-cümle mer'i olmak üzere taife-i mezbureden Rumili ve Özi eyaletlerinde mutavattın olanlar her senede altı ay ve Anadolu'da eyalet-i sairede mutavattın olanlar dahi beher sene altı ay münavebe tarikiyle gelüb, Asitane-i Saadetimde zabitleri marifetiyle iktiza iden hidemat-ı aliyyede bulunmak üzere bundan akdem şeref-yafte-i sudur olan evamir-i şerifem mucebince Rumili ve Özi eyaletlerinde olanlar müsillü sair yerlerde sakin olan gedüklüler için dahi fermanım sadır olmuştur." I would like to thank Özer Ergenç who gave me permission to use this source from his personal archive.

[33] Zeynep Kurt, "13 Numaralı Ve 1727–1730 Tarihli Mühimme Zeyli Defteri (Değerlendirme-Transkripsiyondizin)" (MA diss., Fırat Üniversitesi, Elazığı, 2005): 186; "Sivas Eyaleti'nin elviye alaybeylerine hüküm ki: Birkaç seneden berü düst.r-ı mükerrem müşir-i mufahham nizamu'l-'alem hala Gence muhafızı vezirim Mustafa Paşa edamallahu te'ala iclalehunun ma'iyyetinde iktiza iden hidemat-ı din ü devlet-i 'aliyyemde sancaklarınızın zü'ema ve erbab-ı timarlarıyla bezl-i tab ü tüv.n eyleyüb ve hala hallerinize za'f tari olmağla vilayetlerinize izin ve ruhsat virilmek üzere vezir-i müşarun ileyh tarafından 'arz ve i'lam olunub fi'l-hakika dört beş seneden beru ehl ü 'ıyalinizden dur ve hidemat-ı 'aliyyede tahsil-i rıza-yı hümayunum için bezl-i makdur itmeniz ile sa'yeleriniz mebrur ve meşkur olmağla hallerinize merhameten vilayetlerinizi 'avdete izn-i hümayun erzani kılınmışdır imdi işbu emr-i şerifim ile vüs.lünde vezir-i müş.run ileyhin ma'rifetiyle bi'l-cümle sancaklarınızı zü'ema ve erbab-ı timarıyla vilayetlerinize 'avdet eylemeniz babında ferman-ı 'alişanım sadr olmuşdur, buyurdum ki …."

suffering from being away from their families for four to five years. A change in the current rule was thus made, not only introducing flexibility into this practice but also legitimizing this legal flexibility by reference to the emotional code of compassion (*hallerinize merhameten*). The sultan's compassion in such cases was used as a tool to legitimize changes in current rules and regulations regarding the sultan's delegated agents.

The continuity in the expected display of compassion by each sultan as part of emotionology was apparent even in cases dating from the early nineteenth century. For example, an imperial decree from 1828 was issued with respect to an Armenian woman in Kumkapı, Istanbul, who worked as a midwife.[34] The woman had previously performed illegal acts, such as the termination of pregnancies without legal permission, and therefore had been expelled to Kütahya to be disciplined. Pregnancy termination was illegal in Islamic law, and it was considered an act against social norms. The midwife had lived in Kütahya for a long time, suffering from defenselessness and old age.[35] The midwife's daughter appealed to the Imperial Council, asking that her mother be forgiven and released. We may infer from her request that she believed that her mother had already paid for her crime by living in Kütahya for a long time and that she needed to be protected because of her age and thus deserved the right to request the sultan's compassion. The midwife was pardoned, as she was believed to have renounced her previous evil practices and was determined to practice her profession in an honorable way. The sultan's order emphasized, however, that she had been forgiven "out of [the sultan's] compassion [for her condition]." Compassion, in this case, may also be interpreted as a consideration of the proportionality of the punishment to the crime.

---

[34] Mustafa Yavuz, "Kütahya Şer'iye Sicilleri 15 Numaralı Defterinin Transkripsiyonu ve Değerlendirilmesi" (MA diss., Dumlupınar Üniversitesi, Kütahya, 2009): 111; "... Kumkapıda mütemekkin ermeni gariplerinden Küpeli ebe iskat-ı cenin misüllu hilaf-ı rıza harekete ictisal eylediğine mebni bundan akdem sadır olan emr-i şerifim mucibince li-eclü't-te'dib Kütahyaya nefy ve icla olunmuş ise de mersumenin nefy tazi hayli müddet olarak fukara ve ihtiyarlık sebebiyle müzdarib ve perişan ve vucuh-ı merhamet ve şefaate şayeste ve şitayan olduğundan bahisle afv ve ıtlak olunması hususu mersumenin zevciyle kızı taraflarından bu defa südde-i saadetime arzuhal takdimiyle istirham olunmaktan naşi hususu mezbur seredi bayı hassamdan olan Rum ili kazaskeri esbak a'lamü'l-ulemai'l-mütebahhirin mevlana Mustafa Behçet edamallahü teala fezailehuya havale olundukta mersume adeti reddiyeye sabıkasından vucuh ile kabil terbiye olduğu tahkik gelindiği beyanıyla ıskat-ı cenini hımarından fima ba'd kefyed ve feragat ile sanatında arzıyla meşgul olmak ve ba'de'l-yevm iş bu kar-ı şer' eylediği mesmu olunduğunda te'dibinde diğer vecihle muamele olunmak şartıyla merhameten afv ve ıtlakı babında emri şerifim suduruna havi ilam etmekle ilamı mucibince mersumun afv ve ıtlak olunması fermanım olmağın ...."

[35] "hayli müddet olarak fukara ve ihtiyarlık sebebiyle muzdarib ve perişan."

According to another decree from 1828, the *mufti* of Aydın was also banished to Kütahya as punishment for having acted illegally.[36] His wife, children, and other family members officially sought the sultan's pardon, asking for his mercy. They based their request on their father's good behavior from the first day of his banishment and on the desolate and wretched conditions they'd suffered because of their father's absence. The *mufti* was pardoned, since his family had also been indirectly penalized for his crime, and as in the previous case, the sultan's pardon was legitimized by the phrase "out of [the Sultan's] compassion [for the condition of the mufti of Aydın]."

Compassion, as shown by the documents discussed above, served as an emotional code indicating a shared understanding of when, how, and in which cases it was appropriate for rulers to express compassion and to translate this expression into action to sustain order and ensure the rulers' legitimacy. The feeling of compassion was also hierarchical: only the superior could show compassion; while the subordinate would have the right to demand compassion in certain contexts. There were also well-understood conventions as to when it was appropriate for subjects to display discontent and ask for compassion. These displays of discontent and the linguistic representations of such displays were reflected in imperial decrees issued in response to subjects' political petitions, which also make it possible to hear the voices of subjects. The subjects' petitions for compassion in the cases just discussed reflect their changed perceptions of the sultan, who, as a just and legitimate ruler, was expected to have protected his subjects with compassion. Likewise, the imperial orders issued in response to such petitions represented the sultan's efforts to reverse his subjects' perceptions and legitimize his rule. The linguistic expressions of compassion leading to specific political actions offer further evidence that displays of compassion legitimized the political actions of Ottoman rulers and served to account for seemingly arbitrary decisions. Conversely, the subjects' demand for compassion justified their political claims.

These petitions usually represented cases in which subjects perceived that the protection offered by customary legal means had failed, with subjects losing their emotional (*müreffehü'l-bal*) and material prosperity (*asude-hal*)

---

[36] Mustafa Yavuz, "Kütahya Şer'iye Sicilleri," 101; "Kütahya naibi mevlana zide ilmuhu tevki-i refi-i hümayun vasıl olucak malum ola ki bundan akdem Aydın kazasında mezunen bi'l-ifta olan hilaf-ı rıza hareketi ibtidarına mebni Kütahyaya nefy ve icla olunan Ahmed Rafiin mütteti nikaından beri memleketinde olan iyi hali ve evladı bi-kes ve perişan kalarak vucuhla merhameten şayan olduklarından bahisle merkumun afv ve ıtlakı hususuna müsaade-i aliyyem erzan kılınması iyi hal ve evladı taraflarından arzuhal takdirleriyle istida istirham olunmaktan naşi merkumun merhameten afv ıtlakı babında emr-i şerifim suduruna...."

and entering a state of being dispersed and scattered (*perakende ve perişan*). In these cases, protection was no longer associated with the emotional code of compassion in the subjects' minds. Subjects, then, would demand a change. In doing so, however, they would refer to commonly shared concepts that would enable them to justify their claims.[37] The subjects' demands for compassion also functioned as social signals, implying that the sultan's legitimacy as a protective ruler was in jeopardy, thus requiring the sultan to take political action. The strategic use of emotions in political language thus helped both parties attain their short- or long-term political goals. Emotions, thus, had performative power.

Tracing linguistic expressions of compassion and several other terms linked to it in archival sources shows the value the Ottomans ascribed to compassion, and how and when they regularly practiced it. In Reinhart Koselleck's terms, they constitute a part of political iconography that also encompassed the form of ceremonies, state imagery, and architecture as well.[38]

Uniting with the Hearts of the Subjects
(*telif-i kulüb* and *istimalet*)

How did subjects feel when listening to or hearing about the decree itself from their fellows? In other words, how did subjects experience the protection of their sultan? Indeed, Pernau, as I already mentioned in the introduction, suggests a

---

[37] Oğuzhan Samıkıran, "138 Numaralı Edirne Şer'iyye Sicili H.1119–1161/M.1707–1748" (MA diss., Fırat Üniversity, Elazığı, 2006): 652. See, for example, the decree of the sultan copied in the *kadı* court records of Edirne in the mid-eighteenth century: "vakf-ı mezbur mürtezika fukaralarına gadr-i küllı olduğu tarafımıza arz ve mahzar birle ilam ve istida-yı merhamet itmeleriyle…" (with their petition to us, they asked for compassion reporting that they suffer oppression…).

[38] Hakan T. Karateke, "Legitimizing the Ottoman Sultanate," in *Legitimizing the Order: The Ottoman Rhetoric of State Power*, ed. Hakan Karateke and Maurus Reinkowski (Leiden: Brill, 2005): 16. Karateke suggests a framework for analyzing the legitimacy of the Ottoman sultan and the Ottoman state and the strategies that Ottoman sultans and the ruling elite devised to keep the subjects content. In this framework, the construction of a legitimate authority has a normative and a factual aspect. Factual aspects constitute the concepts of justice, order, and the welfare of the subjects. A normative schema on the other hand, according to Karateke, determines the color of the political rhetoric and symbolism, shapes the ceremonies, the state imagery, the architecture and the sermons. The state ideology is achieved by propagating symbols of power, one of them being the symbolism of the language in Ottoman official documentation. Reinkowski, on the other hand, analyzes the political idiom of Tanzimat and states that "the aim of creating a state ideology is achieved by propagating symbols of power, one of them being the symbolism of language in Ottoman official documentation, which are valuable clues as to how the Hamidian bureaucracy conceptualized such matters as the relationship of the ruler and the ruled," arguing that routine Ottoman bureaucratic correspondence can also be an excellent resource for understanding the Ottoman political idiom and rhetoric of power. Maurus Reinkowski, "The State's Security and the Subjects' Prosperity: Notions of Order in Ottoman Bureaucratic Correspondence (19th Century)," in Karateke and Reinkowski, *Legitimizing the Order*, 198.

theoretical model for answering our question.[39] Relying on Koselleck's investigation of the contested and changing meaning of concepts, Pernau claims that focusing exclusively on language excludes materiality and bodily sensation and thus does not fully capture the richness of emotional expression, arguing that language is not the only way to conceptualize the world.[40]

For example, a decree is an official form of documentation associated with a ritualized and elaborate style, the material onto which it was written, its impressive size and embellished calligraphy, and perhaps even the authoritative tone in the voice of the state agents who visited towns across the empire to read the order of their protector. This, along with recurrent related concepts and contexts, can be considered multisensory inputs for interpreting the content of the decree and the concepts contained within it. These can provide historians with complex layers of meaning-making mechanisms. We know that literacy was low, and knowledge was mostly transmitted orally, which indicates a hierarchy among the senses.[41] Members of Ottoman society prioritized hearing to interpret the world, rather than reading visually, but this did not make them any less competent in interpreting their world.

According to Pernau's model, the senses are at once individual and social. Moreover, sensual experience itself is socially framed. It does not start with the moment of the sensual impact, but builds on incorporated memories of previous experiences and their interpretations. Experiences evoke previous experiences, but they are equally built on expectations.[42] This view is also consistent with experiment-based neuroscientific research, from which we have learned that simulations are our brains' guesses as to what's happening in the world. Our brain uses past experiences to construct a hypothesis—the simulation—then compares this simulation with the cacophony perceived by our senses.[43] In this manner, simulation allows our brains to impose meaning on the noise, selecting what is relevant and ignoring the rest. Scientific evidence shows that what we see, hear, touch, taste, and smell are largely simulations of the world, not reactions to it, according to Lisa Feldman Barrett, and this is a common mechanism not only for perception but also for understanding language, feeling empathy, remembering, imagining, dreaming and many other psychological

---

[39] Pernau and Rajamani, "Emotional Translations."
[40] Ibid., 47.
[41] Nil Tekgül, "Reflections of an External World in the Ottoman Mind: The Production and Transmission of Knowledge in 18th-Century Ottoman Society" (MA diss., Bilkent University, Ankara, 2011).
[42] Pernau and Rajamani, "Emotional Translations," 51.
[43] Barrett, *How Emotions Are Made*, 27.

phenomena.⁴⁴ It is the default mode for all mental activity and one of the basic universals about how the brain works.⁴⁵ Our brains continually predict and simulate all the sensory inputs from inside and outside of our bodies, so they understand what these inputs mean and how to respond to them. Every moment that we are alive, our brains use concepts to simulate the outside world.⁴⁶

Tracing metaphors and metaphoric expressions in the Ottoman language can help us understand subjects' multisensory experiences, since these expressions bring language and image together and may be integrated into historical semantics.⁴⁷ One of the most frequently used metaphors for the relationship between the sultan and his subjects, in which the sultan offers compassionate protection, is the expression "winning the hearts of the subjects," literally expressed as "uniting with the hearts" (*te'lif-i kulûb*) of the subjects. Other synonymous terms are used within different contexts that literally mean "prospering,"⁴⁸ "calming,"⁴⁹ "attracting,"⁵⁰ "consoling,"⁵¹ or "conquering the hearts of the subjects."

The eighteenth-century palace historian Raşid Efendi, whom we previously mentioned, further illuminates the meaning of the concept *te'lif-i kulûb* with an anecdote from his work.⁵² In this story, the Ottoman envoy talks with the Persian shah, and the shah asks the envoy questions about how the Ottoman sultan spends his spare time, whether he is having fun or hunting. No, says the envoy, my sultan doesn't hunt. The shah asks whether he is not even "hunting for

---

⁴⁴ Ibid.
⁴⁵ Ibid., 28.
⁴⁶ Ibid.
⁴⁷ Pernau and Rajamani, "Emotional Translations," 57. Pernau and Rajamani propose not only to analyze verbal images but also look at concepts in metaphors within and across different media and sign systems.
⁴⁸ "terfih-i kulub-ı reaya."
⁴⁹ "tatmin-I kulub-ı reaya."
⁵⁰ "celb-i kulub-ı reaya."
⁵¹ "tatyib-i kulub-ı reaya."
⁵² Özcan et al., *Tarih-i Raşid*, 2: 1260; "'… Hünkar hazretleri şimdi makarr-saltanatlarında eğlenürler mi yohsa sayd ü şikar ederler mi?' 'Hayır şahım, etmezler.' 'Şikar-ı kuh dahi etmezler mi?' dedüklerinde, 'şikar-ı şükuh ederler' dedim. Güldüler, 'ya anların valid-i macidleri ve birader-i emcedleri sayd ü şikara mailler idi. Bunlar n'içün etmezler? Hususâ sayd ü şikar müluk-i izamın şanındandır gerek idi, edeler.' Bu kulları cevab verdüm ki, 'şahım bizim şevketlü Padişahımız şehzadeliğinde tahsîl-i ma'arife gayet sa'y edüp, hususâ tevarihe ve müluk-i eslafın asarına hayli tetebbu'ları var idi. Bir gün tevarih mütala'a ederken, bir mahalle gelmişler ki, Nuşirevan-ı Adil Büzücmihr Hakim'e sual eylemiş ki, 'sayd ü şikar makulesinden kangı sayd ü şikar leziz ve faidelüdür?' Büzücmihr demiş ki, 're'aya vü ahalinin kulubunu sayd etmek cümle saydlardan lezizdir. Ve ahirette intifa'ı ziyadedir' demiş. Ve bu keyfiyyete vakıf oldukdan sonra, 'eger Hakk te'ala taht-ı ali-baht-ı Osmani'ye cülus etmeyi bana müyesser ederse, kat'a sayd ü şikar hevasında olmayup re'aya vü ahalinin ta'mir-i kulub ve terfih-i ahvalleri ile olayım' deyü derununda cenab-ı Bari ile ahd etmiş. Şimdi ol ahde vefa ile daima niyyet-i sâdıkaları celb-i kulub-ı re'aya vü ahalidir."

mountains," a reference to the sultan searching for new lands to conquer. The envoy replies that his sultan hunts for magnificence only. The shah then asks why he does not hunt, since the sultan's ancestors were fond of doing so as a means of signifying their glory. The envoy, in his reply, says that when his sultan was a prince, he had great respect for knowledge and was especially interested in studying history and the influences of his ancestors. One day, he met a wise man and asked what kind of hunting would give both pleasure and benefit. The wise man replied that "hunting the hearts of the *reaya*" is that which gives the most pleasure and the most benefit. The sultan then said that if God allowed him to be the Ottoman sultan, he would have no desire to hunt animals, and would rather always seek to gain the hearts of the *reaya* and make them prosperous.

Cemal Kafadar, a prominent Ottoman historian, examined the *gaza* (Islamic holy war) ideology of the early Ottomans of the fourteenth century, in his groundbreaking book *Between Two Worlds*, by utilizing warrior epics and hagiographic sources. What *gaza* meant for the early Ottomans is still disputed in Ottoman historiography; while some historians interpret the term to denote a radical Islamic holy war ideology that Ottomans used to convert conquered peoples, others interpreted it as an ideology, not necessarily radical, used to legitimize their new political power, influenced by nomadic Turkish Oğuz traditions and a syncretic understanding of the Islam of Sufi dervishes. Kafadar, in his conceptualization of *gaza* ideology of the early Ottomans, argues that

> the people of the marches did not see a contradiction between striving to expand their faith and engaging in conciliatory gestures from members of the other faith. One insight gained from the hagiographies of dervishes like Sarı Saltuk is that an atmosphere of "tolerance" and symbiosis or "improvisation" in Greenblatt's vocabulary, does not preclude a desire to gain converts.[53]

He further asks, "Is it not more intelligent to be conciliatory, whenever possible, in gaining hearts and minds of others?"[54] adding that *gaza* ideology, among other things, was an attempt to gain hearts and minds.[55]

Ottoman chronicles are replete with texts showing *te'lif-i kulûb* as a principal tool for good governance. We come across frequent examples of this principle as we read a range of Ottoman texts. For example, the Ottoman political principles

---

[53] Cemal Kafadar, *Between Two Worlds: The Construction of the Ottoman State* (Berkeley: University of California Press, 1995), 72.
[54] Ibid., 72.
[55] Ibid., 82.

to be implemented for governing Egypt after its conquest were explained in a chronicle after its conquest by Yavuz Sultan Selim in 1517.[56]

The chronicle first emphasizes that taking charge of Egypt's governance would be harder than conquering it. The sultan, while authorizing the talented Yunus Paşa to govern Egypt, also demanded that he conform to Ottoman law and value justice. However, Yunus Paşa did not succeed in his expected mission and was dismissed from office, to be replaced by Hayırbay. The main reason for Hayırbay's assignment to this position was his ability to unite the hearts of the Çerkes and Bedouins, who were the Egypt's native inhabitants before the conquest. It is apparent that the first requirement for establishing affective ties between the ruler and the ruled was based on the metaphorical expression of *telif-i kulûb*. Furthermore, the chronicle reported that the sultan left Egypt after giving the necessary suggestions to Hayırbay. It is also added that the sultan's insight about Hayırbay's potential for success was borne out by subsequent events, owing to his capacity to perceive and understand with his heart (*şah-ı dana-dil*).[57] Indeed, in the Quran, the heart is a prominent theme, not as a physical organ, but as a locus of understanding. The text indicates that Hayırbay's governance was based on the principles of uniting hearts as a metaphorical expression, providing a verbal image of the linguistic interpretation of good governance and thus protection.

---

[56] Hoca Saadettin Efendi, *Tacü't-Tevarih* (İstanbul: Matba'a-i Amire, h.1279/1862), 2:374–5."Cün diyar-ı Mısriyyenin zabtı teshiri gibi asir ve çerakise ve a'rab serkeşleri meyanında hükümet gayri yesir idi. Daver-i durbin bu fikri seza gördü ki mevkeb-i zafer-karin rücuundan öndin erkan-ı batemkinden birin imtihan içün Mısır hükümetine tayin ide. Eger, zabt ve muhafazatı müyesser olursa izi ü ikbal ile Darü's-saltanasına gide. Ve li-heza vezir-i azam ve sair erkandan mukaddem olan Yunus Paşa'yı bendegan-ı pişin ve devlet-hahan-ı dirin adadından olub, hususen bu sefer-i zafer-rehberde asar-ı celadet ve secaati zuhur bulup hidemat-ı şayestesi sezavar-ı tahsin olmağın Mısır hükümetine ta'yin ve kamet-i ikbalin teşrif-i hüsrevane ile tezyin idüb, hall ü akd-i umuru zabt u rabt-ı mesalih-i cumhuru keff-i kifayetine tefviz ve aynin-i şeref-karin-i Osmani muktezası üzerine icra-yı merasim-i adl ü dade tahriz buyurdu. Amma ol şah-ı dil-agahın adet-i saadet-gayeti bu mimval üzere idi ki vulat ve hükkam aktar-ı ahvalinden hemvare istihbar eyler idi. Ve cair olanları girdab-ı gazabında hayır ve muğak-ı hasretde dair idüb tığ-i kahrından necat bulanı har ve ruz-ı ruşeni çeşm-i ibret binine tar eyler idi. Güş-ı huşu istima'-ı ahval-ı hükkam içün küşade ve şimşir-i berk tesiri zulmet-i vücud-ı zaleme def'i içün amade idi. Tığ-i berranı irtişa yedin makdu ve bed-şedidü'l ahzı setm dırahtını beyhinden maklu itmiş idi. Yunus Paşa ile dahi seiyye-i ma'rufe ve adet-i me'lufeleri üzere muamele idüb, eğeçi mücamele suretin izhar buyurdular. Amma eyyam-ı hazar ve seferlerinde mücari-i ahval ve imalinden istihbar buyurdular. Sifariş buyurdukları üslub bi'l-külliye hatırından meslub olup, cem'i male ve tahsili amale hırs ve tehalüki ve bab-ı tamada adem-i temalükü ma'lum-ı şerifleri ve ümera-yı çerakise avradından cebr-i aniv ve tehdit ve tahvif ile mebaliğ-i kesire alduğu ve meşayiğ-i Arab'a tekalif-i şakka ile emval-i azime salduğu ma'ru'z-ı zamir-i ilham-ı halifleri olıcak, ol makule hükümet-i gayrı makbule ile Mısır zabtı müyesser olmadığına cazim ve hükümet-i Mısrı Hayırbay'a tevfize azim oldular. Çün Hayırbay ruşen-i rey'in sadad-ı hali ve hüsn-i efal ve amali ve bab-ı muhalledü'l ikbal-i sultaniye kemal-i sadakati ve hükümet-i Mısır'a liyakatı daver-i ferhunde ferzamirine zahir ve damen-i ismeti levs-i tamadan tahir idi. Ve ol diyarı ahvaline vukuf-ı taamı ve te'lif-i kulüb-i çerakise ve a'raba iktidar-ı 'ammı olmağla ol mansab-ı celilü'l-kadre mezid istihkakı bahir ve etvar-ı hamide ile hidemet-i pesendide edasında mahir idi."

[57] "ol emir-i akil, hükümetinde bir vech ile mu'amil oldu ki, şah-ı dana-dil zannını tasdik ve fikr-i dakiki ve tedbir-i anifini tahkik eyledi."

The sultan's obligation to win the heart of his subjects was also reflected in an eighteenth-century chronicle, *Raşid Tarihi*, in which non-Muslim subjects in the newly conquered island of Morea were exempted from tax obligations.[58] Islamic law places non-Muslim subjects of a Muslim ruler in the category of *zimmi*, as those who are subject to a guarantee of protection in exchange for the payment of a special poll-tax, called *cizye*, paid by adult male non-Muslim subjects. A land survey of the island of Morea, made to determine the tax-paying subjects and thus the potential income of the island, was completed immediately upon its conquest. However, since it had been newly conquered, the land survey could not be made with the necessary degree of accuracy. The *reaya* of the island were exempted from not only other taxes but also *cizye* taxes for two years, to prevent any possible adverse consequences of a hastily made land survey and "to win the hearts of the *reaya*." A new officer was appointed to the island to regulate the *cizye* tax obligations since the exemption period had expired, and was told to be cautious and refrain from any act that could arouse hatred.

Apart from the metaphoric expression of "*telif-i kulüb*," *istimalet* (gentle persuasion or gaining hearts) is a related term that we often encounter in primary documents. Historians at times use the term *istimalet* to indicate a policy of gentle persuasion of non-Muslim subjects only. The root of the Arabic word *istimalet* is *meyl*, which means affection, love, and propensity; and *istimalet* was also commonly used as a policy "to win the hearts of the subjects." Ilgürel claimed that in Ottoman chronicles, *istimalet* was usually used to mean showing tolerance to or looking after the rights of the subjects, with special focus on non-Muslim subjects, or as cherishing one's subjects and nourishing them, following the principle of "love of *reaya*" (*raiyyetperverlik*).[59]

İnalcık was one of the first historians to emphasize the importance of *istimalet* as a policy that facilitated Ottoman conquests. He claims that Ottomans practiced *zimmi* law, in its widest sense, without differentiating between non-Muslim and Muslim subjects, protecting their lives and properties as the rule of God. He further claims that this policy of tolerance, which is also revealed

---

[58] Özcan et al., *Tarih-i Raşid*, 2:1142; "Nizam-ı ahval-i cezire-i Mora ve tahrir-i cedid Mora ceziresi feth ü teshir olundukda egerçi ber-vech-i müsara'at tahrir olunup, lakin henüz feth olunmak takribiyle tahririnde gereği gibi dikkat olunmak mümkin olmadığından ma'ada te'lif-i kulub-ı re'aya için tekalif-i saire değil iki senelik cizyeleri bile afv olunmuş idi. Hala müddet-i afv münkazi olmak takribiyle ahval-i cizyeye nizam verilmek yüzünden cezire-i Mora voyvodası nasb ü ta'yin ve maslahat- ı melhuzayı tahrirde teneffür-i re'ayaya ba'is olur hareketden gâyet ihtiyat üzre hareket eylemek hususu lisanen kendüye tezkir ü telkin olundu."

[59] Müctebe İlgürel, "istimalet," in *DİA*, ed. Türkiye Diyanet Vakfı (İstanbul: Diyanet Vakfı, 2001): 362–3.

as "*telifü'l-kulüb*" in the Quran (et-Tevbe 9/60), was reflected in the Ottoman sources as the policy of *istimalet*.[60]

In a recent study on the concept of *istimalet*, Elias Kolovos discusses its place and history in the Ottoman political vocabulary with reference to several historical texts.[61] He also shows how Ottoman historians interpreted the concept; Heath Lowry, for example, in *Nature of the Early Ottoman State*, claims that *istimalet* was "typified by a flexible tax system which preserved earlier practices," thus helping ensure that "the ensuing new Ottoman order must have looked particularly attractive to a Christian peasantry long abused during the preceding centuries of Byzantine decline."[62] Karen Barkey, in her *Empire of Difference*, has also theorized the concept of *istimalet* as a "strategy for the stabilization of power."[63] Kolovos locates the earliest reference to *istimalet* in the Ottoman chronicles of the fifteenth century, and it was very frequently used in the later Ottoman sources of the sixteenth and seventeenth centuries. In a fifteenth-century chronicle narrated by Oruç Bey, *istimalet* was exemplified by the following policies:

> the Ottomans did not harm the infidels of the neighboring areas in the peninsula of Gallipoli; on the contrary, they won them over as allies, promising that they and their families would be safe and sound.

Kolovos argues that *istimalet* was basically an Ottoman policy of "carrots" that would be replaced by "sticks" if subjects did not agree to it. Kolovos further claims that it was sometimes applied through the distribution of robes of honor (*hil'at*),[64] sometimes gentle persuasion of Ottoman soldiers to participate in the campaign, or salary increases, promises, and concessions promised to soldiers to persuade them to fight.[65] He points out that it addressed both soldiers and prospective subjects of the Ottomans. For example, during the Cretan War, Deli Hüseyin Paşa, the general of the Cretan campaign, had gently persuaded his soldiers to follow him into the conquered fortress of Merambello, where he granted privileges to the conquered *reaya*.[66] Although Kovolos interprets *istimalet* as an accommodationist policy towards not only non-Muslim but also

---

[60] Halil İnalcık, "Türkler ve Balkanlar," in *Balkanlar*, ed. Ortadoğu ve Balkan İncelemeleri Vakfı (OBİV) (İstanbul: Eren Yayınları, 1993): 16–18.
[61] Elias Kolovos, "İstimalet: What Do We Actually Know About It?," in *Political Thought and Practice in the Ottoman Empire*, ed. Marinos Sariyannis (Rethymno: Crete University Press, 2019): 59–70.
[62] Ibid., 60.
[63] Ibid.
[64] Ibid., 65.
[65] Ibid., 67.
[66] Ibid., 69.

Muslim subjects and soldiers in the campaigns by likening it to a carrot-and-stick policy of concessions and material benefits, he implicitly assumes that only the pursuit of material interests, more particularly economic interests, could motivate people, without mentioning emotions. However, we know emotions translate knowledge into actions and practices, thereby providing the motivation and the necessary drive.[67] Moreover, both emotions and cognitions are involved in the interface between the world and its interpretation. Material benefits could provide the emotional motivation and the necessary drive for subjugated people to accept or embrace Ottoman sovereignty or for Ottoman soldiers to fight. Perhaps these motivators could have been feelings of security, safety, or perhaps a desire for trust or peace, since they would be part of an empire and entitled to protection from the ruler regardless of their faith; they would be considered *vedayi-i halik-i kibriya*, bringing a change in their status. Or maybe it was their feeling of relief from fear about their future. Granting privileges to soldiers could potentially elevate their status, providing feelings of honor. The carrot-and-stick approach also implicitly assumes that the Ottoman rulers, in utilizing this policy, consciously tried to deceive their subjects. However, it would be both difficult and hurtful to assume that (for example) non-Muslim subjects of the empire were deceived for over 300 years into showing their deference to the sovereign because of the "carrots" proposed. Would it not be more plausible to approach this policy of gaining hearts and minds and the feelings of deference of the subjects as a policy of reconciliation, which demands a mutual agreement? Reconciliation indeed demands emotional unity. Would it not be more convenient to come into a mutual understanding for both sides? Perhaps it was emotional well-being, as much as the material well-being, that both the subjects and the rulers sought. In the remaining part of this chapter, I will focus on another emotion, namely love (*mahabbet*), by examining the related parts of Kınalızade's advice manual of the sixteenth century as an excellent source for exploring the emotional norms of love in political relations.

The Path of Love (*mahabbet*)

The book of ethics *Ahlak-i Ala'i*, the first volume of which (titled "The Science of Ethics") has been explored in the first chapter in terms of emotion knowledge, has been the topic of much research attempting to explore the Ottoman state

---

[67] Pernau, "Feeling Communities," 7.

and political thought, and has frequently been used as a reference to formulate the concept of the "circle of justice" (*daire-i adalet*).⁶⁸ The essence of order in the political context is referred to by Kınalızade as "executing the rules of justice and upholding the authority of the Sultanate."⁶⁹ The Ottoman understanding of good governance was formulated under the basic concept of *daire-i adliyye* (circle of justice), which was frequently referred to in the texts of pre-Ottoman and Ottoman *siyasetname* literature.⁷⁰ Yet, Kınalızade suggests another means of good governance that he ranks even higher than justice: "the path of love" (*mahabbet*):

> It is apparent that individuals are in need of socializing to achieve order and acquire happiness and perfection. Socializing, however, encompasses the mischief of hindering and striving to surpass the other. There are two paths to overcome this mischief. The first path is achieved by executing the rules of justice and upholding the authority of the Sultanate, as has already been shown. The second path is the path of love (mahabbet). If there exists love among the members of society, there is no need for justice.⁷¹

Mahabbet may roughly be translated into English as mutual love, affection, or friendship, and should be differentiated from passionate love (*'aşk*). I will be using "love" as the translation of the word *mahabbet* from now on. Although the main theme of Kınalızade's work is justice and harmony in society, he also highlights love, whose absence demands justice. In other words, the absence or the distortion of love drives people to demand justice. Kınalızade offers examples of distorted love.

---

[68] Fahri Unan, *İdeal Cemiyet İdeal Devlet İdeal Hükümdar* (Ankara: Lotus Yayınevi, 2004), XXVI.
[69] Koç, ed., *Ahlak-i Ala'i*, 413: "icra-yı kavanin-i adalet ve ihkam-ı saltanat u iyalettir ki işaret olundu."
[70] For further details see Ergene, "On Ottoman Justice," 57; Ergene points out Kınalızade's formulation of "circle of justice"; "Adldür mucib-i salah-ı cihan /Cihan bir bağdur divari devlet /Devletin nazımı şeriatdür /Şeriate olamaz hiç haris, illa mülk /Mülk zabt eylemez, illa leşker /Leşkeri cem" idemez, illa mal /Malı cem' eyleyen raiyyetdür /Raiyyeti ku ider padişah-ı aleme adl." (It is justice which is necessary for the World; the World is a vineyard and its wall is the state; the state is governed by the sheria; the sheria cannot be maintained without a king; the king cannot govern without soldiers; he cannot compile soldiers without wealth; it is the reaya who accumulate wealth; and it is justice which makes reaya the servants of the sultan of the universe). Hasan Kafi formulates justice as "Padişahlık ve sultanlık olmaz, illa erler ile olur, yani asker ile olur, asker ise olmaz, illa mal ile olur; mal ise olmaz, illa vilayet mamur olmak ile olur; vilayet ise olmaz, illa adalet ile dahi hüsn-i siyaset ile mamur olur." (The sovereign cannot rule without troops. He has no troops without money. There is no money if the land is not prosperous. The land would not prosper without good and just government. Therefore one cannot reign except by justice").
[71] Koç, ed., *Ahlak-ı Ala'i*, 413: "Çün zahir oldu ki efrâd-ı insân intizâm-ı ahvâl ve tahsîl-i sa'âdet ü kemâl etmekte ictimâ' u te'ellüfe muhtâc ve ictimâ' u te'ellüf dahi mazarrat-ı müzâhame vü mugâlebeyi müştemildir Ve bu mazarratın def'i iki tarîkle mutasavverdir: Birisi icrâ-yı kavanin-i adâlet ve ihkâm-ı saltanat u iyâlettir ki işaret olundu... İkinci tarîk tarîk-i mahabbettir... Amma bir cema'at içinde tarîk-i mahabbet olsa, mümkindir ve mahabbet olıcak tarîk-i adalete ihtiyâc kalmaz."

In one lengthy chapter,⁷² Kınalızade defines the different kinds of love, which vary in their intensity and in the motives underlying the relations between the parties to several superior–subordinate relationships, such as God–believer, father–son, husband–wife, and ruler–subjects. He states:

> There are two kinds of love: natural and voluntary. While the love of a mother for her child is natural, the love of a novice for his/her master is considered an example of the voluntary kind.⁷³

He then continues by classifying voluntary love into four sub-forms in terms of their durability:

> the one that is swift to contract and dissolve, the one that is slow to contract but swift to dissolve, the one that is swift to contract and slow to dissolve, and the one that is slow to contract and to dissolve.⁷⁴

The ideal form is that which is swift to develop and slow to dissolve. Furthermore, he defines the motives underlying love as pleasure (*lezzet*), benefit (*nef'*), and good (*hayr*).⁷⁵

In Kınalızade's virtuous city, where order is established, *hayr* is the motive behind the noblest and highest love and has no underlying selfish expectation of reward or material gain; furthermore, it is swift to contract and slow to dissolve. It mirrors the term *fi-sebilillah*, used in Ottoman daily language, which means "in the name of God" with no expected compensation. Love with a motive of pure good is further divided into four types.

> The first one is love for God, the source of which is goodness and happiness. The second one is love for one's own master, as masters teach righteous behavior and good ethics. The third one is love for one's parents and ancestors because they are the reason for one's existence and the source of one's values, either inherited from or taught by them. The fourth is love of a subject for his/her ruler. For some people, the last one can rank even higher than a son's love for his father.⁷⁶

---

⁷² Tezcan, "The Definition of Sultanic Legitimacy," 94–95. Tezcan argues that although this section on love is placed within the political part of the book by Kınalızade, as well as by Devvani and Tusi, it was originally part of Miskawayh's *Tezhibü'l Ahlak*. Tezcan's comparision of the three texts shows that Kınalızade closely follows Tusi and Devvani in his discussion of love.

⁷³ Koç, ed., *Ahlak-ı Ala'i*, 415: "Amma insanda olan mahabbet iki nev'dir: Biri tabi'i, biri iradidir: Tabi'i, maderin ferzendine mahabbeti gibi. Mahabbet-i iradi, müte'allimin mu'allimme, müridin şeyhine mahabbeti gibi."

⁷⁴ Ibid.

⁷⁵ Ibid.: "Ve sebeb-i mahabbet dahi üç nesnedir. Evveli lezzet, ikincisi nef, üçüncüsü hayrdır."

⁷⁶ Ibid., 433.

However, for Kınalızade, deviations from the ideal always exist. Love that is not induced by pure good requires the intervention of justice. He gives several examples of relations in which either the motivations of the parties are different or relationships consist solely of pleasure and benefit. He offers the following example:

> If one party's love is induced for pleasure while the other's is for benefit, the relation would incur complaints and reprimand, and that is why this kind of love is termed "reproachful love" (*mahabbet-i levvame*). If [the] love between the sultan and his subjects, the rich and the poor, the servant and the served belongs to this type, the relation may not be free of complaints and oppression, since each party would want to benefit from the other. The oppression and complaints of the one who is being served would demand continuous service.[77]

In another section, Kınalızade explains the reasons for a subject's submission:

> The source of love of subjects for their ruler may be to obtain their prosperity through the sultan's benevolence and favors. Love and loyalty of subjects for those rulers who do not oppress and transgress is apparent. It is especially apparent for those sultans who decorate their crowns of wisdom with good government. If a sultan conjoins this with justice and kindness, refrains from oppression, unites with his subjects in their faith, protects the weak, and is a friend of dervishes, subjects' love would transcend simple love (*mahabbet*) and reach a deeper level of love (*meveddet*), and they would become as submissive to their sultan as are God's slaves.[78]

In its normative and idealized form, then, subjects' submission to their rulers, as Kınalızade highlights, should mirror their love of God, as if they were God's slaves. In such cases, a subject's love reaches the level of *meveddet*, which also means love, but apparently denotes a different and a deeper one.

---

[77] Ibid., 428–9: "Bir tarafdan menfa'at, aherden lezzet sebebi olan mahabbete şekva vü itab çok olur ... Ve bu makule mahabbete 'mahabbet-i levvame' derler, levmden hali olmadığı için. Ve padişah u rai'yyet ve gani vü fakir ve hadim ü mahdum aralarında mahabbet bu kısmdadır. Şekva ve tazallümden hali değildir, zira her biri aherden bir nev' menfa'at ister. Muradı üzere olmıycak şekva vü tazallüm zahir olur. Ve adalet ri'ayet olmayınca bu şekva vü tazallüm mürtefi' olmaz. Mahdum, hadimden hidmette devam ve hazrette kıyam ve ihmal ü tekasülden gayet ictinab ve fehm-i garaz ve tahsil-i meramda nihayette ihtimam ister. Hadim riayet-i me'akil ü melabis ü merakibinde nihayet-i inayet tama' eder."

[78] Ibid., 431: "Re'ayanın selatine mahabbeti saye-i inayetlerinde müreffehü'l hal ve fevazıl-ı in'amlarından müna'amü'l-bal oldukları içindir. Ve selatin—ki ifrat-ı cevr ü zulmle mevsuf olmayalar—re'ayadan anlara ifrat-ı mahabbet ve nihayet-i sadakat mukarrerdir, hususen ki bir nesl-i şerif nice zeman vilayetde tac-ı hikmetlerini gevher-i hükumetle murassa' etmiş ola. Eğer, ziver-i adl ü insafla ittisaf ve mezheb-i zulm ü i'tisaftan inhiraf edip mezheb-i hakk ri'ayetinde re'ayasıyla hem-kiş ve zu'afa-yı zir-destlerini hıfz u hiraset edip mu'in-i gani ve muhibb-i derviş ola, mahabbet dayiresinden geçip sıdk-ı rıkıyyet ü meveddet mertebesini koyup hakk-ı ubudiyyet üzere olurlar."

Kınalızade's text details not only the expected moral behavior of rulers and subjects in his virtuous city, where political order has been achieved, but also the expected emotion of *mahabbet* to be felt and displayed by political actors towards one another, although not with the same intensity or in the same manner. In this sense, it mirrors the concept of Stearn's "emotionology." From the perspective of emotionology, in an idealized political order, the motives underlying love are therefore expected to be pure good for both parties, and the absence of such good must be remediated by justice. The emotion of love was codified into the reciprocal relationship between superiors and subordinates as mirroring the relationship between God and believers. Indeed, emotions were central not only to the Ottoman Empire but to all early modern monarchies.[79] They constituted the basis for the relations between rulers and subjects in early modern monarchies because the fatherly love of the ruler for his subjects mirrored God's love for His believers; and subjects and believers had a reciprocal duty to love God and their ruler.[80]

Concluding Remarks

In this chapter, I have shown that the emotion of compassion provided the meaning of the concept of protection. Compassion was a hierarchical emotion, always expressed by superiors to subordinates, and for subordinates there were norms specified as to when and in which cases it was appropriate to demand compassion from their protector. In the early modern setting of the Ottoman Empire, in which the state was personified with the body of the ruler, emotional codes of compassion (*merhamet*) and mutual love (*mahabbet*) were culturally and historically significant during the period between the sixteenth and the nineteenth centuries. Each of them had its own norms as to when, to whom, and how it should be displayed, and also acted as a tool to formulate political relations of domination and subordination. Both emotions provided

---

[79] See for example, Alejandro Caneque, "The Emotions of Power: Love, Anger and Fear, or How to Rule the Spanish Empire," in *Emotions and Daily Life in Colonial Mexico*, ed. Javier Villa-Flores and Sonya Lipsett-Rivera (Albuquerque: New Mexico University Press, 2014) for emotions in colonial Mexico and how emotions of love, anger, and fear played a decisive role in the polity. Caneque also highlights that it was the mutual love between the ruler and the ruled that was seen as the emotion fundamentally defining political relations, as an emotion that most guaranteed the peace, tranquility, and security of the community in the setting of early modern Spanish Empire.

[80] Helen Watanabe-O'Kelly, "Monarchies," in *Early Modern Emotions: An Introduction*, ed. Susan Broomhall (London: Routledge, 2017): 179–82.

the contested meaning of protection and it seems that the Ottomans not only considered them as innate but also believed that they could be trained and disciplined. Compassion and love were both political and social.

To capture the experience of being protected, I also took an etic approach in this chapter. We know that the experience of reality is multisensorial. In other words, without being seen, heard, touched, tasted and smelled, material reality cannot be interpreted.[81] Like written and spoken languages, images, sounds, smells, tastes, and movements are cultivated into meaningful sign systems that form the media through which concepts are communicated, shaped, and changed. The metaphoric expression of "uniting with the hearts" of the subjects (*telif-i kulüb*) provided the verbal image of the concept of protection and thus a multisensory experience to the concept of "protection," making it more plausible. The term *istimalet* was another emotion meaning affection, sincerity, and propensity and indeed related to the metaphor of uniting with the hearts of the subjects. *İstimalet*, too, was one of the emotional codes of protection. As this chapter has confirmed, drawing on archival sources, expressions of emotions did not appear only as a rhetoric to persuade or sometimes deceive the subjects. All of the terms also manifested themselves in the political undertakings of the state. The emotional codes consisted of compassion, love, and affection in political relations between the ruler and the ruled, with metaphors providing the sensations of this relationship. Regarding the question of what it *meant* and how it *felt* like to protect and be protected, these emotion codes provided the meaning of protection.

---

[81] Pernau and Rajamani, "Emotional Translations," 49.

3

Emotions in Intracommunal Relations: *Rıza* and *Şükran*

In this chapter I focus on communal relations in neighborhoods as spatial communities and in guilds as occupational communities, again in an attempt to understand what it *meant* and how it *felt* to be protected by community members. How did Ottoman neighborhood and guild communities in the seventeenth and eighteenth centuries conceptualize communal relations in a world of differences in social and legal status, wealth, faith, ethnicity, and settlement practices? How could they themselves bridge the pre-existing boundaries, be they spatial, legal, religious, ethnic, or occupational? How did they define the boundaries of their own communities? What was the common principle bonding the members of each community? What was the key to the co-existence of members with different secondary identities in one community, be it a neighborhood community (*mahalle cemaati*) or a guild community (*esnaf taifesi*)? I start with a brief explanation of sub-communities in the Ottoman Empire and discuss how historians interpreted intracommunal relations so far.

Since the judicial court case records indicate that people recurrently expressed in the testimonies either the presence or absence of *rıza*, and *şükran*, whether in answers to questions about the conduct of their fellows or in collective demands for the expulsion of their fellows from their communities, in the next section I carry out a lexicological and contextual analysis of these two terms. I claim that both neighborhood and guild communities resemble Rosenwein's "emotional communities," defined as "social communities who share the same or similar valuations of particular emotions, goals, and norms of emotional expression."[1] This term is a useful analytical starting point for exploring how community

---

[1] Rosenwein and Cristiani, *What Is the History of Emotions?*, 4.

members themselves configured their communal relations.[2] Rosenwein proposes that scholars "uncover these systems of feeling that they value, and seek the evaluations that they make about others' emotions, the nature of the affective bonds between people that they recognize, and the modes of emotional expression that they expect, encourage, tolerate, and deplore." In other words, emotional communities were (and are) groups of people who share the same or similar valuations of particular emotions, goals, and norms of emotional expression.[3] I will therefore call Ottoman neighborhood and guild communities "domains of gratitude" as a starting point, and use it as a heuristic device to better understand the emotional dimension of intracommunal relations. Both Ottoman neighborhood and guild communities prioritized feelings of gratitude in configuring their communal relations. In the next section, I analyze another commonly used term, *kendü halinde olmak*, which may roughly be translated from modern Turkish as *being on one's own*, which I claim represented sensations underlying their understanding of protection, which evidences that sensations were also important in drawing the boundaries of their communities. Then I analyze cases of expulsions from the communities that provide insights as to how the societies themselves regulated intracommunal relations. Cases of expulsion, from a backward reading, also enable one to trace the norms and understand the processes before appealing to courts for expulsion. In the final section, I discuss emotions as practices, giving examples from judicial court records, and claim that emotions were represented in their practices, which provided meaning to their particular understanding of protection.

Sub-communities in Ottoman Society

Ottoman society was composed of different sub-communities labeled either *cemaat* or *taife*, depending on their legal, religious, ethnic, spatial, and occupational identities. Both of the terms, *cemaat* and *taife*, mean *community*, *assembly* or *a body of people*, and the terms could be used interchangeably. *Rum cemaati* refers to the Greek community, *mahalle cemaati* to a neighborhood

---

[2] Rosenwein, *Emotional Communities in the Early Middle Ages*, 25. She further argues that "they are in some ways what Foucault called a common 'discourse': shared vocabularies and ways of thinking that have a controlling function, a disciplining function, and are also similar as well to Bourdieu's notion of 'habitus'; internalized norms that determine how we think and act and that may be different in different groups."
[3] Rosenwein and Cristiani, *What Is the History of Emotions?*, 4.

community, *efrenc taifesi* to Europeans, *nas taifesi* to females, and *taife-i zükur* to males. The terms were revealing for any type of community. Although any community would be referred to as *cemaat* or *taife*, the terms *millet* or *fırka* could also be used, especially in reference to religious identities. The main spatial settlement unit in the cities were neighborhoods (*mahalle*) and the subjects of such communities (*mahalle cemaati*) were spatially identified by their neighborhood. Occupationally, city residents' identities depended on the specific non-agricultural production unit or guild (*hirfet*) to which each belonged (for example, the bread-baking community, *ekmekçi taifesi*).

These communities, however, were not isolated from one another. Any Ottoman subject could simultaneously be a member of more than one community. People of different faiths could be members of the same residential settlement, *mahalle*. A Muslim, a Christian, or a Jew could at the same time be a member of a specific occupational group. Throughout their lives, Ottoman subjects would pray in their place of worship with other members of their faith in the morning, then work in the afternoon as a part of a specific production unit along with colleagues from different faiths. Thus, one's religious identity did not determine one's occupational or spatial identity. In this respect, we may regard Ottoman society as transitive, allowing room for mobility within various overlapping and intertwined sub-communities. Moreover, both residents of a neighborhood and the members of a guild were expected to act as sureties for one another. Acting as surety included both a guarantee for the value of a thing (*kefil bi'l mal*) representing the material guarantee, and also a security for the person of another (*kefil bi'n nefs*) representing a guarantee for another's character and behavior. Since community members were expected to act as each other's sureties, the community had the right to expel members of a community. Indeed, judicial court registers are filled with cases in which community members came to court to demand the expulsion of other community members; this has been a topic of interest for many Ottoman historians.[4]

Historians have long tried to attribute co-existence either to the successful promulgation of the rules and regulations of the state or to the state's flexible and

---

[4] See, for example, Özer Ergenç, "Osmanlı Şehrindeki Mahallenin İşlevleri ve Nitelikleri Üzerine," in *Osmanlı Tarihi Yazıları Şehir, Toplum, Devlet*, ed. Derya Önder (İstanbul: Tarih Vakfı Yurt Yayınları, 2012): 75–85; Andre Raymond, *Osmanlı Döneminde Arap Kentleri*, trans. Ali Berktay (İstanbul: Tarih Vakfı Yurt Yayınları, 1995); Nurcan Abacı, *Bursa Şehrinde Osmanlı Hukukunun Uygulanması (17. Yüzyıl)* (Ankara: Kültür Bakanlığı Yayınları, 2001); Özen Tok, "Kadı Sicilleri Işığında Osmanlı Şehrindeki Mahalleden İhraç Kararlarında Mahalle Ahalisinin Rolü (XVII.ve XVIII. Yüzyıllarda Kayseri Örneği)," *Sosyal Bilimler Enstitüsü Dergisi* 18, no. 1 (2005): 155–73; James E. Baldwin, "Prostitution, Islamic Law and Ottoman Societies," *Journal of the Economic and Social History of the Orient* 55 (2012): 117–52.

pragmatic approach to its diverse population. A purely structuralist approach to history would assume that people followed and internalized the rules of the state. Some historians, on the other hand, focused on communities' social norms. While individuals were free to follow their own religious practices, it was expected that they would conform to the social norms of their community, which were monitored closely by the community itself. Each community had its distinct norms prescribing righteous behavior. For the guilds, apart from orally transmitted standards, there were also written manuals of conduct, *fütüvvetname*s, which also served as standards for becoming an exemplary member. *Fütüvvetnames* include topics ranging from guiding principles for complete and utter selflessness, unlimited generosity, hospitality, and tolerance of other people's faults to guild rules, regulations, and rituals. They acted as a moral and spiritual guide for the members of the community.[5] Social norms of neighborhoods, on the other hand, were transmitted orally from generation to generation with no written records; however, residents were well aware of these norms. According to this narrative, individuals followed these prescriptions, since any deviation could result in discipline, punishment, or social exclusion. One was either born into a neighborhood community or started one's early career as an apprentice in a guild, which would demand years of hardship devoted to learning the secrets of a specific craft. Members of communities would learn the legal, religious, and social norms throughout their lives and act accordingly within these pre-existing structures. Moreover, historians assumed that individuals obeyed social norms for their own material and political interests only.

Two things are missing in this structuralist approach to history. First, the link between norms and actual behavior is not clear. Why and how did people follow norms? Secondly, this approach assumes that material interests alone motivate human behavior. Such an approach tends to ignore emotions, regarding them as irrational brute reflexes, without any effort to understand whether emotions had an impact on how people understood, interpreted, and instantiated these norms. There is no room for emotion in a structuralist narrative, mirroring what Lisa Feldman Barrett identifies as a "classical view" of emotions.[6]

If we put aside the dichotomy between emotion and reason, however, and take a closer look at communal relations by starting to take words of emotions

---

[5] Ines Asceric-Todd, "The Noble Traders: The Islamic Tradition of 'Spiritual Chivalry' (*futuwwa*) in Bosnian Trade-guilds (16th–19th centuries)," *The Muslim World*, volume 97 (2007): 159–173, http://doi.org.10.1111/j.1478-1913.2007.00168.x.

[6] Barrett, *How Emotions Are Made*, xi.

into consideration, we find a richer view of our current understanding of communities, and a better explanation of how they defined the boundaries of their communities. Such an approach enables one to understand what it *meant* and how it *felt* to be a protected (or not) member of their communities, since one's survival depended on being a protected member of their communities.

Neighborhoods and Guilds as "Domains of Gratitude"

In a case dated December 28, 1683,[7] some neighborhood community members approached a court and claimed that they no longer wanted to share their communal space with an individual named Ahmed. Ahmed had been accused of deviating from the social norms of his community through his misconduct and intrigues, and his failure to comply with community standards was expressed in the form "we do not have *rıza* and *şükran* to this Ahmed" (*rıza ve şükran üzere değilleriz*). People recurrently expressed either the lack or the presence of "*rıza* and *şükran*" for their fellow members in their testimonies.

Although the term *rıza* in modern Turkish refers to approval only, in a religious context, it is interpreted to mean satisfaction or perfect contentment with God's will or decree. According to Annemarie Schimmel, the author of *Mystical Dimensions of Islam*, *rıza* is closely related to *şükran*, or gratitude, another virtue within Islam.[8] Apparently the term suggested a sense of being pleased and satisfied, unlike today's meaning. Indeed, in court records, the word *hoşnud*, which literally means a feeling of being pleased, is used interchangeably with *rıza*.

Şükran or *şükr*, on the other hand, means thankfulness, gratitude, and acknowledgment; it also carries the meaning of praise, which is the verbal expression of gratitude. As a religious and mystical concept, it refers to an internal state and its external expression. *Şükr* on the part of God signifies "requiting and commending [a person]," "forgiving" a man: or "regarding" him "with content, satisfaction, good will," or "favor": and hence, necessarily, "recompensing," or "rewarding him." As a factor in public life and as a legal principle, in early Arabic, the term seemed to refer to a public proclamation of gratitude or debt. In later Arabic, the term also referred to the affective state of

---

[7] Hülya Taş, "XVII. Yüzyılda Ankara" (PhD diss., Ankara Üniversitesi, Ankara, 2004): 251. Quoted from Ankara Judicial Court Records (JCR) 64: 167.
[8] "Rida," *Encyclopedia of Islam* (2nd edn) (Leiden, The Netherlands: Brill, 2010).

feeling grateful, which is usually tied to the concepts of *nimet* (benefaction) and *rıza* (contentment/satisfaction).[9]

Both terms, which were always expressed together, refer to feelings of being thankful, pleased, grateful, contented and satisfied. Members of both neighborhoods and guilds defined the boundaries of their communities themselves and included some members, while excluding others, and it seems that they expressed either the presence or absence of their communal feelings of pleasure and gratitude linguistically in the judicial court records. These terms, however, never appeared in court cases as personal expressions of feelings, but rather as communal feelings directed towards either one or more members of their own community. Even if asked by the judge, the word "I" does not appear in the response. Rather, the community refers to itself collectively as "we," as in "*we* do not feel contentment, *we* do not feel gratitude." Mirroring Rosenwein's "emotional communities," I label neighborhoods and guild communities as "domains of gratitude." These feelings seem to be the most important element in a community's emotional script. In this sense, Ottoman neighborhoods and guilds were pre-existing structures whose members valued, encouraged, and enacted expressions of contentment and gratitude when cultivating communal relations.

Reconstructing any emotion in history means contextualizing the expression of emotions, understanding the cultural significance and meaning of emotional concepts, and recognizing the signs that characterize the emotional script of a society or group. The court records elaborated on the social meaning of emotional terms and the contexts in which it was appropriate for community members to express either the presence or absence of gratitude towards their fellows. What was the role of such emotional expression and when, where, and to whom was it appropriate to express it? What were the constraints imposed by being someone whom other members of the community were thankful to and pleased with?

We encounter the phrase *rıza ve şükran* frequently, not only in spatial communities such as neighborhoods, but also in guilds. This was also an expression widely used by the guild members about those who were considered to be a part (or not) of their community. From an Istanbul court record dating from the seventeenth century, for example, we learn that Hacı Ahmed, a member of a guild for makers of *şariye* (a kind of cloth made of animal hair—*kıl*) in İstanbul, came to court and demanded that his own conduct be investigated and cleared, since the leader of his guild had shut down his workshop and prohibited

[9] Ibid., "Shukr."

him from practicing his occupation. Witnesses from his own guild and several other individuals from different guilds (most likely, spatially adjacent ones) confirmed that Ahmed offended no one, showed expertise in his craft, and thus posed no harm to others. Moreover, they stated that they all felt contentment and gratitude towards Hacı Ahmed (*şakir ve razılarız*).[10]

Judicial court cases show that protection by one's community was crucial for one's survival. This mirrors the concept of a ruler's protection of his subjects as those entrusted to him by God, the Almighty, as discussed in the previous chapter. The norms for being a pleasing and gratifying member were so strict that anyone who deviated could face multiple penalties including expulsion, demotion from leadership positions, false allegations, the loss of support of the community in the event of oppression by government officials, or the loss of credibility in the eyes of one's neighbors. In other words, being a member of an emotional community and demonstrating a willingness to conform to community standards served as a protective shield. Thus, the emotions of *rıza* and *şükran* provided meaning to the concept of protection.

For example, in a case record dating from the seventeenth century,[11] the non-Muslim members of a *dimici* (a tightly woven cotton fabric) guild, Geromi, Yani,

---

[10] Timur Kuran, ed. *Mahkeme Kayıtları Işığında 17. Yüzyıl İstanbul'unda Sosyo-Ekonomik Yaşam.* V:1. *Esnaf ve Loncalar, Hıristiyan ve Yahudi Cemaat İşleri, Yabancılar* (İstanbul: İş Bankası Kültür Yayınları, 2010): 266–7. Quoted from İstanbul JCR 16: 92a/4; "Mahmiyye-i İstanbul'da olan şa'riyeci taifesinin ihtiyarlarından Hacı Ahmed bin Hacı Ali nam kimesne meclis-i şer'de takrir-i kelam ve ta'bir-i ani'l-meram idüb ben kendi halimde olub san'atımda kusurum olmayub kimesneye zararın yok iken halen kethüdamız olan Hacı Uhyel nam kimesne bi-gayr-ı vech mahmiyye-i mezburede Tahte'l-Kal'a'da vaki karhanemi kapayub beni işlemeden men' itmişdir keyfiyet-i halim etrafımda olan dekakin ashabı ve taife-i mezbureden sual olunub haberleri tahrir ve yedime hüccet virilmek muradımdır didikde mezbur Hacı Ahmed'in keyfiyet-i hali etrafında olan dekakin ahvalinden olup hazirun-ı bi'l-meclis olan attar el-Hac Abdi bin Yusuf ve tabib es-Seyyid Ahmed Çelebi ibn es-Seyyid Şaban ve ... Mehmed bin Hacı Ali ve bazarcı Mehmed bin Ebubekir ve Attar Hacı Mehmed bin Yusuf ve fesci Mehmed bin Hacı Ahmed ve attar Mehmed bin Cafer ve taife-i mezbureden Hacı Ali bin Ömer ve Hacı Ali bin Hamza ve Hacı Ahmed ve Hacı Ahmed bin Hacı Mehmed ve Hacı Selim bin hacı Mehmed ve Hacı Mehmed bin Ivaz ve Hacı Mehmed bin Şaban ve Ömer bin Şehab bin Cezzar ve Hacı Cemal ibn el-Hac Şehade ve Ali Hacı Ali ibn Sultan nam kimesnelerden mezbur Hacı Mehmed'in keyfiyet-i hali sual olundukda her biri mezbur Hacı Ahmed içün kendi halinde olub san'atında kusuru ve kimesneye zararı olmayub her vechle halinden şakir ve razılarız deyu hüsn-i hal virdiklerinde ma-vaka'a bi't-taleb ketb olundu fi'l-yevmi'l-işrin min Saferi'L-hayr li-sene sitte ve sebine ve elf."

[11] Taylan Akyıldırım, "259 Numaralı Şeriyye icili Defterine göre Galata (Metin ve Değerlendirme)" (MA diss., Mimar Sinan Güzel Sanatlar Üniversitesi, İstanbul, 2010): 374–5. Quoted from Galata JCR 281: 32; "Mahrusa-i Galata ve tevabiinde vaki dimici taifesinden Geromi veled-i Melike ve Yani veled-i Manol ve Melike veled-i Geromi ve Vesnci veled-i Bati ve Corci veled-i Cani ve Frankovi veled-i Todori ve Anton veled-i Pepi nam zimmiler ve sairleri meclis-i şer'de hala beynlerinde kethüda nasb ve tayin eyledikleri işbu rafiü'l-rakim Yani veled-i Manol nam zimmi muvacehesinde her biri ikrar ve takrir-i kelam ide idüb kadimü'l-eyyamdan bu ana gelince umurumuzu rü'yet içün beynimizde bir kethüda nasb u tayin olunageldüb ve hala kethüdamız olan işbu hazırbi'l-meclis Nikola veled-i Manol nam zimminin evza u etvarından cümlemiz hoşnud ve razılar olmadığımız cihetle merkum Nikola'yı ihrac ve yerine merkum Yani'yi beynimizde bi'l-ittifak kethüda nasb u tayin ve ihtiyar eyledik dediklerinde merkum Yani dahi ber vech-i muharrer kethüdalığı kabul ve mahallinde hidemat-ı lazımesini ikamete taahhüd itmeğin ma-hüvel-vaki bi'l-ibtiga ketb olundu. Fi'l-yevmi's-sani ve'l-işrin min Zi'l-kadeti'ş-şerife li sene 1137."

Melike, Vesnci, Corci, Frankovi, and Anton came to the court, and in the presence of Yani, who was their chosen leader, alleged that although Nikola had been their chosen leader for some time, they were no longer pleased with him and did not feel contentment. Therefore, they demanded that Nikola be expelled from his post as administrator and Yani be appointed as their new and unanimously elected leader. The group requested that the decision be recorded when Yani agreed to become their leader and carry out the requirements of his new duty. Court registers are full of similar cases providing evidence of group members demanding the dismissal of their leaders and the subsequent expression of their emotions of contentment and gratitude while doing so.

In a case record dated February 28, 1736,[12] community members in Konya witnessed the good conduct of one of their members, while also declaring the misconduct of a woman from another community. In this case, Hadice, who was a visitor to Konya from the village of Gök Osmanlı, made a claim against Gökman Osman, Demirci Mehmed, and Kibaroğlu Mehmed and stated in their presence that the preceding day, while she was passing through the cemetery, these three men had forcefully seized her and taken her to their house in the Sadırlar quarter, where they held her overnight. She wanted them to be questioned in the light of the law and asked that their conduct be examined. For the inquiry into the men's character, witnesses from their own quarter were questioned. The witnesses, however, verified that they were pleased with them and had feelings of contentment and that they could act as guarantors for their conduct. The

---

[12] İzzet Sak and İbrahim Solak, *53 Numaralı Konya Şer'iye Sicili (1148–1149/1736–1737) Transkripsiyon ve Dizin* (Konya: Selçuk Üniversitesi, 2014): 47. Quoted from Konya JCR 53: 20/5; 'Medine-i Konya sancağında Gök Osmanlı Karyesi'nden olub medine-i mezburede misafirenten sakine ve zatı bi'l-marifet-i şer'iyye muarefe olan Hadice bint-i Hüseyin nam hatun meclis-i şer'-i hatıra refi'iyyü'l-kitab Gökman Osman bin Mehmed ve Demirci Mehmed bin Mehmed ile Kibaroğlu Mehmed nam kimesneler mahzarlarında üzerlerine dava ve takrir-i kelam idüb tarih-i kitabdan bir gün mukaddem menzilhane kurbunda mezaristandan geçüb giderken mezburan Osman ve Mehmed ve diğer Mehmed beni cebren ve kahren ahz ve mezbur Demirci Mehmed ve diğer Mehmed'in Sadırlar Mahallesi'Nde vaki menziline götürüb bir gün ve bir gece habs ve tasarruf eylediler sual olunub mezburunun keyfiyet-i ahvalleri mahalleleri ahalisinden istihbar olundukda mezburun Demirci Mehmed ve Gökman Osman ve Kibar Mehmed kendü hallerinde eyü ademlerdir ve cümlemiz kendülerinden hoşnud ve razılarız ahvallerine dahi tekeffül ideriz deyu mezburun Demirci Mehmed ve Gökman Osman ve Kibar Mehmed'in hüsn-i hallerini ve mezbure Hadice Konya ahalisinden olmayub ahardan kazadan fuhş ile meşhure ve na-mahremden ictinabı dahi olmamağla tarih-i mezkurede mahalle-i mezbure Sadırlar'da vaki mezbur Demirci Mehmed'in menzlinden mezbure Hadice'nin hurucunu bi'l-muayene müşahede eyledik deyu mezbure Hadice'nin su-i halini mahalle-i mezbure ahalilerinden olub zeyl-i vesikada muharrerü'l-esami müslimin ala tariki'ş-şehade haber virmeleriyle ma-hüve'l-vaki hıfzen li'l-makal bi't-taleb ketb olundu. 15 şevval 1148/28 February 1736.'

witnesses further stated that Hadice, the plaintiff was not from Konya, but had come from another district and was notorious for her prostitution, and that she did not resist those who were defined canonically as strangers. They also stated that they had witnessed her leaving the defendants' house. In this case, it is apparent that the community members considered the defendants to be blameless and good people. Their emotions were again linguistically expressed with the combined phrases of gratitude and feelings of contentment. We do not know whether Hadice, who was from another district, was indeed a prostitute or not. However, this case indicates that as an outsider, she was excluded from their domain of gratitude and that one could encounter false allegations in a community outside of one's own domain of gratitude.

A case dated February 25, 1736[13] confirmed the importance of being a part of a domain of gratitude and the dangers of wandering outside one's domain. Şerife Fatıma, a woman from the quarter of Şekerfürüş, brought a claim in court against Şatıroğlu Süleyman, a resident of the Abdülaziz quarter, making the following allegation: "This Süleyman invited me to his house and requested me to tailor for the wife of İnce Mustafa, who was not present in the court. When I entered Süleyman's house in the quarter of Abdülaziz, they both approached me, and I screamed. When the neighbors came to help me get out of the house, Süleyman and Mustafa ran away." However, the defendants denied her claim. The judge then questioned community members about the defendants' conduct. The witnesses, however, said only that they had witnessed Şerife Fatma leaving the house and the defendants escaping from the roof of

---

[13] Sak and Solak, *53 Numaralı Konya Şer'iye Sicili*, 38. Quoted from Konya JCR 53: 17/1; "Mahmiye-i Konya'da Şekerfürüş Mahallesi sükkanından zatı bi'l-marifeti'ş-şer'iyye muarefe olan Şerife Fatıma bint-i Mehmed Beşe nam hatun meclis-i şer'-i hatir-i lazımü't-tevkirde Abdülaziz Mahallesi sükkanından Şatıroğlu Süleyman nam kimesnenin mahzarında üzerine da'va ve takrr-i kelam idüb mezbur Süleyman gayib-i ani'l-meclis İnce Mustafa nam kimesnenin zevcesi benim esvabım vardır kesiverin deyu mahalle-i mezbure Abdülaziz'de vaki menziline beni davet edib ben dahi mezbur Mustafa'nın menziline vardığımda mezbur İnce Mustafa ile benim üzerime gelib ben dahi feryad eylediğimde mahalle-i mezbure ahalileri gelib beni menzil-i mezburdan çıkarub ve mezburan Süleyman ve Mustafa firar eylediler idi sual olunsun didikde gıbbe's-sual mezbur Süleyman mezbure Şerife Fatma'nın takrir-i meşruhunu bi'l-külliye inkar idicek mahalle-i mezbure Abdülaziz ahalisinden merkum Süleyman ile gayib-i merkum İnce Mustafa'nın keyfiyet-i ahvalleri sual olundukda ber-vech-i muharrer merkum Süleyman ile gayib-i merkum İnce Mustafa menzil-i mezburun damından firar eylediklerini ve mezbure Şerife Fatıma'nın dahi menzil-i mezburdan hurucunu bi'l-muayene müşahede eyledük deyu mahalle-i mezbure Abdülaziz ahalisinden olub zeyl- vesikada muharrerü'l-esami müslimin haber virmeleriyle mezbur Süleyman ile merkume Şerife Fatma'nın tazirine tenbih bir le ma-vaka'a bi't-taleb ketb olundu. 12 şevval 1148/25 February 1736."

the house. The judge then demanded that both Süleyman and Şerife Fatma be punished. It seems that Şerife could not successfully prove that she was indeed a praiseworthy member of her own community, since she was attacked outside of her domain of gratitude. However, another court case report from the same day reported on the same dispute, providing further details about the episode.[14] In this second case, Şerife Fatma, having been found guilty, now demanded that her own conduct be questioned by both members of her own community as well as residents of the Abdülaziz quarter, who emphasized her status as a skilled craftsperson in tailoring. These witnesses offered testimony that she was a pious, respectable, honest, upright, and good person. We do not know for sure, but it is likely that after having validated her good conduct, Şerife Fatma would have escaped the legal sanctions arising from her previous case. This case shows that one was protected only within a domain in which one had established affective ties. Once outside one's domain of gratitude, one would be vulnerable to accusations of false allegations.

For community members, the expression of feelings of gratitude and contentment was like a secret code, with everybody well aware of its rules. At the same time, expression of the emotions of *rıza* and *şükran* were tools for effective communication. A domain of gratitude represents an imagined domain where affective ties are established among members, and the presence of such ties are linguistically defined, labeled, and named as expression of feelings of contentment and gratitude. Expressing the presence (or absence) of feelings of contentment and gratitude for any member of the community would officially symbolize the community's acceptance (or rejection) of that member, and thus recognize them as being under protection of the community.

---

[14] Sak and Solak, *53 Numaralı Konya Şer'iye Sicili'*, 42. Quoted from Konya JCR 53: 18/4; "Mahmiye-i Konya'da Şekerfüruş Mahallesi sakinelerinden zatı bi'l-marifeti'ş-şer'iyye muarefe olan Şerife Fatıma bint-i Mehmed Beşe nam hatun meclis-i şer'-i hatırda takrir-i kelam idüb, tarih-i kitabdan bir gün mukaddem Abdülaziz Mahallesi sakinlerinden İnce Mustafa nam kimesnenin zevcesi benim esvabım vardır kesiverin deyu beni menziline davet edib benim dahi terzilik sanatım olmağla menzil-i mezbura vardığımda mezbur İnce Mustafa ile Şatıroğlu Mustafa benim üzerime gelib ben dahi feryad eylediğimde mahalle-i mezbure ahalileri feryadıma yetişüb beni tahlis ve mezburan Mustafa ve Süleyman firar eylemişler idi mahalle-i mezbure ahalilerinden ve benim mahallem ahalilerinden keyfiyet-i ahvalim sual olunub takrirleri tahrir olunmak matlubumdr didikde mezbure Şerife Fatma'nın mahallesi ahalisinden el-Hac Abdullah bin Osman Efendi ve el-Hac Ahmed bin Hacı Mahmud ve İmam Molla Said ve Ali Bey nam kimesneler li-ecli'l-ihbar meclis-i şer'a hazırun ve istihbar olunduklarında fi'l-vaki mezbure Şerife Fatma'nın yedinde terzilik sanatı olub kendü halinde ehl-i ırz dindar ve müstakime eyü hatundur deyu mezburun ve mahalle-i mezbure Abdülaziz mahallesinden olub zeyl-i vesikada muharrerü'l-esami müslimin mezbure Şerife Fatma'nın hüsn-i halini her biri ala tariki'ş-şehade habir virmeleri ma hüve'l-vaki bi't-taleb ketb olundu. 12 şevval 1148/25 şubat 1736."

Sensations and Drawing the Boundaries of Communities: *Kendü halinde olmak*

What is also striking in judicial court records is the recurrent use of the phrase *kendü halinde olmak*, which would be interpreted in contemporary Turkish as someone who is detached, who does not interfere with others, and perhaps who is careful to mind their own business. Some historians have translated the term as *law-abiding*, some as *trustworthy*, *well-behaved*, or *virtuous*. None of these translations, I would argue, give the right meaning. Contextualization of the phrase shows that this term referred to neither being detached from the world, nor law-abiding.

In a case record from Bursa, a city in northwest Anatolia, the expulsion of a member of a guild was demanded since he was not *kendü halinde*, was frequently familiar (*ülfet*) with those who were vile (*erazil*) and disgraced (*nikbet*), and was usually walking around drunk with a weapon in his hand and could not escape being vicious (*alet-i harb ile sekran geşt-i güzar ve fısk ve fesaddan hali olmamağla*).[15]

A case recorded on August 16, 1698, in the judicial court register of Bursa,[16] offers insight into the relationship between a woman and the residents of the quarter she lived in. In the case, Mehmed Emin Efendi, who was the *imam* (religious leader) of Zağfiranlık quarter of Bursa, and several others from the same quarter came to the court and claimed that a certain woman from the same quarter, Edibe, was not *kendi halinde* (chaste) and did not refrain from associating with those who were canonically defined as strangers (*namahrem*), adding that she was also long-tongued (*medidü'l-lisan*). Despite several previous warnings by community members, she would not correct her behavior. Thus, they collectively demanded her expulsion from their quarter.

---

[15] Bursa JCR B166: 61/4.
[16] Bursa JCR B166: 60; "Medine-i Brusa'da Zağfiranlık mahallesi ahalisinden işbu ashabü'l-kitab imam Mehmed Emin Efendi ibn El-Hac İbrahim ve Abdullahzade İbrahim Ağa ve Abdülkadir bin Cafer ve Molla İbrahim bin Mehmed ve Molla Abdullah bin Mustafa ve Es-Seyyid Molla Bektaş bin Es-Seyyid Hüseyin ve Molla İbrahim bin Ali ve Molla Mehmed bin Mahmud nam kimesneler ve sairleri meclis-i şer'-i hatir-i lazimi't-tevkirde yine mahalle-i mezbure sakinelerinden Edibe bint Ali muvacehesinde herbiri takrir-i dava ve tasvir-i müddea idüb, mezbure Edibe mahalle-i mezburede kendi halinde olmayıb ve na-mahremden dahi ictinabı olmadığından maada medidü'l-lisan olmağla bundan akdem kendi halinde olmak üzere kendüye tenbih-i ekid olundukda mütenebbih olmamağla mezbure Edibe'nin mahalle-i mezbureden ihracına tenbih birle ma vakıa bi't-taleb ketb olundu."

In another case dated November 27, 1692,[17] many people from the quarter of Şeyh Şemseddin-i Tebrizi in Konya came to court with allegations against Kassab Osman and his wife Satı:

> Satı is not *kendü halinde*, she stays in her house only once a week. On the remaining days, she habitually visits the houses of bandits while playing the drum and tambourine. Her brigandage (*şekavet*) and fraud (*fesadat*) have become habitual. Her husband, although aware of his wife's misconduct, has not prevented her from continuing her behavior; rather, he has remained silent.

Repeated entreaties from neighborhood members remained futile; thus, they demanded the expulsion of both husband and wife from the neighborhood, adding that if the couple were not expelled, members of the community would be dispersed and scattered. In this context again, being *kendü halinde* denotes chastity.

The court cases show that *kendü halinde* usually meant being inoffensive (especially for men) and physically harmless to others; describing those who were not a source of feelings of physical pain or carrying the risk of being so. People pursued their corporal interests in defining their communities and rejected those who caused offense or harm. Thus, a sense of what hurts or what pleases drove decisions about who to include (protect) or exclude.

For women, on the other hand, the term *kendü halinde olmak* usually denoted chastity and modesty (*her biri cevablarında mezbur Aişe kendü halinde, afife, ve mesturedir deyü*).[18] In some cases, especially for guilds, a member towards whom they felt gratitude was someone who had occupational expertise (*sanatında kusuru olmayıb*).[19] Women who had occupational talents such as tailoring also

---

[17] İzzet Sak and İbrahim Solak, *38 Numaralı Konya Şer'iye Sicili (1103–1104/1692–1693) Transkripsiyon ve Dizin* (Konya: Selçuk Ünviversitesi, 2014), 327. Quoted from Konya JCR 38: 198/2; "Mahmiye-i Konya'da merhum Şeyh Şemseddin Tebrizi mahallesi ahalisinden ashab-ı haze'l-kitab Molla Yahya bin Hasan ve.... nam kimesneler meclis-i şer'-i hatir-i lazımü't-tevlirde yine mahalle-i merkume sükkanından Kasab Osman bin Abdurrahman ve zevcsi Satı bint-i Rıdvan nam kimesneler mahzarlarında her biri takrir-i kelam ve tabir-i ani'l-meram idüb merkume Satı kendü halinde olmayıb haftada bir gün kendi menzilinde olub sair günlerde def ve düplek ile ehl-i fesad eşkiya ve fıska evlerin gezmeyi mu'tad dinüb ve sair bunun emsali fesad eşkıya ve şekavet üzere olub ve zevci merkum dahi merkumenin şekavet ve fesadatı malumu iken sükut idüb nice def'a men ve nasihat olunub her biri amil olmadıkları ecilden her birinin bu makule hilaf-ı şer' evza'ına tahammülümüz kalmamıştır mezburan Osman ve Satı ile bir mahallede ma'iyet üzere olmağa her birimiz razı değilleriz mezburlar mahallemizden ihrac olunmaları matlubumuzdur eğer ihrac olunmazlarsa her birimiz perakende ve perişan olmamız mukadderdir deyüb her biri mezkuranın su'-i hallerini ihbar itmeğin min bad mahalle-i merkumede durmayıb menzillerinden çıkub gitmeğe mezkuran Osman ve Satı'ya tenbih bir le ma vaka'a bi't-taleb ketb olundu. fi'l-yevmi's-samin aşer min şehr-i Rebi'ül-evvel li-sene erbaa ve mie ve elf' (18 Rebi'ü'-l-evvel 1104/November 27, 1692)."

[18] Ankara JCR 78: 76.

[19] Kuran, *Mahkeme Kayıtları Işığında*, 266–7. Quoted from İstanbul JCR 16: 92a/4.

contributed to feelings of pleasure (*Şerife Fatıma'nın yedinde terzilik sanatı olub kendü halinde ehl-i ırz dindar ve müstakime eyü hatundur deyu*).[20]

James Baldwin, for example, an Ottoman legal historian, in his extensive research, examined the treatment of prostitution in several genres of Ottoman legal writing, such as manuals and commentaries of Islamic jurisprudence, fetwas, and *kanunnames*, and questioned how prostitution was addressed in practice by using judicial court records. Usually, the solution in cases of prostitution was either banishment or expulsion from a neighborhood. He argued that expulsion of prostitutes from a neighborhood reflected the concerns of the plaintiffs, who were local residents unhappy living in close proximity to vice. They were, in other words, he argued, less interested in seeing the offenders punished than in the ways prostitution impinged on the rights of Ottoman subjects and disrupted Ottoman societies. If people were less interested in seeing offenders punished, but rather wanted to establish distance from any vicious behavior that would disrupt their societies, I would argue that it may also be associated with their sense of moral pain. It was a sense that hurt, and they thus tried to keep themselves away from it as much as possible.

Morality and emotions have been a topic of interest among historians of emotions. Katie Barclay for example, basing her claims on empirical evidence from Scottish legal sources from the eighteenth century, also discusses morality and emotion in neighborhoods.[21] She describes *caritas* (a form of love), the root of the modern term *charity*, different from the passionate love, as an "emotional ethic" designed to promote a particular type of community relation, encompassing feelings, embodied actions informed by a set of moral principles.[22] It was a duty to be performed and demanded a normative behavior. She claims that *caritas* provided the framework for ethical and emotional neighborly relations.[23]

Rob Boddice, on the other hand, in his book *The History of Emotions*, but more particularly in its final chapter titled "Morality," for example, discusses the link between morality and emotions. He argues that emotions are the fundamental meaning-making mechanisms in human life. Moreover, "they are part of cognitive processes, undergirding social relations, coloring in reasoned discourse and providing a sense of what hurts and what pleases,

---

[20] Sak and Solak, *53 Numaralı Konya Şer'iye Sicili*, 42, quoted from Konya JCR 53: 18/4.
[21] Barclay, *Caritas*.
[22] Ibid., 3.
[23] Ibid., 9.

what feels good and bad, and what feels right or wrong."[24] Yes, he says, "what humans strive to feel is closely aligned to, or resistant to, the power structures that lay out the prescriptions of what humans should feel." "But, there's also moral relevance in this universal framework" he continued, asking, "what is a feeling of accord except a sense of appropriateness, or a feeling of rightness or wrongness?" The emotional repertoire thus necessarily comes loaded with moral value, experienced as a moral sense. He argues that morality, as an abstract moral code, does not necessarily lead to acceptance of an individual on a societal level. Moral codes would be worthless without the social and cultural instruments of power and influence that give meaning to them.[25] He suggests that only by understanding the moral element of emotional prescription can we understand why people follow norms, or why they struggle to resist them.[26] But more importantly, he states that "rights and wrongs can be codified and introduced in abstract terms, but rights and wrongs are experienced, always, as sensory and affective as well as intellectual phenomena." Moral economy,[27] which includes structures of power, the dynamic interaction within and across boundaries, and construction of taboo, he argues, is constructed through the sensory and emotional particularities of a given place at a given time.[28] He states that the moral compass exists in the realm of feeling, which includes emotions and sensations.

I would argue that a close reading of Ottoman sources shows that a person who is "*kendü halinde*," accepted by the community to be under their protection, refers to someone who is not perceived as a potential threat to physical or moral pain, which again is associated with senses, either pleasure or pain. More concisely, it described those who were not a source of feelings of physical or moral pain or who carried the risk of being so. People pursued their corporal and moral interests in defining the borders of their communities. Thus, a sense of what hurts or what pleases drove decisions about who to include or exclude—or better put, who to protect.

---

[24] Boddice, *The History of Emotions*, 191.
[25] Ibid., 193.
[26] Ibid., 196.
[27] Ibid., 196. According to Boddice, moral economy is defined as "a web of affect-saturated values that stand and function in well-defined relationships to one another, in which, moral refers to the psychological and the normative, to the valorisation of objects and actions (practices) with emotion. The word economy refers to a regularized sytem that is explicable but not always predictable."
[28] Ibid., 202.

Expulsions from Domains of Gratitude

Let's take a closer look at judicial court records addressing exclusion from one's community, which represent cases in which a member of their communities ceased to be under the protection of their fellows. The question of what the conditions are for being a member in good standing of a neighborhood community would be considered as a contested knowledge. Whatever the norms are, be they religious, moral, or judicial, people assign meaning to them not only through reasoning but also through their emotions, which doesn't necessarily make them irrational. For example, if a member of a community violates Islamic law by being close to those who are canonically forbidden to them, according to religious norms, we would expect community members to demand that member's immediate expulsion. Yet, this is not what we see in the records.

For example, in a case dated May 26, 1776 from Bursa,[29] male and female residents of the İmaret-i İsa Bey quarter came to court and made a claim against Es-Seyyid Mehmed and Şerife Fatma. Es-Seyyid Mehmed was living in the rooms of Sultan Mustafa Inn, which was probably located in the same quarter. In their allegations, the plaintiffs accused Şerife Fatma of not being *kendü halinde* (drawing on my discussion of the term from the previous section, in this context the term refers to chastity and modesty) by allowing Es-Seyyid Mehmed, whose merits and familial ties were unknown, to stay in her house, along with his brother. Community members demanded that both Es-Seyyid Mehmed and Şerife Fatma be expelled from the community. This case is an example

---

[29] Bursa JCR B-166: 62; "Medine-i Brusa hısnı dahilinde İmaret-i İsa Bey mahallesi ahalisinden işbu eshabü'l-kitab Mustafa Çelebi bin Osman ve Es-Seyyid Süleyman Çelebi ibn Mehmed Çelebi ve Salih bin Mustafa ve Mehmed bin Süleyman ve Osman bin Abdullah ve Ali bin Mehmed ve Hasan bin El-Hac İbrahim ve Mehmed bin Yahya nam kimesneler ile nisa taifesinden Saliha bint-i Ali ve Aişe bint-i Ali ve İhsan bint-i Mustafa diğer Aişe bint-i Mehmed ve Saliha bint-i Mehmed ve Hatice bint-i Mehmed nam hatunların meclis-i şer'-i hatır-i lazımü't-tevkirde mahalle-i mezburede Sultan Mustafa odaları dimekle ma'ruf odalarda sakin Es-Seyyd Mehmed bin Es-Seyyid Numan ile Şerife Fatma nam kimesneler mahzarlarında her biri takrir-i kelam ve dava' ve tasvir-i müddea idüb mezbure Şerife Fatma mahalle-i mezburede kendi halinde olmayıb bu esnada diyar-ı aherden gelen hasebi ve nesebi meçhul işbu mezbur Es-Seyyid Mehmed'i li-ebeveyn karındaşı beraber olmak üzere menzilinde beytutet ittirdiğinden maada kendi daileri ile mukayyed olan hatunları izlal kaydında oldundukda mütenebbih olmayub ef'al-i kabihada ısrar üzere olduklarından emniyetimiz meslub olmağla mahalle-i mezbureden ihrac olunmaları matlubumuzdur deyü muvacehelerinde su-i hallerini haber virmeleriyle mezburan Es-Seyyid Mehmed ve Şerife Fatma'nın mahalle-i mezbureden ihraclarına tenbih birle mavakıa bi't-taleb ketb olundu. fi'l-yevmi's-sabi min şehr-i rebiü'l-ahir sene tısın ve mie ve elf."

of community members demanding the removal of two members from their domain of gratitude. However, my main interest in the case is not the expulsion but rather the phases of the process. The plaintiffs stated that they had repeatedly and sternly warned Es-Seyyid Mehmed and Şerife Fatma to stop their wrongful behavior. However, the two refused to comply and insisted on continuing with their wrongful acts. The warning, then, was a step before the formal demand of expulsion in the court. This case thus shows that being expelled from one's domain of gratitude was not an instantaneous process. Community members tried to resolve the problem first amongst themselves by trying to persuade the wrongdoers to change their behavior. The process thus included a phase of admonition. The established affective ties, in other words, did not break down at once. A closer look at the terms and concepts used offers us clues about the events and run-up to the court case.

A case dated May 1752 illustrates another phase in the process of leaving a domain of gratitude.[30] In this case, El-Hac Mehmed and Es-Seyyid El-Hac Hasan, who were residents of Ankara castle, came to court and made the following allegation against their next-door neighbor, Es-Seyyid Osman:

> This Osman is a habitual debaucher and drinks wine. The night before the date of the case, he invited over some men regarded as brigands living in a foreign quarter outside the castle, and while drinking, acting immorally, and shouting, they annoyed community members. His mother, Zahide, kept him company. We tried to prevent and forbid their wrongdoings by kindly counseling both Es-Seyyid Osman and his mother. However, they did not listen to us and defended their misbehavior by cursing us. We demand that their conduct be judged by community members and that they be expelled from our quarter.

---

[30] Ankara JCR 135: 155/6; "Medine-i Ankara hısnı ahalilerinden baisü hazi'l-kitab El-Hac Mehmed bin İlyas ve Es-Seyyid El-Hac Hasan nam kimesneler meclis-i şer'-i şerif-i enverde car-ı mülasıkları Es-Seyyid Osman bin Es-Seyyid Osman bin Es-Seyyid Mehmed nam kimesne mahzarında her birileri üzerine dava ve takrir-i kelam idüb mezbur Es-Seyyid Osman daima kendi halinde olmayub şürb-i hamr ve fısk-ı fücur adet-i müstemiresi olmağla işbu gice haric kale sakinlerinden eşkiya makulesinden birkaç nefer kimesneleri menziline davet ve alet-i lehva ile adet-i melufeleri üzere şürb-i hamr ve fısk-ı fücura meşgul oldukları halde halt-ı kelam savt-ı sekranı izhar ile bizleri ve sair civarını iza ve taciz eylediklerinde bizler dahi gerek mezbur Es-Seyyid Osman ve gerek validesi gaibe ani'l-meclis Zahide nam hatunu men' ve zecrleri üzere hayırla tavsiye ve fiil-i mekruh-ı mezkurdan fariğ olmak içün nasihat eylediğimizde mezburlar adem-i kabullerinden naşi herbirilerimize şetm-i galiz ile şetm ve atale-i lisan eylediklerinden maada meşgul oldukları fiil-i kerihde ısrar ve devama ikdam itmeleriyle mezburların keyfiyet-i ahvalleri ahali-i mahalle ve sükkan-ı kal'adan sual ve istihbar olunub takrirleri tahrir ve muceb-i muktezası bade'l-icra mahallemizden huructarı matlubumuzdur didiklerinde... fi evail-i receb bil ferd sene hamse ve sittin ve mie ve elf."

When the other community members were questioned, they claimed they had witnessed Es-Seyyid Osman's and his mother's misconduct, emphasizing that such acts were habitual for them. They both emphasized that the wrongdoing was continual, perpetual, and long lasting, thus habitual. This constituted yet another phase in the expulsion process itself and revealed the phases of the process more clearly. Community members, long before demanding their expulsion, had made an effort to correct the behavior of the accused and had proffered their advice to them. However, their continued acts of misconduct required community members to finally demand their expulsion. Court cases, then, show only the very last phase of the deterioration of relations and affective ties between community members.

These cases provide important clues about the process of moving out of one's domain of gratitude. What they all show is that if community members posed a risk to other members of the community or engaged in misconduct, the offending members were first counseled and admonished, not once but usually repeatedly, to correct their behavior. This was the first stage of the disciplinary process. The second phase started when offenders chose either to return to the domain of gratitude, feeling regret for their actions, or chose to continue their behavior, rejecting the wishes of their community. If community members chose to return to their domain, we would probably be unable to detect it, since there would be no documented demand for expulsion. The third stage was that in which offenders persisted in habitual misconduct, in which case community members would engage in surveillance, monitoring the offenders' actions. Only then, once other community members had confirmed that the wrongdoing had become habitual, would they appeal to the court, representing the final phase of the process.

Another thing that we should keep in mind is that we only have access to cases that had already escalated to the final irreversible phase, although we may still be able to discern clues about the preceding phases of the process. However, we do not know how many cases occurred in which community pressure succeeded in correcting wrongdoers' behavior. It is quite probable that most cases were resolved within the community without resorting to the courts. Indeed, a community's demand for the expulsion of one or more members appears to be the final and irreversible phase of the process. Yet, a closer look at the case records suggests even this may not always be so; some court cases showed that even after the judge had ruled that an offender was to be expelled from the community, the offender could still continue to live in that community, an example of which is given below.

In this case,[31] es-Seyyid Hüseyin, Mehmed Efendi, Alaaddin the religious leader, Mehmed Efendi the religious scholar, and several others, who were all the residents of the Tabbah Yunus quarter, came to the court and made a claim against Sema Hatun, who was from the same quarter:

> This Sema Hatun is in the habit of mischief. Additionally, there are always people entering her home who are regarded canonically as strangers. If she continues to stay in our community, malice in our community would be inevitable. Although she has been legally ordered numerous times to be expelled, she has not left this quarter and still lives in our neighborhood. We demand that she be expelled again.

Sema Hatun subsequently requested a period of delay to leave the community on her own volition, and the judge ordered that she leave the quarter within three days. This case showed that even though Sema Hatun was expelled from the community and was legally ordered to leave several times, she still managed to live in the same quarter for a period of time. Thus, what looks like the last phase of expulsion of a community member from a domain of gratitude may not have been the very final phase.

Being expelled from one's domain of gratitude was a long process. However, the conditions for being regarded as a community member in good standing and the length of the expulsion process differed for each community. The amount of time allowed for counseling and warning and the time frame used to define habitual acts could differ from one community to the next. These cases demonstrate that both the boundaries of the domain of gratitude and the degree of tolerance for pushing the boundaries may differ for each community; but they show something else, too. It is emotions that make a rule, be it judicial, social, or religious, plausible. Enforcing a rule should feel right. It seems that expulsion was demanded only if the misconduct was determined to be habitual. If law and

---

[31] İstanbul JCR 03 v.13: 316, İSAM, "Mahmiye-i İstanbul'da Tabbah (debbağ) Yunus mahallesi sakinlerinden işbu hafızu'l-kitab es-Seyyid Hüseyin b.es-Eyyid Ramazan ve Mehmed Efendi b. Alaaddin el-imam ve Mehmed Efendi el-müderris ve Ali Subaşı b. mezbur Hüseyin Çelebi ve Mehmed Çavuş b. Kasım ve Hüseyin Bey b. Memi ve Mehmed Bey b. Mustafa el-cündi ve Behram b. İbrahim ve Osman Çelebi ve el-Hac Şehabettin ve sairleri bi isrihim meclis-i şer'a, yine mahalle-i mezbureden Sema Hatun bt. Mehmed'i ihzar ve mahzarında takrir ve dava edip, mezbure Hatun evinde daima fesad üzredir olduğundan gayrı evine na-mahrem girip çıkmaktan hali değildir, mahallemizde bu üslub üzre sakine olursa fesad olmak mukarrerdir, kiraren mezbureye mahallemizden çıkmaya tenbih olunmuş iken ahar mahalleye çıkmak ile mukayyed değildir, hala mezbureyi mahallemizden ihrac olunmasını talep ideriz dediklerinde, mezbure Hatun dahi rızasıyla çıkmaya istimhal etmeğin, tarih-i kitabdan üç güne değin ahar mahalleye nakl olunmak için mezbureye tenbih olundu. Hurrie fi 24 Cemaziyelahir fi-tarihi'l-mezbur."

punishment were the only considerations in enforcing community rules, then it would be expected that members would immediately demand expulsion of wrongdoers.

Emotions as Practices

As I have discussed in the first chapter, within the philosophical framework of Ottoman society, emotions were conceptualized as practices, either as emotion-vices or emotion-virtues, relevant only in terms of relationships. In some case records, although there are not any terms of emotion expressed, one may trace emotions as bodily practices, realized in their social relations.

In a judicial court record of Aleppo dating from 1663,[32] fifteen Muslim and eleven Christian subjects who were residents of the same neighborhood came to the court, reporting that they had previously collectively borrowed 520 *guruş* from Hamza Ağa to meet the neighborhood's tax obligations, and he was now seeking repayment. Considering that one 17 *guruş* was equivalent to 120 *akçe*, and the cost of a loaf of bread was 1 *akçe*, 520 *guruş* was a significant amount of money, perhaps enough to buy a big pension, or more than the total collective tax obligations of a couple of villages. Over the course of the seventeenth century, taxes called *avarızhane*, which were normally only collected in extraordinary times of war, became regularized.[33] One unit of this tax obligation was allocated to a number of households in the same neighborhood. This could cover three, five, seven or nine real households, depending on the taxpayers' economic means. We do not know for sure how many real households formed a single tax unit, or *avarızhane*. In other words, the allocation of this accrued tax was determined by the communities themselves. In this case, both Muslim and Christian residents from the same neighborhood testified to the court that the current tax obligation of certain homeowners could not be collected. They collectively demanded that

---

[32] Charles L. Wilkins, *Forging Urban Solidarities: Ottoman Aleppo 1640-1700* (Leiden: Brill, 2010), 104.
[33] For *avarızhane* tax see Ömer Lütfü Barkan, "Avarız," *İA* 2: 13-19; Özer Ergenç, *XVI. Yüzyılda Ankara ve Konya* (2nd edn) (Istanbul: Tarih Vakfı Yurt Yayınları, 2012) especially on the functions of *avarız akçesi vakfı*, ibid., 205; Süleyman Demirci, "Demography and History: The Value of the Avarızhane Registers for Demographic Research. A Case Study of the Ottoman Sub-Provinces of Konya, Kayseri and Niğde, c. 1620s-1700," *Turcica* 38 (2006): 181-211; Wilkins, *Forging Urban Solidarities*; Eunjeong Yi, *Guild Dynamics in Seventeenth-Century Istanbul: Fluidity and Leverage* (Leiden: Brill, 2004); Linda Darling, *Revenue-Raising and Legitimacy: Tax Collection and Financial Administration in the Ottoman Empire, 1560-1660* (Leiden: Brill, 1996); Oktay Özel, "Population Changes in Ottoman Anatolia during the 16th and 17th Centuries: The 'Demographic Crisis' Reconsidered," *International Journal of Middle East Studies* 36 (2004): 183-205.

the judge give permission to collect from the financially able residents, in a single sum, the tax amount to cover both the debt to Hamza Ağa and the remaining tax arrears. This would allocate the burden of the tax liability to those in the neighborhood who could afford to pay, representing a case in which community members protected their fellows from the financial burden of tax payments, and emotions in this case are realized as practices.

Likewise, in another record,[34] the *kethüda* and the notables of the stone-making (*taşçı*) guild in İstanbul, all of whom were non-Muslims, came to the court to make an unusual petition in the presence of Mahmud Çelebi, the administrator of a *waqf* (social fund) established to collect communal taxes to be used for the Bayezid Ağa neighborhood's shared expenses. The Bayezid Ağa neighborhood was situated within the Topkapı gate of the city walls of Istanbul. From their court application, the Bayezid Ağa neighborhood apparently had nine registered units of taxation (*avarızhane*). However, members of the stone-making guild were voluntarily paying the taxes and other expenses corresponding to the obligations of one taxation unit of the Bayezid Ağa neighborhood with feelings of contentment (*rızamız ile*) for providing sustenance (*imdad olmak üzere*) to the quarter. They now came to court requesting to pay for not one but three units of taxation. It seems likely that the *taşçı* guild was located in close proximity to the Bayezid Ağa neighborhood. This close proximity brought together two different communities, members of the stone-making guild and the residents of the Bayezid Ağa neighborhood. It is apparent that there were also affective ties established between the two, evidenced by the guild's feelings of contentment about their voluntary payment of the other's obligations. It is also worthwhile to note that although the residents of Bayezid Ağa neighborhood were Muslims, the members of the stone-making guild were non-Muslims. This case also shows that their religious identities were not a consideration in their undertaking the

---

[34] İstanbul BAB JCR 03 v. 17: 667, İSAM, "Mahmiye-i İstanbul'da vaki taşçı taifesinin kethüdaları Duka v. Dumo ve ihtiyarlarından Papa Yorgi v. Serafi ve Kiro v. Duka ve Konstantin ve İstefanos ve Liko v. Minho ve Pando v. Duka ve Koka v. Kirov e Fentari v. Dimitri ve Duka v. Dino ve Biço v. Fanka nam zimmiler meclis-i şer'-i serif-i lazımü't-teşrifde mahmiye-i mezbure hısnı ebvabından Topkapı dahilinde Bayezid Ağa mahallesi avarızına mevkufe nukudun bi'l-fiil mütevellisi olan Mahmud Çelebi b. Muharrem ve mahalle-i mezbure imamı Mustafa Efendi b. Ramazan ve ahali-i mahalle-i mezbureden Ahmed Çelebi b. Mustafa ve Hüseyin Çelebi b. Ahmed ve İbrahim Çelebi b. Mustafa ve Ali Bey b. Mehmed nam kimsneler mahzarında her biri takrir-i kelam ve ta'bir-i ani'l-meran idüp mahalle-i mezburenin dokuz hane avarızı olup mukaddema biz rızamız ile bir hanesinin mahalle-i mezbure ahalisine malimizden imdad edegelmişdik bade'l yevm beher sene zikr olunan dokuz hanenin üç hanesini rızamız ile kendi malımızdan ahali-i mahalle-i mezkureye imdad eylemek üzere taahhüd eyledik dediklerinde ma hüve'l-vaki bi't-taleb ketb olundu. Fi'l-yevmi'-sani aşer min Şabani'l-muazzam li sene seb'a ve seb'in ve elf."

obligations of another community. The emotional ties between them, then, acted not only as a shield from outside threats but also as a tool to ease their financial liabilities. In this case, we witness emotions expressed through virtuous acts and behavior and demonstrated by the payment of the taxes of a neighboring group.

We may also apply the practice theory approach to the rituals "as a means of achieving, training, articulating, and modulating emotions for personal as well as social purposes."[35] Rituals such as banquets organized for guild disciples mastering their specific profession were also media for expressing communal gratitude. Emotions in this case are not expressed through language; rather, they are expressed through actions and practices. For example, a case from July 11, 1698 is interesting in the sense that it illustrates the process of becoming a master member of a guild and officially moving into a domain of gratitude.[36] We understand from the accounts of the masters that the tailors organized a banquet for their disciples once they were fully trained and were ready to be promoted to the status of a master. This was a customary ritual involving the participation of tailor guild members along with members of other guilds and friends. The banquet as a ritual of the tailors' guild represented permission for the disciples to practice their craft on their own (*başka çıkmak*) as qualified professionals. In that year, 180 disciples were ready to be promoted, although we do not know how long it had taken them to advance to this point and become masters in their profession. We also do not know whether the period of training was the same for each and every disciple. However, this particular record shows that it was a process, most probably a long one, for the disciples to be trained by their masters, learning the secrets of the profession, and awarded at the end of their perhaps arduous training with a banquet symbolizing their maturation. This was a process in which masters passed on to their disciples not only knowledge about the social and occupational norms of the group, but also its emotional norms. It was this process of training and transmitting knowledge that also

---

[35] Ibid., 210.
[36] Ankara JCR 78: 15; "Medine-i Ankara sukunun dekakininde sakin Hayyat taifesinden Abdi Çelebi ibn Ali ve ... meclis-i şer'de taife-i mezburenin şeyhi ve yiğitbaşısı olan işbu eshabu hazi'r-rakam El-Hac Mehmed bin Mehmed ve Hüseyin bin Zülfikar ve Mehmed bin Ömer nam kimesneler mahzarlarında her biri bi'l-asale ve bi'l-vekale ikrar-ı tam ve takrir-i kelam idüb erbab-ı hiref beyninde kadimden cari mutadımız esnaf ve sair ahbabımıza ziyafet hılalinde 180 şakirdimiz başka çıkmak için cümle olub her birinden müştemian akçe ve eşyayı mezburuna ala tariki'l-emane virüb yevm-i ziyafetde harc ve sarfa cümleye izn virüb mezburun bade'l-harc lede'l-muhasebe beynimizde harcın killet ve kesretine müteallika münazaat-ı ekide vukuunden naşi beynimize müslihun vesatetiyle müctemia olub yevm-i mezburda harc ve sarflarından baki zimmetlerinde makbuz yirmidört guruş ve dört res ağnam ve doksan adet sabunve altı vukıyye piriç ve sekiz makrama üzerine ahedihum aherin zimmetine lazım gelen hukukdan zimmetimizi ibra itmek üzere inşa-ı akd eylediklerinde biz dahi sulh-ı mezburu Kabul ... fi yevmi's-sani min muharremi'l-haram sene 1110."

established affective ties between disciples and their masters. Once disciples had mastered their craft, they were qualified to establish themselves professionally, and only then did they have the right to move into the domain of gratitude of this specific occupational community. This ritual evoked a sense of attachment, a sense of belonging to the community, perhaps a respect for the masters, and a feeling of gratitude as well.

Another court record dating from the seventeenth century[37] also revealed feelings of unity among members of a guild, which were expressed through their actions. When a ship came to Istanbul loaded with fruit, the distribution of the fruit from the ship to the guild members would be overseen by the leader of a guild. At some point, however, contrary to this custom and practice, some guild members started rowing their own boats to the ship to take fruit directly, without leaving any for the rest of the guild members. This was considered an unfair practice, and some guild members declared that this practice could even lead to a riot among members. Members of the guild were quite displeased with this situation and went to the court to verify that they had unanimously decided that not one member of the guild was to row his boat to the fruit ship, and that if even one did, they would all collectively burn their own boats. They wanted this collective decision to be recorded in the court registers to ensure their right to take legal action against anyone who disobeyed it.

This was quite a radical decision by the members to address those who disobeyed the established rules and regulations and thus hindered the fair distribution of raw materials. The promise to collectively burn their boats was not something imposed on the group externally; rather it reflected the will of the guild members themselves. It was a collective decision made with the agreement and consent of all members to solve a community problem, and thus reflected a strong sense of solidarity among the members. No guild

---

[37] Kuran, *Mahkeme Kayıtları Işığında*, 163–4, quoted from İstanbul JCR 3: 29b/1; "Mahmiye-i İstanbul'a ve etrafında vaki yemişciler taifesinden bazarbaşları Mehmed bin Ahmed ve Mustafa bin Abdullah ve Hüseyin ibn Nasrullah ve Süleyman bin Mustafa ve Ömer bin Mahmud ve Hamza bin İbrahim ve El-Hac Himmet bin el-Hac Hüseyin ve El-Hac Ahmed bin ... ve El-Hac İbrahim bin Mehmed ve es-Seeyid Mahmud ve İbrahim bin Nasuh ve Süleyman bin Hüdavirdi ve es-Seyyid Ahmed bin Mustafa ve Yusuf İmalüddin ve Seyyid Ahmed Çelebi ibn es-Seyyid Mustafa ve sairleri meclis-i şer'-i kavim-i lazımü't-tekrimde hazırun olub bast-ı kelam idüb taşradan yemiş gemisi geldikde bazarbaşımız marifetiyle beynimizde tevzi' olunub kayak ile karşulanı gelmiş değil iken halen olıgelene muhalif bazımız kayıkları ile taşradan gelen gemiye karşulamak ile fukaraya hisse değmeyüb külli ihtilale bais olmağın marifetleri yoğiken her kangımız taşradan gelen sefineyi kayak ile karşulayıb zahire alursa şer'le hakkından gelinüb muhkem te'dib ve zabt mümkin olmaz ise kayıklarımız ihrak olunmak üzere terazi ve tevafuk eyledik vech-i meşruh üzere olan ittifakımız tahrir olunub yedimize def' olunmak taleb ideriz didiklerinde ... tahriren fi evaili Cumadelahire sene seb'a ve isrine ve elf."

member resisted the collective decision, even though each put himself at risk of harm by agreeing to it. Committing to individual promises for the good of the community, even if this could cause personal loss, reflected the strong affective ties among the community members. This record does not contain any emotion words. However, it shows a sense of belonging, a sense of unity, expressed through relationships and actions. In this case, they expressed their sense of belonging through their acts, movements, and practices, with no referral to words of emotions.

A judge in Sivas, a city in eastern Anatolia, wrote his verdict in the judicial court register of Sivas on December 31, 1783.[38] Apparently, Meryem, the wife of Istefan, fled her house, perhaps because she could no longer stand her husband's violence. We do not know where she went or where she stayed. Nor do we know how long she stayed away from her home. In the court's decision, Meryem was to be handed over to her husband, who was warned to stop beating his wife, which is considered a violation of Islamic law. More importantly though, the court demanded that someone act as a surety in case Istefan broke his promise; subsequently, Feyzullah Ağa became the husband's surety. Both the Orthodox Christian couple and Feyzullah Ağa were from the same neighborhood, the Uğurlupınar quarter of the city of Sivas. Feyzullah Ağa agreed to be held legally responsible if his neighbor İstefan beat his wife again, even though this could be considered the private and personal affair of a non-Muslim family. One would presume that Feyzullah Ağa and the couple were living in close proximity, since Feyzullah Ağa had to closely monitor İstefan to ensure he kept his promise.

In the communal life of the Uğurlupınar quarter of the city, we can even make a guess at how Feyzullah Ağa and his family were influenced by and even emulated the religious rituals of Meryem and İstefan. In a record dated from the eighteenth century in Amasya, another city not far from Sivas, the *mufti* of the time was asked "whether it was acceptable for Muslims to receive food and Easter eggs from non-Muslims on their religious or wedding days, and the *mufti* expressed his opinion that 'it was.'"[39] Perhaps this question

---

[38] Sivas JCR 134: 6; "Uğurlupınar mahallesi mütemekkinelerinden Meryem binti Kayril nam nasraniyye zevci İstefan veledi Nazar nam zimmiye teslim olunub bir dahi hilaf-ı şer" mesfureyi dövmemek üzere tenbih ve mesfur dahi kabul ve bir dahi dövmemesine Çubukçuzade Kassab Seyyid Feyzullah Ağa ibn-i Hacı Hasan kefil ve zamin olduğu kayd şud. fi 6 safer 1198."
[39] Ali Rıza Ayar and Recep Orhan Özel, eds, *Amasya Fetvâları ve İlk Amasya Şehir Tarihi (Belâbilü'r-Râsiye Fî Riyâz-ı Mesâili'l- Amâsiyye) Mustafa Vazıh Efendi (1764–1831)* (Amasya: Amasya Belediyesi, 2011).

addressed a regular practice, which is why the *mufti* of the time was asked to issue his opinion. Hence, it is not hard to imagine Meryem and İstefan sending food and Easter eggs to Feyzullah Ağa in the Easter of 1783. Once we acknowledge that emotions are also practices, embodied in their bodily acts, being a member of the same residential settlement acted as a protective shield against legal sanctions, expressed not linguistically this time but through behaviors.

Concluding Remarks

This chapter has focused on the intracommunal relations of Ottoman subjects. It showed that Ottoman neighborhoods and guilds were "domains of gratitude" mirroring Rosenwein's "emotional communities," which represents an imagined domain in which people have a common stake, interests, values, and goals, with particular shared emotional phrases and expressions. The presence of affective ties was linguistically expressed as feelings of *rıza ve şükran*, denoting feelings of satisfaction/pleasure/contentment and gratitude. Contextual analysis of the terms *rıza ve şükran* provided further clues to its broader meaning and function in communal relations. Cases indicate that protection by one's community was crucial for survival. One could face multiple penalties, such as expulsion and false allegations, and it was emotions that provided the rules in their decisions of who to protect or not in their communities. Linguistic and contextual analysis of another frequently used term, *kendü halinde*, unlike its meaning in modern Turkish, referred to those who were not perceived as a potential threat of physical or moral pain, indicating that a sense of what hurts or what pleases drove decisions about protection. The analysis of expulsion cases, on the other hand, showed that it was not the state but the communities themselves who regulated intracommunal relations. A close reading of cases indicates that expulsion was the last phase of a long process, including phases of advice, counseling, persuasion efforts, close watch, warning and discipline. Appeals to court tended to be made only when the community members confirmed that the misconduct was habitual, which represented the final phase. This shows that communities were more concerned with amelioration than punishment and it was their emotions of unity and solidarity that provided meaning to protection. In the final section of this chapter, I explored emotions as practices. As per their emotion knowledge, emotions for early modern Ottoman society were realized only if acted upon. I showed that tracing linguistic expressions of emotions is not the only way to capture what people felt. Practices also reflect emotions of solidarity, unity, and belonging, as evidenced in cases such as that of a Muslim acting as surety for his non-Muslim neighbor, residents supporting their less well-off neighbors, and rituals organized by guilds, providing meaning to historically and culturally contingent concept of protection.

4

Regulating Communities by an Emotion: Shame

We have seen in the previous chapter on intracommunal relations that being a part of a "domain of gratitude" ensured protection by one's community members, which was critical for one's survival and acted as a shield of protection. If not protected by their communities, members could be subject to false allegations and face severe penalties including expulsion, dismissal from leadership positions, loss of community support in the event of oppression by government officials, or loss of the personal support and endorsement of their neighbors. Being a member of a community also eased the individuals' financial liabilities. I showed that it was communities themselves, rather than the state, that regulated intracommunal relations. In this chapter, I analyze the emotion of shame, privately felt but collectively constructed, in its relation to sustaining order in "domains of gratitude." I claim that shame, defined as the fear of social disapprobation or fear of being blamed or criticized, provided a willing obedience to social and emotional norms, thereby ensuring sustainability of the communities. I start with a judicial case record in which an expression of shame opens up several questions. In the next section I give examples from different disciplines, which shows the cultural variations of shame. Then I explore shame-words from a variety of Ottoman sources, ranging from travelogues, judicial court records to chronicles. The richness of vocabulary for shame is apparent in the wide range of sources that I utilize, which denote not only linguistic but also an experiential plurality.[1] Then I explore a gendered emotion, *ar*, and how it functioned in societal relations. In the final section, I explore the ways in which individuals shamed others in Ottoman society and claim that shaming was an emotional practice, not necessarily traced as linguistic expressions but also as performatives.

---

[1] Thomas Dixon, "What Is the History of Anger a History Of?" *Emotions: History, Culture, Society* 4 (2020): 29.

In the year of 1659, Hüseyin Hoca, the religious leader (*imam*) of the Poladlar neighborhood of Konya, a city in central Anatolia, came to the judicial court and made a claim against a certain Sefer with the following allegation: "The accusations of Sefer about me for having an illicit sexual relationship with Rahime, the wife of Ebu Bekir, are slander. Shame (*ar*) has stuck to me (*lahık oldu*)." The expression *lahık olmak* literally means *to stick on*, as in the colloquialism "mud sticks." Hüseyin Hoca filed his complaint to emphasize how shameful Sefer's accusations were to him. When Sefer denied making these accusations, the court demanded that Hüseyin Hoca prove his claim, and he presented Mehmed and Halil as his witnesses, both of whom confirmed that Sefer had made the said accusations in their presence.[2]

Although we do not know how the lawsuit was resolved, we may infer that Hüseyin Hoca, the plaintiff, took a copy of the record from the *qadi* and together with the legitimate evidence, demanded that Sefer be penalized by the policing official (*subaşı*). Under Ottoman law, judges did not have the right to execute their own verdicts. Only military officials such as *subaşı* were entitled to execute sentences. We can reasonably assume that Sefer was penalized either by bastinado or fined for his false allegation.

It may be inferred that Hüseyin Hoca, who was a prominent member of his community as their religious leader, was afraid of losing his reputation and power over community members and therefore decided to report the case to the legal authorities. This may have been a matter of honor that was taken very seriously in his community, and if the allegation spread, his reputation would have been seriously tarnished. Indeed, Ottoman historians always considered expressions of shame in court cases in its association with honor.

The case of Hüseyin Hoca opens up many questions about shame in Ottoman society, the answers to which provide us with the meanings ascribed to shame as an individual and social emotion and particularly its role in communal relations. Why did Hüseyin Hoca express his shame in the judicial court? Why did people

---

[2] Konya JCR 10: 134/2; "Mahmiye-i Konya'da .... mahallesi sakinlerinden rafiü'l-kitap İmam Hüseyin Hoca bin Hüsamettin meclis-i şer-i hatir-i lazımü't-tevkirde Poladlar mahallesi sakinlerinden Sefer bin.... mahzarında üzerine dava ve takrir-i kelam idüp, 'mezbur Sefer bana iftira idüp, Ebubekir bin İvad'ın zevcesi Rahime ile muamelesi vardır dimekle bana ar lahık oldu, sual olunsun' didikde gıbbe's-sual ve akibü'l-inkar mezbur Hüseyin Hoca'dan takririne muvafık beyyine talep olundukda, udul-ı müsliminden Mehmed bin Receb ve Halil bin hasan nam kmesneler liecli'ş-şehade meclis-i şer'e haziran olup, istişhad olunduklarında 'fi'l-vaki Sefer bizim huzurumuzda merkum Hüseyin Hoca'ya mezkure Rahime ile muamelesi vardır dedi, biz bu hususta şahitleriz, şehadet dahi ideriz' deyu eda-yı şehadet-i şeriyye eylediklerinde şehadetleri hayyiz-i kabulde vakıa olmağın ma vakıa bi't-talep ketb olundu."

always express their shame in judicial courts using the word *ar*, but not any other emotion words for shame? Was this an honor-based shame, in the sense that Hüseyin Hoca wanted to confirm that he was an honorable member of his society? What was its larger role in community life and its association with the "domains of gratitude," such as neighborhoods and guilds, that we have covered in the previous chapter? Did it have any role in social cohesion? How effective was shame in regulating communal relations? How was it linked to subjects' feelings of protection?

Any analysis of shame, or any other emotion, demands an interdisciplinary approach. How a specific emotion is defined by a given society or a given language has been the object of much research so far not only in history, but also anthropology, social psychology, sociology, and linguistics.[3]

Shame in Different Cultures

Although sources are rather silent on the personal experience of shame, they tell us much about its role in public relations and public order, since shame emerges in response to some kind of wrongful act and violation of standards. Aristotle, for example, saw shame as fundamental to ethical behavior.[4] Muslim thinkers also saw shame as the most fundamental emotion for proper social functioning and adherence to law. Marion Holmes Katz, a scholar of Middle Eastern and Islamic Studies, analyzes *haya*, which may be roughly translated to English as "shame," understanding it as the fear of moral and social disapprobation, in ethical and legal works of scholars of the Shafi legal school in the eleventh to early twelfth centuries. Her study focuses on the works of Shafi jurists Mawardi (d.1058) who lived under Buyid rule, Ghazali (d.1111), and Juwayni (d. 1085), whose works flourished under the Selçuks.[5] She illustrates a changing understanding of shame's role in Islamic societies.

---

[3] See for example Nader Al Jallad, "The Concept of '*Shame*' in Arabic: Bilingual Dictionaries and the Challenge of Defining Culture-Based Emotions," *Language Design* 12 (2010): 31–57; Marry H. Kayyal and James A. Russell, "Language and Emotion: Certain English–Arabic Translations Are Not Equivalent," *Journal of Language and Social Psychology* 32 (2013): 261–71; Anna Wierzbicka, *Emotions Across Languages and Cultures: Diversity and Universals* (Cambridge: Cambridge University Press, 1999).

[4] Ibid., 20.

[5] Marion Holmes Katz, "Shame (Haya) as an Affective Disposition in Islamic Legal Thought," *Journal of Law, Religion and State* 3, no. 2 (2014): 139–69.

Emotion words in one language rarely have an exact translation in any other language. Psychologists Marry Kayyal and James Russell, for example, research whether twelve emotion words in English (happiness, sadness, anger, fear, interest, relaxation, embarrassment, disgust, contempt, surprise, perplexity, and hesitancy) had equivalent words in Arabic. They use a translation–back-translation method to obtain the best available Arabic translation for each word. This method is defined as the process of translating a previously translated document or text back to its source language. Unlike ordinary translation, its starting point is the translation itself. They discover that out of twelve words, only one translation (happiness—*ferah* in Arabic) passed the tests of equivalence, while the remaining eleven words differed across cultures and languages. Evidence seems to be mounting that when we translate a word, we risk changing its meaning. This is why emotion words demand a broader explanation in their translation, keeping in mind that they usually bear different meanings in different contexts. Shame is among the emotions that show a high degree of variability among cultures, which confirms it to be a social construction. It also exists on a continuum, with different shame-related emotion words expressing different intensities of feeling.

Al Jallad, on the other hand, provides a linguistic framework for analyzing, understanding, and describing the emotion of "shame" in contemporary Arabic by proposing a specific linguistic, cognitive, and cultural apparatus to define the emotion.[6] His study of six different emotion words used in contemporary Arabic (*hacal, haya, hishmah, ayb, faziha,* and *ar*) includes a contextual analysis, and he argues that there are basic differences in the semantics, grammar, and cultural aspects of shame between Arabic and English. While all six Arabic shame-like words are translated into English as "shame," each Arabic word differs in its scale and meaning. It is therefore necessary to understand the culture in which the emotion of shame is being expressed to better understand its meaning. For instance, no kind of shame in English is praised, recommended, or respected, he argued. In Arabic, however, *haya* is almost like a moral power that guides one's behavior, while *hacal* is more internal, personal, and self-oriented. *Hishmah* means being highly sensitive to shame-inducing situations and represents a value that is recommended and praised. *Hismah*, as he defines it, recalls the word "shamefast," which Stearns argues in his work *Shame: A Brief History* had been used in the West to refer to the kind of anticipatory

---

[6] Al Jallad, "The Concept of '*Shame*' in Arabic," 31–57.

emotional discipline that would steer an individual away from bad behavior. The term "shamefast" suggested extreme modesty or bashfulness that would serve as emotional constraint.[7]

Likewise, in her ethnographical study based on fieldwork conducted among settled Bedouin nomads living west of Alexandria, called Awlad Ali, Lila Abu-Lughod, in her seminal work *Veiled Sentiments*, conceptualizes honor and modesty in a Bedouin society.[8] She argues that one of the most complex concepts in Bedouin culture is *hasham*, whose meaning depends on the context. Although it means *modesty*, the concept transcends that meaning. It involves both feelings of shame in the company of the more powerful and the acts of deference that arise from these feelings. Various words formed from the trilateral root *hashama* have been translated as modesty, shame, and shyness. In its broadest sense, it means "propriety" (*adab*). Abu-Lughod's linguistic approach to the word *hasham*, which had differing meanings in different contexts, is especially important for understanding how such culturally constructed concepts in societies may serve to regulate social relationships. *Hasham* was distinctive to the Awlad Ali community and had its own social and political functions for this Bedouin society. It is interesting to note that *hasham*, or *haşmet* in Ottoman Turkish, has more than one meaning. It refers to shame, modesty, or bashfulness, but also to anger, irritation, and grandeur. Most of the time, in Ottoman sources, *haşmet* refers to magnificence, or is related to one's retinue of followers and servants, and is not frequently used as an expression of any kind of shame.

Stearns's *Shame: A Brief History* concentrates on East Asia and the West and compares and contrasts the two cultures in terms of their understandings of shame and the values they ascribed to it. The Confucian idea of shame emphasized a type of boundary crossing or violation of accepted patterns of social behavior and social relationships. Illustrations of shame thus frequently involved references to inappropriate clothing, food, or material goods more generally. However, both Greek and Chinese philosophers strongly connected shame with ethical conduct, in discipline and anticipation alike. The prominence of shame in Greek and Chinese philosophy, argues Stearns, both reflects and explains the importance of emotion in actual community life. Thus, significant research confirms that shame was and still is defined differently by different societies and in different time periods.

---

[7] Peter N. Stearns, *Shame: A Brief History* (Urbana: University of Illinois Press, 2017), 41.
[8] Lila Abu-Lughod, *Veiled Sentiments: Honor and Poetry in a Bedouin Society* (Berkeley: University of California Press, 1986).

Shame in Ottoman Sources

Many words were used to express feelings of shame in Ottoman sources, varying in meaning by context and differing in their intensity: *hacal* (being or becoming confused with shame); *haşmet* (anger, irritation, shame with annoyance, modesty, or bashfulness); *şerm-sar* (a word of Persian origin for bashfulness or embarrassment); *haya* (a feeling of shame, modesty or bashfulness, to feel ashamed of); *fazihat* (shame, disgrace, or infamy); *ayıb* (a fault, flaw, defect; anything looked upon as shameful, a breach of manners, or shameful); and *ar* (a cause of shame, a shameful act or quality, bashfulness, or shyness) constitute only some of the different expressions of shame. All these words had different connotations and were used in different contexts. *Haya*, for example, refers to ingratitude caused by a socially shaped conscience that monitors one's actions. This in turn differs from either *ayıb* or *ar*. *Fazihat* is defined as *rezil rüsva olma hali*, or losing face. This is experienced when one's faults come to be known by others or when a secret is exposed. It is other-oriented and different from *haya* or *hacal*. All these words are broadly similar but differ subtly in their use.

The sensation denoted by *ayıb*, for example, was not as intense as that denoted by *ar*. One is expected to feel *ayıb* for violating proper rules of behavior. Robert Dankoff conducts both a linguistic and a historical analysis of the term *ayıb* using a seventeenth-century travelogue *Seyahatname* (Book of Travels) by Evliya Çelebi, which showed that within the Ottoman lands, different societies had different understandings of shame.[9] He also explores different words for shame, each having a different meaning in different contexts. He emphasizes that the concept of *ayıb* changed geographically, revealing it to be a culturally constructed concept. For example, according to Evliya, while it was considered to be *ayıb* (disgraceful) for women to go about in the marketplace in Ayntab (*çarşu u bazarda gezmeleri gayet ayıbdır*), this was not the case for women in Istanbul.[10] The women of Cairo, on the other hand, "never go out in the street during the day, except when it is an emergency and then they do it secretly. But at night, they light torches and visit their relatives attended by their servants, otherwise it is shameful for women to go about in marketplaces (*avret bâzârda gezmek gâyet ayıbdır*)."[11] But in Peshpehil, Evliya writes, "men and women do

---

[9] Robert Dankoff, "Ayıp Değil! (No Disgrace)," *Journal of Turkish Literature* 5 (2008): 77–90.
[10] Ibid., 77.
[11] Ibid., 78.

not flee from each other and women may go outdoors without their husbands' permission and even sit and chat and drink with us Ottomans, and none of this is considered shameful, and they have behaved in this disreputable fashion ever since the time of the Virgin Mary."[12]

Ayıb then, refers more to social norms in Evliya's *Book of Travels*. In this sense *ayıb*, similar to the Confucian idea of shame, emphasized a kind of boundary crossing or violation of accepted patterns of social behavior and social relationships. The shame denoted by *ar*, on the other hand, represents the most intense feeling of shame and is experienced when committing an act that is in extreme opposition to moral values or social norms, often with sexual connotations. This may be the reason why we always encounter the expression *ar* in judicial court cases as a linguistic expression of feelings of shame, rather than any other shame word. Contextual analysis of the expression *ar* in judicial court records shows when and in which cases it was used.

In a case record dating from 1736, for example, es-Seyyid Molla made a claim against Ebubekir, stating that the previous day, Ebubekir had called him a pimp (*puşt ve dip satan*).[13] In this case of defamation, Seyyid Molla stated that shame stuck on him (*ar lahık oldu*) and thus demanded that his accuser be punished. Although Ebubekir denied the accusations, Seyyid Molla proved his case with the help of witnesses who confirmed Ebubekir's slander. The judge then decided that Ebubekir was to be punished, which would either be a fine or bastinado, to be executed by the military official of the town.

---

[12] Ibid., 81. "Peşpehil'de ise erleri ve avratları birbirlerinden kaçmayıb bizim Osmanlı ile avratları bir yerde oturub ayş u işret etdükte kocası birşey demeyüb kapudan taşra gider, ayıb değildir, zira bu Kafiristan'ın cümlesinde hüküm avratındır, ta Meryem Ana'dan berü ayin-i bedleri böyle olagelmiştir."

[13] Sak and Solak, *53 Numaralı Konya Şer'iye Sicili*, 32, quoted from Konya JCR 53: 14/3; "Mahmiye-i Konya'da Sadırlar Mahallesi sükkanından rafi'ü'l-kitab imam es-Seyyid Molla İbrahim bin Ahmed nam kimesne meclis-i hatir-i lazımü't-tevkirde yine mahalle-i mezbureden Ebubekir bin Mirza nam kimesne mahzarlarında üzerine dava ve takrir-i kelam idüb, tarih-i kitabdan bir gün mukaddem mahalle-i mezburede huzur-ı müsliminde alenen bi'l-muvacehe mezbur Ebubekir bana puşt ve dip satan deyu şütum-ı galize ile şetm idüb, bana ar lahık olmağla sual olunub mucib-i şer'isi icra olunmak matlubumdur didikde gıbbe's-sual ve'l-inkar ve bade't-taleb-i beyyine udul-ı ahrar-ı rical-i müsliminden Abdurrahman bin Mehmed ve İbrahim bin İbrahim nam kimesneler li-ecli'ş-şehade meclis-i şer'e haziran olub eserü'l-istişhad fi'l-vaki merkum Ebubekir tarih-i kitabdan bir gün mukaddem mahalle-i mezburede bizim huzurumuzda bi'l-muvacehe merkum es-Seeyid Molla İbrahim'e puşt ve dip satan deyu şütum-ı galize ile şetm eyledi biz bu hususa şahitleriz, şehadet dahi ideriz deyu her biri eda-i şehadet-i şer'iye eyledikelerinde gıbb-ı riayeti şerayitü'l-kabul mucibiyle mezbur Ebubekir'in zabiti marifetiyle tazirine bade't-tenbih ma-vaka'a bi't-taleb ketb olundu fi'l-yevmi's-sani aşer min Şevvali'l-mükerrem li sene seman ve erba ve mi'ete ve elf" (12 Şevval 1148/25 Şubat 1736).

In another case,[14] Molla Abdullah Halil bin Abdülehad made a claim against es-Seyyid Mehmed bin Seyyid Ahmed, stating in his allegation that the day before, es-Seyyid Mehmed had struck his neck without any reason and cursed him by saying "*büyük tersek yersin*" (you will have a big shit on your head) and thus shame stuck on him (*ar lahık oldu*). He demanded that es-Seyyid Mehmed be questioned and face the legal repercussions. However, when es-Seyyid Mehmed denied the claim, evidence was requested from the plaintiff to prove his case. Some of the Muslim members of the community testified as witnesses on behalf of the claimant. It was one of the emotional norms of the community members to express their intensive feeling of shame.

In another case,[15] Mevlud bin Mehmed brought a claim in court against his brother Ebubekir with the aid of a military officer (*subaşı*). Mevlud made the following allegation: "Four days ago, this Ebubekir defamed my wife Ayşe by calling her a bitch (*kahbe ve rusbik*). Shame stuck on me (*bana ar lahık oldu*). I demand that he be questioned and the legal requirement implemented." He claimed that his brother had defamed his wife, which, in turn, had compromised her chastity. Mevlud's feeling of shame must have been quite intense, since he accused his own brother and even asked for help from the *subaşı* to make sure that his brother was questioned. His insistence that his brother be punished revealed how grievous he perceived the insult to be. It seems that he felt obliged

---

[14] Sak and Solak, *53 Numaralı Konya Şer'iye Sicili*, 181, quoted from Konya JCR 53: 77/5; "Mahmiye-i Konya'da Sarıyakub Mahallesi sakinlerinden rafi'ü'l-kitab Molla Abdullah Halife bin Abdülehad nam kimesne meclis-i şer'-i münirde es-Seyyid Mehmed bin Seyyid Ahmed nam kimesne mahzarında üzerine dava ve takrir-i kelam idüb, tarih-i kitabdan bir gün mukaddem Külahçılar Suku'nda mela-i nasda mezbur Seyyid Mehmed bi-gayrı vech benim yakama yapışışup başından büyük tersek yersin deyu bana şütüm-i galize ile şetm etmekle bana külli ar lahık olmuştur sual olunub takriri tahrir ve mucib-i şer'isi icra olunmak matlubumdur didikde gıbbe's-sual ve'l-inkar ve bade'-taleb-i beyyine udul-ı ahrar-ı rical-i müsliminden Osman bin Hacı Ömer ve Müsli bin İbrahim nam kimesneler li-ecli'ş-şehade meclis-i şer'e haziran ve istişhad olduklarında fi'l-vaki tarih-i kitabdan bir gün mukaddem Külahçılar Suku'nda mela-i nasda merkum Seyyid Mehmed müdde-i mezbur Molla Abdülhay Halife'nin bizim huzurumuzda yakasına yapışışup başından büyük tersek yersin deyu şütüm-i galize ile merkum Molla Abdülhay Halife'ye şetm eyledi biz bu hususa şahitleriz, şehadet dahi ideriz deyu her biri eda-i şehadet-i şer'iye eylediklerinde bade't-tadil ve't-tezkiye şehadetleri makbule olmağın mucibiyle merkum Seyyid Mehmed'e tazir lazım gelmekle tazirine tanbih bir le ma-vaka'a bi't-taleb ketb olundu fi'l-yevmi'l-hamis ve'l-işrin min Zi'l-hicce li-sene seman ve erba'in ve mi'ete ve elf (25 Zi'l-hicce 1148/7 Mayıs 1736)."

[15] Konya JCR 35: 121/2; "Bi'l-fiil eyalet-i Karaman'a mutasarrıf olan.... izzetlü saadetlu Mehmet Paşa hazretlerinin mütesellimi olan fahrül-akran Abdurrahman Ağa tarafından husus-ı ati'ül-beyana mübaşir tayin olunan Mehmed Ağa müzaheretiyle mahmiye-i Konya kazasına tabi Sahra nahiyesinde Damköy sükkanından Mevlud bin Mehmed nam kimesne meclis-i şer'-i hatir-i lazımü't-tevkirde karındaşı Ebu Bekir nam kimesneyi ihzar ve mahzarında üzerine dava' ve takrir-i kelam idüp, 'tarih-i kitabdan 4 gün mukaddem mezbur Ebu Bekir zevcem Ayşe'ye kahbe ve rusbi deyu şetm idüp, bana ar lahık olmuştur, sual olunub, muceb-i şer'isi icra olunması matlubumdur,' didikde, gıbbe's-sual mezbur Ebu Bekir cevabında tarih-i kitabdan 4 gün mukaddem ben mezburun zevcesi Ayşe Hatun'a kahbe ve rusbi deyu şetm eyledim deyu tavi'an ikrar ve itiraf itmeğin ma vakıa bi't-taleb ketb olundu."

to express his feelings of shame and how deep his feelings of shame were in court. Ebubekir accepted the accusation and confirmed that he had defamed his brother's wife, Ayşe.

Likewise, in a case dating 1737,[16] El-Hac Abdülkadir Halife demanded the expulsion of Fatma, a newcomer to their community. Abdülkadir stated that the state officials had required that all community members should either be mutual guarantors to one another or that the members should be aware of who others' guarantors were. Therefore, they asked Fatma who her guarantor was. Fatma, however, in her reply swore at Abdülkadir, and threatened that if they did not feel content with her presence in their quarter, she would let her brother, who was a Janissary, take possession of Abdülkadir's wife or burn down his house. Because of Fatma's degrading language about his wife, Abdülkadir expressed his shame in court, demanding Fatma's expulsion from their community. Even though it was not him but his wife who was targeted by the insult, it was Abdülkadir who expressed his shame, which reveals the gendered use of *ar*. The witnesses also confirmed Fatma's utterance, and the judge passed a verdict that Fatma would be penalized (*tazir*), which would probably be either bastinado or fine. But later on, the judge demanded that Fatma's conduct be questioned by the community members, and they stated in their testimonies that they did not feel contentment and gratitude for Fatma (*rıza ve şükran*) and demanded her

---

[16] Sak and Solak, *53 Numaralı Konya Şer'iye Sicili*, 600, quoted from Konya JCR 53: 247/1; "Mahmiye-i Konya'da Şeyh aliman Mahallesi sakinlerinden işbu rafi'ü'l-kitab el-Hac Abdülkadir Halife ibn Ahmed nam kimesne meclis-i hatir-i lazimü't-tevkirde zatı bi't-tarifi'-şer'i muarefe olan Fatma bint-i Abdullah nam hatun mahzarında üzerine dava ve takrir-i kelam idüb, merkume Fatma'nın bizim mahallemizde mülk menzili olmayub vali ve hükkam-ı kiram taraflarından bizlere mahallerinizde kefilsiz kimesne koymayasız deyu tenbihe binaen mezbure Fatıma'ya tarih-i kitabdan bir gün mukaddem senin dahi kefilin var mıdır deyu sual eylediğimizde mezbure Fatma ben mütevelli izniyle geldim eğer sen razı olmazsan karındaşım yeniçeri Kabakulağ'a gice ile senin avradın tasarruf ve menzilin ateş yakdırırım deyu bana mezbure Fatma itale-i lisan itmekle ol vecihden bana ar lahık olmuşdur sual olunub mucib-i şer'isi icra ve keyfiyet-i ahvali mahalleden istihbar ve mahalle-i mezbureden ihrac olunması matlubumdur didikde gıbbe's-sual ve'l-inkar ve ba'de talebü'l-beyyine udul-ı ahrar-ı rical-i müsliminden Hacı Ebubekir bin Himmet ve Ali bin Hüseyin nam kimesneler li-ecli'ş-şehade meclis-i şer'e haziran olub eserü'l-istişhad fi'l-hakika tarih-i kitabdan bir gün mukaddem merkum el-Hac Abdülkadir merkume Fatıma'ya bizlere vali ve hükkam-ı kiram taraflarından mahallerinizde kefilsiz kimesne koymayasız deyu tenbih vardır senin dahi kefilin var mıdır deyu sual eyledikde merkume Fatıma merkum el-Hac Abdülkadir'e ben mütevelli izniyle geldim siz razı olmazsanız karındaşım yeniçeri Kabakulağ'a gice ile senin avradın tasarruf ve menzilin ateş yakdırırım deyu bizim huzurumuzda merkum Hacı Abdülkadir'e itale-i lisan eyledi biz bu hususa şahitleriz, şehadet dahi ideriz deyu her biri eda-i şehadet-i şer'iye eylediklerinde bade't-tadil ve't-tezkiye şehadetleri makbule olmağın mucibiyle merkume Fatıma'nın tazirine tenbihden sonra mezbure Fatıma'nın keyfiyeti ahali-i mahalleden istihbar olundukda zeyl-i vesikada muharerrü'l-esami müslimin mezbure Fatıma'nın dilazar ve halkı ta'ciz ve ızrar adet-i müstemeresi olub bir vechle kendüden razı ve hoşnud değilleriz deyu her biri mezbure Fatıma'nın su-i halini haber virmeleriyle mucibiyle mezbure Fatıma'nın mahalle-i mezbureden hurucuna tenbih bir le ma-vaka'a bi't-taleb ketb olundu fi'l-yevmi's-sabi min Şevvali'l-mükerrem li-sene tis'a ve erba'in ve mi'ete ve elf' (7 Şevval 1149/8 Şubat 1737)."

expulsion from their communities since she hurt their feelings (*dilazar*) and was habitually annoying and harmful (*halkı taciz ve ızrar adet-i müstemeresi olub*) to community members. The judge then demanded her expulsion.

These cases show us the emotional norms of Ottoman communities regarding what to feel and when and to whom. Cultivating these feelings of shame in community members and communicating shared concepts of shame helped preserve domains of gratitude and protected community members from threats, be they moral, religious, or social. Although the cases differ in the cause of the feeling of *ar* as intense shame, they all serve the same purpose: to discourage behaviors that community members considered undesirable and to preserve the values of the "domain of gratitude." It also highlights the emotion's role in social discipline.

Shame encourages a willing obedience to social and emotional norms, thereby functioning to ensure the sustainability of the domain of gratitude. It operates with the assumption of an audience, and various social groupings play their own roles in defining and deploying shame, regardless of individual experience.[17] Since shame demands the presence of an "other" to be experienced, one would not feel ashamed unless there is at least one "other" besides oneself. Thus, shame acts as a tool to sustain social order by motivating a willing obedience to social and emotional rules.

Gendered Emotion of Shame: *Ar*

But more importantly, in all the cases that have been identified, it was always the men who expressed their shame in court with the phrase *bana ar lahık oldu*. This also shows that the emotional norms also not only dictated what to feel, when, and to whom, but also by whom. Women such as Ayşe or the wife of Abdülkadir in the previously mentioned cases must have felt ashamed as well; however, they were not expected to express it as such. Rather, it was their husbands or male members of their families who were expected to express their or their family members' shame and humiliation. How are we then supposed to explain the fact that only men expressed their feeling of shame as *ar* in court and not women? Although it would require separate and in-depth research to answer this question, we may try to make some assessments based on a lexicological analysis.

---

[17] Stearns, *Shame: A Brief History*, 12.

Muru'a, which is a complex and elusive Arabic concept,[18] appears as *mürüvvet* in Turkish and is defined as a manly virtue. Fruma Zachs examines the ways the modern Arab discourse of masculinity made use of the pre-Islamic concept of *muru'a* during the late nineteenth century.[19] As a complex term first adopted by Arab tribes during the pre-Islamic period but which underwent significant modification in the succeeding centuries, it retained much of its persuasive powers into the nineteenth century. Both *muru'a* in Arabic and *mürüvvet* in Turkish are derived from Arabic *mar'*, which means "man" and also denotes properties such as bravery, generosity, chivalry, or the cultivation of a perfect man. Although it was originally a gendered term, in time it became a neutral term used as a property of human nature (*insaniye*) in general, especially in reference to generosity or acting humanely. However, it also continued to be used to describe masculine traits. In other words, men had to have *muru'a* in Arabic and *mürüvvet* in Ottoman Turkish to be considered praiseworthy to others in their society.

Ar and *haya* in this sense remained as a man's fear of losing his *mürüvvet*, thereby facing social disgrace. The term's close associations with manliness may be one reason why only men expressed feelings of *ar*. Since men were the ones who were usually in the public sphere, responsible for representing the honor of both themselves and their wives, it was always men who were obliged to either display or linguistically express their emotion of *ar* in public. It was also men who were expected to protect the honor of all family members, including their wives. This also shows that *ar* had a mostly sexual connotation. The use of the term by men only may also be interpreted as demonstrating their obligation to protect and discipline their wives, which I will cover in the next chapter when exploring family relations. Sources indicate that there were implicit rules about when to feel shame, to whom to express feelings of shame and, most importantly, how to express them. Because of its intensity and its implicit association with the protection of honor, only the feeling of *ar* would be expressed and justified in court.

---

[18] Ibid., 148.

[19] Fruma Zachs and Sharon Halevi, *Gendering Culture in Greater Syria: Intellectuals and Ideology in the Late Ottoman Period* (London: I. B. Tauris, 2015), 66. Zachs argues that scholars mostly agree on the two conjoined meanings of *muru'a*: "It describes the physical qualities of a man (such as strength, bravery, fortitude, military prowess, and leadership abilities) and his moral virtues (such as loyalty, chastity, dignity, politeness, hospitality, compassion, religious observance, resolve, truthfulness, and generosity)."

Shaming Others in Ottoman Society

Other cases showed that members of Ottoman society, either personally or collectively, had particular modes of shaming others to express the community's displeasure. The close relationships established between community members in traditional societies facilitated not only strong friendships but also envy and hostility. Therefore, parties in legal disputes frequently either supported false allegations or denied imputations of such, which were often labeled *töhmet* or *isnat*, or if rumors, as *goft u gû, kil ü kal, dedikodu* or *hadd-i tevâtür*. For example, in another court record dating from 1592, from the city of Bursa, a certain Sefer claimed in court that a letter had been left at the door of his house, and that it was full of words of immorality (*fuhşiyat*) about him and his legal wife and was against the law (*şer-i şerife muhalif*).[20] Sefer was suspicious of Ali, and blamed him for writing the degrading letter to him. He stated that his "suspicion is based on the grounds of hostility (*adavet-i dünyeviyye*) established between himself and Ali" and demanded that he be questioned. Although no linguistic expression of shame appeared in this court record, it is apparent that Ali left the letter in front of Sefer's house to shame him. It seems likely that this was a customary practice among the community members and shows differences in how individuals expressed their feelings of displeasure towards one another. Whether or not the accusation was true, the letter seems to show how members of society used different tools to shame others. Leaving an anonymous letter at someone's door either to slander or to embarrass them, either because of personal hostility or as a warning that other community members were aware of the addressee's misbehavior, was just one way of expressing displeasure.

In most cases, the shamers were anonymous, and their acts most likely reflected the community's evaluation of the targeted member. Moreover, different actions were used to shame others, such as spreading tar on someone's door (*kapısına katran sürme*) or hanging a horn on someone's door (*boynuz asmak*). In these cases, they shamed a community member by expressing their hostility not linguistically but by performance.

---

[20] Bursa JCR B-7: 37/6; "Mahrusa-i Bursa'da Mücellidi mahallesinden Sefer bin Kamber nam kimesne meclis-i şer-i şerifde Ali bin Abdullah mahzarında takrir-i kelam idüb hala mahalle-i mezburede sakin olduğum menzilimin kapısına mektub bırağılıb içinde bana ve hala taht-ı nikahımda olan zevceme müteallik fuhşiyat ve şer-i şerife muhalif bazı kelimat yazılmış mezbur Ali ile beynimizde adavet-i dünyeviyye zikr olunan fiili merkumdan sudur itti zannederin sual olunsun didikde gıbbe'l-istintak ve bade'l-inkar mudde-i mezburdan müddeasına mutabık beyyine taleb olundukda ihzarından aciz olıcak müdde-i merkum talebiyle mesfur Ali'ye'e zikr olunan fiil kendüden sudur eylemeyüb ve kimesneye dahi ittürmediğine yemin teklif olundukda yemin bi'llahi'l-a'lai'l-a'la ittikde ma hüvel vaki bi't-taleb ketb olunub yedd-i talibe vaz' olundu. tahriren fi evahir-i muharremi'l-haram sene ihda ve elf. Late muharrem 1001."

In a court record dating from July 27, 1692,[21] Katip Yusuf Efendi, who was responsible for the judicial investigation, brought the non-Muslim Simaven to the court and stated that somebody had spread tar on the door of Simaven's house (*kapısına katran çalma*). He demanded that the conduct of Simaven and his family be investigated by community members. In his reply, Simaven verified that tar had been spread on his door and added that he did not know who had done it. He also indicated that his family members were all *kendü halinde* and honorable (*ehl-i ırz*). When Simaven and his family were investigated, witnesses from the community all attested that the family members were honorable, upright, honest, and *kendü halinde*, and they did not entertain any visitors who misbehaved. They added that until the day of the case, they had heard nothing about them that might necessitate the intervention of legal officials. The judge made his verdict that Yusuf Efendi would be prohibited from harassing Simaven with further false allegations.

Spreading tar on someone's door was a common practice in Anatolia. Although there was no mention of shame in the aforementioned court case records, it is clear that this was a case of public shaming. Özer Ergenç was the first to bring the topic of *katran sürme* to the attention of historians.[22] Several historians later added to our knowledge about the practice by increasing the number of cases identified in various locations.[23] Ottoman historians have so far emphasized that this practice either functioned as a social sanction or as a tool for slander, and recent research shows that it was a widespread practice in Ottoman

---

[21] Sak and Solak, *38 Numaralı Konya Şer'iye Sicili*, 114. Quoted from Konya JCR 38: 74/2; "Bi'l fiil eyelet-i Karaman'a mutasarrıf olan düstur-ı mükerrem müşir-i mufahham vezir-i ruşen-i zamir izzetlü saadetlü Halil Paşa edamellahü te'ala iclaluhu hazretlerinin mütesellimi olan fahrü'l-emasil ve'l-akran Seyyid Mehmed Ağa tarafından husus-ı atiyyül'l-beyana mübaşir tayin olunan Katip Yusuf Efendi meclis-i şer'-i şerife mahmiye-i Konya'da Şükran mahallesi sükkanından hamil-i haze's-sifr Simaven veled-i Kirkor nam zimmiyi ihzar ve mahzarında takrir-i kelam ve tabir-i ani'l-meram idüb tarih-i kitap gicesi merkum zimminin zokak kapusuna katran sürmüşlerdir merkumun menzilinde olan iyalinin keyfiyet-i halleri ve mazınnası sual ve istihbar olunması matlubumdur didikte gıbbe's-sual merkum zimmi cevabında tarih-i kitap gicesi benim zokak kapusuna katran sürülmüş lakin faili malumum değildir ve iyalimde olanlar ehl-i ırz kendi hallerindedir didikten sonar mahalle-i mezbure ahalisinden el-Hac Seyyid Mustafa ibn el-Hac Osman ve ... nam kimesneler li-ecli'l-ihbar meclis-i şer'a hazirun olub eserü'l-istihbar mezbur Simaven kendi ve zevcesi ve iyalinde olanlar bi'l-cümle ehl-i ırz müstakim kendü hallerinde kimesnelerdir ve haricden dahi yaramaz makulesinden gelür gider yokdur bu ana gelince hükkam-ı kiram tarafından dahl olunmak icab eder halleri mesmuumuz olmamışdır deyu her biri habir virmeğin mübaşir-i merkumu mu'arazadan men bir'le ... (13 Zi'l ka'de 1103/July 27, 1692)."

[22] Ergenç, "Osmanlı Şehrindeki Mahallenin İşlevleri ve Nitelikleri Üzerine."

[23] See for example Cemal Çetin, "Anadolu'da Kapıya Katran Sürme Vak'aları: Konya Şeriyye sicilleri Işığında Hukuki, Kültürel, Toplumsal Boyutları 1645–1750," *Turkish Studies* 9, no. 1 (2014): 133–56; Abdulmecid Mutaf, "Osmanlı'da Zina ve Fuhuş Olaylarına Karşı Toplumsal Bir Tepki: Kapıya Katran Sürmek ve Boynuz Asmak," in *Osmanlı'dan Cumhuriyete Balıkesir*, ed. Bülent Özdemir-Zübeyde Güneş Yağcı (Balıkesir: Yeditepe, 2007): 93–104; Zübeyse Yağcı, "Osmanlı Taşrasında Kadına Yönelik Cinsel Suçlarda Adalet Arama Geleneği," *Kadın 2000* 3, no. 2 (2005): 51–81; Fikret Yılmaz, "Zina ve Fuhuş Arasında Kalanlar, Subaşıya Karşı," *Toplumsal Tarih* 220 (2012): 22–31.

neighborhoods.²⁴ Indeed, it was not a practice only limited to Muslims; it was practiced regardless of one's religious identity. For example, in a recent study, out of fifty-two cases of spreading tar on doors from 1645–1750 in the city of Konya, forty-four of the accused were Muslims, thirteen were Christians, and one was an Armenian, with this distribution mirroring the religious populations of the country.²⁵ Whatever their faith was, they communicated with one another with the same emotion concepts, with the same mode of expression. It was among the practices usually used to denounce an illicit sexual relationship (*zina*), since because these relationships were often not possible to verify and it was not easy to publicly testify in Islamic law, false allegations of illicit sex could lead to severe punishment. Gestures of shaming were also used as a message to a community member implying suspicion about their chastity and honor. Shame thus had a role in sexual discipline.

Performances of public shaming such as spreading tar, hanging a horn on someone's door, or leaving an anonymous degrading letter were intended as a warning to the targeted group member. Such warnings demanded that one behave if one wanted to return to the domain of *rıza ve şükran*. Such public shaming served both as an admonition to the wrongdoer and a wider public message that others may fear and be ashamed.²⁶ These warnings were crucial for motivating willing obedience to social and emotional norms and helping enforce community standards.

Sources also indicate that the two geographically adjacent but competing empires communicated with each another using the same emotional concepts, to which they both ascribed the same values. The same understanding of shame and its association with honor was held by the rulers as well. A letter written by the Ottoman Sultan Yavuz Sultan Selim to Şah İsmail of the Safavid Empire during the Çaldıran expedition (1514), the full text of which is in *Tevarih-i Ali Osman Li-Lütfi Paşa*,²⁷ does not include any emotion words at all. However, it

---

²⁴ Çetin, "Anadolu'da Kapıya Katran Sürme Vak'alari," 133–56. According to Çetin, several cases were identified in the cities of Balıkesir, Bursa, Manisa, Ankara, Konya, Karaman, Antep, and Kayseri that evidence its use for accusations of illicit sex.
²⁵ Ibid., 146.
²⁶ Ibid., 44.
²⁷ Lütfi Paşa, *Tevarih-i Ali Osman Li-Lütfi Paşa* (İstanbul: Matba'a-i Amire, 1341/1925): 217: "padişahların taht-ı tasarrufunda olan memleket menkuhesi mesabesindedir, reculiyyetten (manliness) hissesi ve fütüvvetden (used as valor) behresi belki derununda fi'l cümle zehresi olan kimesneler kendüden gayrı bir ferd ana taarruz ittiğüne tahammül etmek ihtimali yokdur, öyle olsa bunca gündür ki, asakir-i nusret-measirim memleketine dahil olub kamranlıklar iderler, henüz senden ne nam ve ne nişan peyda ve ne vücudundan eser hüveydadır. Hayatın mematın ale's-sivadır."

implicitly represents a display of the sultan's anger, reflecting the Ottoman state's politics of anger in its relationship with its rival, the Safavid Empire. The letter, written by Yavuz Sultan Selim, aims to provoke Şah İsmail to fight. It challenges Şah İsmail's manliness, stating that those with valor would fight against those who would abduct their wives. Declaring this code of honor, Yavuz further seeks to incite Şah İsmail to fight against him by comparing his advance into the Safavid lands to the abduction of Şah İsmail's wife. The letter of Yavuz aims to degrade and insult Şah İsmail, to make him feel ashamed in front of his soldiers and his subjects. This passage indicates clearly how the shared emotion concepts were used between two military rivals, showing that they felt the same emotions since they communicated with the same concepts.

Concluding Remarks

In this chapter, I analyzed early modern Ottoman society's understanding of shame and how feelings of shame were named, labeled, defined, expressed, and valued. Sources indicate a rich variety of lexical terms for shame, which reveal not only how shame in all its variations was experienced, but also the importance it played in communal and political relations. Each different word for shame denoted a different degree of intensity or a different source of shame. Cases indicate that the shame-word *ar* appears most frequently among others in court records, and it was the most intense feeling of shame, which was brought on by highly immoral acts, often of a sexual nature. *Ar* was also a gendered emotion, with only men being expected to express it in judicial courts on behalf of themselves, their wives, or their families. It was linked to the uniquely male obligation to protect one's family members, both physically and morally. The emotion of *ayıb*, on the other hand, was felt when an accepted pattern of social behavior was violated, but had no sexual connotations. Shame was an emotion that needed to be cultivated for the good of society, for harmony and order in communal relations, and for moral grounding. More importantly, it functioned as a tool to motivate willing obedience to social and emotional norms regulating social relationships. It helped enforce community standards, or better put, the norms of "domains of gratitude." I also showed that cases of public shaming like tarring a wrongdoer's door or leaving a threatening letter evidence emotions as practices acting as a warning against wrongdoing, highlighting the role of community members and their shared emotional concepts in maintaining community standards. Even if such cases do not have any emotion words, they may be used in tracing how people had felt, once we acknowledge that emotions reveal themselves as bodily practices. On the political level, as we have seen, it also functioned to monitor political relations with one's rivals. As two adjacent empires, evidenced to have a long historical relationship and a cultural resemblance, the Ottoman and the Safavid empires had a shared understanding of protection and shame as codes of honor. The Ottoman sultan's letter to Şah İsmail was written with the aim of appealing to his code of honor, by matching protection of one's land to honor of one's wife. It shows that they had a shared concept of protection with associated feelings of honor and shame and that is how they could communicate with one another.

5

Emotions in the Ottoman Family

In this chapter, I will scrutinize the affective ties between husbands and wives before modernity in an attempt to understand what it *meant* and how it *felt* by women to be protected in a world where they held unequal hierarchical status to men. I will first explore the emotionology[1] of the Ottoman family, the most basic legal and social unit in Ottoman society. I depart from the scholarship produced so far on the Ottoman family,[2] which has mainly focused on the family as a social structure and institution, and will examine the emotional norms of the family, embedded in social values and beliefs. Unlike the European and Ottoman historians who have either implicitly or explicitly assumed that marriages took place more for social, economic, and reproductive purposes and that love marriages only emerged with modernity, I claim that individual fulfillment and affective ties were present in early modern Ottoman families, yet expressed differently. For investigating the emotionology of the family, I refer to the book of ethics by Kınalızade, *Ahlak-i Ala'i*, intended to serve as a manual of conduct, for exploring social and emotional prescriptions, discussed in Chapter 1 and 2 in my analysis of emotion knowledge and the relations between the state and the subjects. Secondly, moving from formal prescriptions, I will

---

[1] Emotionology is defined as "the attitude or standards that a society, or a definable group within a society, maintains toward basic emotions and their appropriate expression and ways that institutions reflect and encourage these attitudes in human conduct." Stearns and Stearns, "Emotionology," 813–36.

[2] There are several studies on the Ottoman family. To cite just to cite a few: Ömer Demirel, "1700–1730 Tarihlerinde Ankara'da Ailenin Niceliksel Yapısı," *Belleten* 54, no. 211 (1990): 945–61; İlber Ortaylı, "Osmanlı Toplumunda Ailenin Yeri," in *Türk Aile Ansiklopedisi*, ed. T. C. Başbakanlık Aile Araştırma Kurumu Başkanlığı (Ankara: T. C. Başbakanlık Aile Araştırma Kurumu Yayınları, 1991): 74–81; idem, *Osmanlı Toplumunda Aile* (İstanbul: Pan Yayıncılık, 2002); Hüseyin Öztürk, *Kınalızade Ali Çelebi'de Aile* (Ankara: T. C. Başbakanlık Aile Araştırma Kurumu Başkanlığı Yayınları, 1990); Alan Duben and Cem Bahar, *Istanbul Households: Marriage, Family and Fertility 1880–1940* (Cambridge: Cambridge University Press, 1991); Abdurrahman Kurt, *Bursa Sicillerine Göre Osmanlı Ailesi (1839–1876)* (Bursa: Uludağ Üniversitesi, 1998); Abdal Rahman Abdal-Rehim, "The Family and Gender Laws in Egypt During the Ottoman Period," in *Women, the Family, and Divorce Laws in Islamic History*, ed. A. E. Sonbol (Syracuse: Syracuse University Press, 1996): 96–112; Mary Ann Fay, "The Ties That Bound: Women and Households in Eighteenth-Century Egypt," in *Women, the Family, and Divorce Laws in Islamic History*, 155–73.

seek to uncover the emotional realities experienced within Ottoman marriages by utilizing Ottoman judicial court records and *fetva* collections and explore the descriptions of emotions in the period of engagement and in divorce cases, focusing on the emotion terms and concepts that they expressed in testimonies.

Emotionology of the Ottoman Family: House of Companionship and Love (*Hane-i Ülfet ve Mahabbet*)

The second volume of *Ahlak-i Ala'i* is entitled "The Science of Household Governance" (*ilm-i tedbirül'l menzil*), and the fifth section of this volume covers "disciplining the household members" (*ehl ü iyal terbiyesi*). Kınalızade gives details on the expected conduct in interactions between husbands and wives and between spouses, their children, and their servants. Its relevant sections on family relations show the rights and responsibilities of husbands and wives embedded in social, religious, and legal norms, but also refer to emotional standards including what to feel, when and how to express such emotions. These emotional prescriptions encompass knowledge passed on from generation to generation and show idealized codes of behavior expected of husbands and wives as members of a family.

Kınalızade uses the phrase *"hane-i ülfet and mahabbet,"* which literally means "a house of companionship and love," when referring to a family. The household (*ehl ü iyal*) was defined as a unit to be taken care of that also includes servants (*hadem*).[3] Indeed, the term *ehl ü iyal* also appears in judicial court records and conduct manuals, where it refers to family members living under the same roof. For example, in a court record from the seventeenth century,[4] a man claimed that the window of his neighbor's house was within sight of his *ehl ü iyal*, disturbing their privacy; he thus demanded that it be demolished. The household members were defined as a community (*cemaat*), whose members constituted the chief pillars of a house where the basics of life take place. He further listed five fundamental elements of a house: the father, the mother, the children, the servants, and their sustenance.[5] "A house as not just as 'a building (*hane*) made up of stone or wood' but rather 'a place' (*mahal*) that embraces all of the five fundamental elements mentioned above," writes Kınalızade.

---

[3] Mustafa Koç, ed., *Kınalızade Ali Çelebi: Ahlak-ı Alâ'i* (İstanbul: Klasik, 2007): 321.
[4] Konya JCR 10: 12/3.
[5] Koç, *Kınalızade Ali Çelebi*, 322.

For Kınalızade, the husband was the chief pillar of the family. However, the wife (*hatun*) was also important, since she produced offspring and took care of them. Additionally, she served as her husband's assistant and protector of their provisions, property, and belongings. He further noted that children needed their parents both for maintenance and education. It was also necessary to have servants in the house.

The next section offers advice on how to discipline (*terbiye*) family members (*ehl ü iyal*). Kınalızade describes the role and the responsibilities of women as fundamental for the well-being of the family unit:

> a suitable wife should act as a companion, an assistant, and a partner of her husband in bringing and maintaining order in the family. In her husband's absence, she should act as the head and the protector of the household. In his presence she should act as her husband's counselor and consultant. She is her husband's confidant in overcoming difficult times and his most intimate companion in his days of sorrow.[6]

Kınalızade continues as follows:

> a most preferable wife has to be wise and pious, chaste and virtuous, respectful and modest providing her husband a deep love, pleasure, and contentment. She should pay attention to her husband's concerns and give utmost importance to protect her honor. The wife should also be grateful and never long-tongued.[7]

It shows that the relations between husbands and wives were complementary, not based on equality. Indeed, in legal terms, as per Islamic law, men and women were not equal and it was a fact of life, immutable.

Kınalızade further elaborated that a wife was to be under her husband's control and governance (*siyaset ü zabt*).[8] He emphasized that the father was to serve as the governor of the household and compared his role to that of a shepherd: Just as the shepherd takes his flock to rich pastures and protects them from predators, the head of the household must provide sustenance for his household and protect its members. This exactly mirrors the relationship between the sultan and his subjects covered in Chapter 2, which is defined and understood

---

[6] Ibid., 344. "… ve hatun-ı muvafık ve karine-i saliha, zevcine tedbir-i menzilde mu'avin ü müşarik ve gaybetinde mal u ıyalini hafız u nayib, huzurunda müşkilat-ı umurunda nasih ü müşavirdir ve şedayid ü nevayibinde gam-güsar u musahibdir."

[7] Ibid., 344. "… ve hatunların efdali vü ekmeli oldur ki akl u diyanet ve iffet ü hasanet ve edeb ü haya ve zevcine mahabbet ü safa ile mevsuf olub rıza-yı zevci kanda ise ehemm-i mehammmı olup hıfz-ı namusu gayet meramında ola. Ve zeban-dıraz u na-hak-şinas olmaya…."

[8] "Ve hatun, erinin siyaset ü zabtında 3 emri riayet ü iktisab ve 3 şeyden taharrüz ü ictinab etmek gerek."

in terms of protection. From the outset, the phrase "control and governance" denoted the deference of wives, who held inferior status both socially and legally, to the indisputable power of their husbands.

The relationship between husbands and wives in its relation to protection may be explained in terms of Ze'evi's "woman-as-an-imperfect-man" model,[9] which provides a different perspective on the unequal relations between husbands and wives. Ze'evi claims that Ottoman medical tradition was influenced by the Galenic-humoral paradigm, which supported the notion of a single-sex continuum. Influenced by the work of Thomas W. Laqueur on the history of Western conceptions of gender, Ze'evi argues that the difference between men and women tended to be seen not in terms of an absolute binary opposition, but as a continuum, in which women were seen as flawed, undeveloped males. He argues that this native medical paradigm was only challenged by the introduction of modern Western medicine in the nineteenth century, when the "imperfect man" model was discarded for the contemporary "two-sex" model. The governance of wives by their husbands may be interpreted as the need for women, as underdeveloped versions of men, to be protected and disciplined by fully developed men. This paradigm was also compatible with the Islamic religious discourse.[10] Yet, attending to emotions associated with protection provides a fuller picture of this unequal relationship in social and legal terms, in which wives were considered to be seen under the protection of their husbands.

In Kınalızade's model of control and governance, he listed three points to be obeyed and three actions that were forbidden in a marriage:

> Firstly, the man has to be the one who holds power (*heybet*) in a family. If the wife neglects his power and does not obey his claims, there would be no order in the family. If the wife gets her own way and demands that her husband fulfill every wish of hers, then the chief and the officer would switch their positions, thus leading to malice, which is a case impossible to resolve. This is the most important rule to be obeyed.[11]

---

[9] Dror Ze'evi, "Changes in Legal-Sexual Discourses: Sex Crimes in the Ottoman Empire," *Continuity and Change* 16, no. 2 (2001): 219–42.

[10] Dror Ze'evi, *Producing Desire: Changing Sexual Discourse in the Ottoman Middle East, 1500–1900* (Berkeley: University of California Press, 2006).

[11] Koç, *Kınalızade Ali Çelebi*, 347. "Riayet olunacak umurun evveli zevci zevcesinden heybet üzerine olmakdır, zira zevc hatunun nazarında mehib olmıyacak imtisal-i evamir ve ictinab-ı nevahisinde ihmal üzerinde olup ahval-i menzile ihtilal arız olsa gerek. Ve bu şart ehemm-i şuruttur. Ve bu şart mefkud olıcak avrat galib ve muradatını calib olup belki zevcini teshir ve kendi hükmüne muti' etmekle amir memur ve muti' muta' olmakla fesadat u fezayih kabahat u şenayi müterettib olur ki def'i na-mümkin ve ref'i na-meysur olur."

> Secondly, the husband should treat his wife with honor and respect to gain her heart and make her feel contented. The wife would then become deeply attached to her husband strengthening the emotional ties between the two. However, the husband should not be too generous in his display of love and affection exceeding its limits, otherwise the wife could perceive herself as superior to her husband.[12]

Thus, as the protector of their wife, a husband was expected to provide for not only their wife's material needs but also their emotional needs, by trying to gain their heart and make them feel contented. However, it is apparent that there were also constraints on display of emotions of *mahabbet* and *meveddet* on the part of husbands, who were expected not to be too generous in their display.

Kınalızade also suggested that husbands should be cautious about letting their wives socialize.

> Thirdly, the husband should not keep his wife idle. On the contrary, he should provide the available conditions to keep her busy with housework, putting the house in order, preparing the food, and worship. In her spare time, she should be encouraged to keep herself busy with either needlecraft or similar preoccupations.[13]

Husbands were expected to prohibit their wives from going to places where women would assemble, such as weddings and similar events. When wives go to such places, he claimed, they may either demand things they had seen in such places from their husbands or feel deprived for not having them, which would diminish their love and respect for their husbands.[14]

---

[12] Ibid., 347. "İkinci oldur ki zevc hatununu tekrim ü riayet eyleye, ol kadar ki mahabbetini isticlab ve meveddetini tahsil ü iktisab eyleye ki hatun ol kerametin zevalini tasavvur edip ita'at u inkiyad ve muhalesat u ittihaddan hali olmaya. Amma bu keramet ü ta'zim hadden birun olmaya ki bu, maglub ve hatun mütegallib olmakla zarar-ı mezkur müterettib olmaya."

[13] Ibid., 348. "Üçüncü emr—ki ri'âyeti vâcib idi—oldur ki hatununu bir şuglle mukayyed edip battal oturmaya komayalar. Eğer zabt-ı menzil ve levazım-ı ma'aş tertibinden ve ibadat-ı mefruza ve mendubesinden fariğ olursa evsat-ı nastan ise gazl-i kutn u kettane ve ekabirden ise zer-duzluk ve ana manend sanayi' azizeye meşgul kılalar."

[14] Ibid., 349. "Ve mümkin oldukça hatunu a'râs ve mecâmi'-i nisâ olan mevâzi'den men' edeler, husûsen bu zemânda ki nisâ arasında esbâb-ı hevâ meşhûr ve birbirine mahabbet—ki mâdde-i emr-i şenîdir—ma'rûf u mezkûrdur, pes ihtimâldir ki ba'z-ı fâsidâta celîs olup umûr-ı fâside canibine tahrîk edeler. Ve ekall-i zararı budur ki kendiden fâyik hulâ vü hulel sâhibelerin görüp tahassür ile gelip zevcine teklif-i umûr-ı mezkûre ede yâ kıllet-i mahabbet ü hurmet-i zevce mü'eddî ola. Ammâ mecâmi'-i ricâlden men' hod farz u vâcib idüği zikr ü beyâna muhtâc değildir."

The most important of the three behaviors from which husbands should refrain is the following:

> Firstly, the husband should not show his love excessively. If he has such a tendency, he should know how to hide his feelings so that his wife would not know his affection. Otherwise, she could demand fulfillment of every wish of hers by feigning reluctance.[15]

Refraining from excessive expression of emotion, especially by men, seems to be one of the most remarkable codes of display of emotions. This is compatible with the Ottoman philosophical framework for emotions, discussed in detail in the chapter on emotion knowledge. In this framework, emotions were to be moderated, and both excessive and insufficient expression of emotion were regarded as moral vices. Moreover, emotions were not always expressed linguistically but also expressed through practices.

For example, in the travelogue of Evliya Çelebi, when Melek Ahmed Pasha, Evliya's kinsman and patron, covered himself with dirt at the grave of his beloved wife, Kaya Sultan, the grand vizier Köprülü scolded him, saying that he should be ashamed of himself for crying for the sake of a woman.[16] Dunkoff correctly noted that such extreme displays of grief on the part of the Ottoman elite were considered disgraceful. So great was the importance of restraint in a man's display of love for a woman that weeping for a much-loved wife was regarded as a shameful act. Crying for a woman represented a different mode of emotional display, not through linguistic expression but physical acts.

Kınalızade then described the second and the third most important prohibitions for husbands:

> Secondly, the husband should not reveal all important affairs to his wife, and should not unveil his secrets to her.[17]
>
> Thirdly, the husband should govern his wife in such a way that she should be prevented from going to public places where she could see other good-looking men and to places where she could listen to stories of lovers and the beloved. Wives should be prevented from taking old women home and from letting them interfere in their personal affairs.

---

[15] Ibid. "Evvelkisi oldur ki gayet-i mahabbet izhar eylemeye. Eğer mihnet-i mahabbete mübtela dahi olmuş ise setr ü ketm eyleye ki zen, mahabbet-i zevce vakıf olıcak muhkem naz u idlal etmeğe azim olup ne derse imtisal olunmaya cazim olsa gerek. Bu kesret-i idlal kesret-i izlale mü'eddi olmak mukarrerdir."

[16] Dankoff, "Ayıp Değil!," 79.

[17] Koç, *Kınalızade Ali Çelebi*, 349. "İkincisi oldur ki mesalih-i azime ve umur-ı külliyede anlar ile müşavere etmeye ve cemi'-i esrar u hafaya-yı umuruna muttali' kılmaya."

In this section, Kınalızade also cited a story and advised husbands not to let their wives listen to love stories such as *Yusuf and Züleyha*, since these might arouse their passions. Likewise, he offered another warning:

> Wives should refrain from drinking wine because it may cause women to lose their sense of shame and provoke sexual desire.[18]

This clearly shows that ideally, marriage was not considered fully purposeful or rational. Wives were expected to remain under the control and governance of their husbands, but this does not imply an absence of affective ties between the two. On the contrary, although husbands were expected to be the pillar of their families, they were also expected to respect and honor their wives and endeavor to win their hearts and make them feel contented. A man's wife, on the other hand, was expected to be his assistant and companion in his days of sorrow; she had to be virtuous with a deep love for her husband. Thus, there should be mutual affection and love between them. Although we know that husbands were legally superior to their wives, their power at home did not originate solely from legal superiority. It was only made possible through the establishment of a mutual understanding built on affection, in this rather complementary relation.

Another important code of behavior involved the limitations on the public behaviors of women and the public places that they were permitted to visit. A record from another genre, namely the *fetva* collections, also reflects the restrictions placed on women:

> Question: The young girls of Amasya wore nice outfits, had makeup on, were perfumed and wore jewelry while going to public places such as *namazgah* or attending public events such as sermons. They even covered their faces and heads with thin veils, enabling them to show their beauty. Wiggling and jiggling along their walk through the crowded streets, they even let their faces show by opening and covering their veils intentionally. For all such reasons, should they be restrained from attending such public events through the aid of judges and administrators?
>
> Answer: Yes, it is appropriate to restrain them.[19]

---

[18] Ibid., 349. "Üçüncüsü oldur ki havâtîni mebâdî'-i ömrden zabt edip melâhî istimâ'ından ve ricâl ve sâhib-cemâl cüvânlar müşâhede olunacak mevâzi'den ve âşık u ma'şûk hikâyetlerinden Hüsrev ü Şîrîn gibi, Veys ü Râmîn gibi ve hezl kitâbları tilâvetinden ve istimâ'ından men' edeler, belki temâm bilmedikleri acûzu kat'â menzile koymayalar ve mehârime karıştırmayalar.İbn Arabşâh Tevârîh-i Timûr'da zikr eyler ki 'Cihânbaht Begüm—ki duhter-i Timur'dur—ibtidâda afîfe vü sâliha idi. Bagdâdiyyelerden ba'z-ı fâsideler ana ittisal edip anı ifsâd eylediler. Hâla andan hikâyât-ı sû' ve tevârîh-i bed nakl olunur.' Ve ba'z-ı ahbârda vârid olmu.tur ki 'Hatunlarınıza Yûsuf kıssasın ta'lîm eylemen, ya'nî ışk-ı Züleyhâ ve cemâl-i Yûsuf mülâhazası tahrîk-i silsile-i hevâ eylemeye.' Ve şarâb içmekten be-gâyet tahzîr eder, zîrâ keyfiyyet-i şarâb hayâyı re'f ve şehveti tehyîc ve inkıâd ve semâhat-ı tab' verir. Ve bu hısâl hatunlarda cem' olıcak fesâd-ı azîm ve fitne-i külliyye peydâ olur."

[19] Ayar and Özel, *Amasya Fetvâları ve İlk Amasya Şehir Tarihi*, 17.

The *fetva* was copied in the nineteenth century; however, it may have originally been issued much earlier. The context of the *fetva*s within this collection reveals that they were most probably issued in the late seventeenth or the early eighteenth century. This *fetva* shows how the prescriptions regarding the prevention of women from entering public spaces were reflected in women's daily lives. It also reflects a stance against social norms and an attempt to expand the limits defined by men in a male-dominated society. The women's behavior became the subject of a *fetva* because their actions themselves did not explicitly violate any religious or administrative law; rather they were recognized as pushing the established limits of acceptability. If an improper act could be proven to be a violation of the law, it could have been easily punished. However, the women described in this *fetva* were attempting to establish a new interpretation of acceptable modesty without technically violating the law. That is probably why it wasn't a subject of a case in a judicial court, but the subject of a *fetva* to determine its compliance with or violation of religious law. Although the *mufti* ruled against those women, this case also reveals an expansion of women's boundaries of freedom in the late seventeenth and early eighteenth centuries.

Although the *fetva* did not contain any textual mention of emotions, once we regard emotions as practices and understand that they are always embodied, "we may have an access to emotions by looking at other practices on which emotion-as-practice is dependent and intertwined."[20] The practice of "wiggling and jiggling along their walk through the crowded streets, letting their faces show up by opening and covering their veils intentionally" seems to instantiate what Scheer calls "doings," acts in which emotion-as-practice are dependent and intertwined. Restraints on their actions would perhaps prevent them from expressing their joy and happiness and even their desire to publicly show off their beauty.

The sources quoted above reflect an "emotional regime," in Reddy's vocabulary, defined as "the codes of expression and repression created and enforced by societies and governments." Both men and women were required to moderate their emotional expression. While husbands were restricted from excessive displays of love for women, women were restricted from going to public spaces with their fellow women, where they might accidentally hear love stories that could arouse their sexual desires. The women were to be trained and disciplined by men in an attempt to govern and protect them.

---

[20] Scheer, "Are Emotions a Kind of Practice?," 209.

Expressions of Emotions in Engagement

In the next section, I will scrutinize how both men and women expressed their feelings in familial relations, particularly in two phases of marriage. While the first stage is the *namzedlik* (engagement) period, the second is the *hul* (divorce) period, since the records in judicial court registers are most revealing about how both women and men spoke of or displayed their feelings in disputes regarding engagement and divorce.

On the path to establishing a family, men and women usually had a period of engagement (*namzedlik*) before getting legally married. (*Namzed* literally means "a candidate.") The presence of many court records from across the Ottoman Empire describing disputes involving engaged couples or writs (*hüccet*) for termination shows that *namzedlik* was a prevalent practice in Ottoman society, not only for Muslims but also for non-Muslims. Abdal Rahman also argued that marriage in Egypt in the Ottoman era almost always took place after an engagement period.[21] Many non-Muslims also appealed to Islamic judicial courts either to settle disputes about their engagements or to authorize their termination.[22] However, this does not mean that every girl had a chance to choose her husband. Families would frequently arrange marriages for their sons and daughters, acting on their behalf as their legal representatives when they were young. But in such cases, the marriage would officially start only when the children reached maturity, although there was no defined age. It was expected for both the girl and the boy to be mature enough to have the mental capacity to make discernment (*akl-i baliğ*) as per Islamic law. Therefore, the girl had the right to reject any marriage when she reached puberty. But it is hard to know how much they could exercise their right. We know only from the cases that ended up in judicial courts showing that at least some could indeed do so.

In Islamic law, *namzedlik* was termed *hıtbe* (a request that a girl be given in marriage). It was a request initiated by the man, his family, or a proxy, to marry

---

[21] Abdal Rahman Abdal-Rehim, "The Family and Gender Laws in Egypt During the Ottoman Period," in *Women, the Family, and Divorce Laws in Islamic History*, 96.

[22] İzzet Sak, "Osmanlı Toplumunda Namzedin (Nişanın) Bozulması ve Sonuçları: Konya Örneği (18. Yüzyılın İlk Çeyreğine Ait Konya Şeriyye Sicillerine Göre)," *Selçuk Üniversitesi Sosyal Bilimler Enstitüsü Dergisi* 16 (2006): 519–21. For example, in the presence of her non-Muslim (*zimmi*) *namzed* Hacetor veled-i Müyesser, the Christian (*nasraniyye*) woman Penbak bint-i Andon stated in the court that she felt contentment at marrying her *namzed*. After her declaration and the contentment of her *namzed* their marriage was officially registered ("merkum Hacetor nam zimmi benim bundan akdem namzedlim olmağla hala üçer kat melbusat ve 1 sim kuşak mehr-i muaccel ve beynimizde malum mehr-i müeccel ile ayin-i batılamız üzere nefsimi tezvice izin verdim"; quoted from Konya JCR 45: 47/4).

a girl, and the couples would get engaged (become *namzed* to each other) if the man's request was approved either by the girl herself or her family. In other words, the parties involved had to be in mutual agreement. However, since it was not regarded as a legal marriage contract, it was not legally binding and imposed no obligation for registration in the judicial courts. It was considered to be only a promise to marry (*tezevvüc vaadi*), which could be rescinded by either party. The court records that we encounter are related only to the termination of *namzedlik*. There were two main reasons for bringing such cases to trial or getting a *hüccet* from the court for its termination. One was to settle a dispute about the retrieval of the goods exchanged between the parties during the *namzedlik* period before the engagement ended.[23] The second reason was just to authorize the termination of the engagement, which would allow the woman to marry another man, since it was religiously forbidden (*haram*) to marry a woman who was still engaged to another man. However, registration of engagement in the judicial court was not obligatory.

The court records provide us with significant clues about how the institution of engagement was practiced.[24] Research into these records shows that the parents usually initiated the practice of *namzedlik* before their sons and daughters reached puberty. Probably for this reason, engagements could last for five, ten, or even twenty years. A court record dating from April 16, 1747 indicated that the non-Muslim, İlya bt. Aslan, had been engaged to Hanna for twenty-two years, for thirteen years of which period Hanna had lived in a different town.[25]

---

[23] There are also several judicial opinions (*fetvas*) given by the *müftis* regarding the exchange of the gifts during the engagement period. Bünyamin Karadöl, "Şeyhülsilam Minkarizade Yahya Efendi'nin Nikah Akdi/Evlilik ile İlgili Fetvaları" (MA diss., Çukurova University, Adana, 2006): 104: "Mesele: Zeyd Hind-i bikre namzed oldukda tarafından hediye tarikiyle bazı eşya irsal olunup her biri istihlak itdikten sonra nikah müyesser olmasa ol hedaya tarafından tazmin olunur mu? El cevap: Olunmaz." In one such *fetva* issued by Şeyhülislam Minkarizade Yahya Efendi, it was decreed unacceptable for both sides to demand the return of goods sent as gifts during the engagement, even if the marriage had not been finalized and the goods had already been consumed. A contradictory opinion, however, is given by the Şeyhülislam Ebussuud, in which he claims that the gifts should be given back, as shown in his *fetva*. Pehlul Düzenli, "Osmanlı Hukukçusu Şeyhülislâm Ebussuud Efendİ ve Fetvaları" (PhD diss., Selçuk Üniversitesi, Konya, 2007): 115: "Zeyd Hind'in kızı Zeyneb'e bir kaç yıl namzed oldukdan sonra Hind Zeyneb'i Zeyd'e vermez olıcak Zeyd-i mezbur nişan deyu ve bayramlık deyu Zeyneb'e verdiği esbabın kıymetin Zeyd almaya kadir olur mu? El-cevab: Nişan kalın makulesindendir, kalanı dahi öyle ise olur. Hediye makulesinden olanın baki olanı iki tarafdan alınır. Halik tazmin olunmaz."

[24] Sak's research drawing on judicial court registers is the most comprehensive study on the practice of *namzedlik*. His article draws on 158 writs from fourteen judicial court registers of Konya (register numbers 10, 11, 39–50) recorded in the seventeenth and eighteenth centuries.

[25] Ahmet Kankal and Kenan Z. Taş, eds, *252 Nolu Mardin Şer'iye Sicili Belge Özetleri Ve Mardin* (İstanbul: Mardin Tarihi İhtisas Kütüphanesi, 2006), 101–2. Quoted from Mardin JCR 252:101/268.

However, upon reaching puberty, either member of the couple could break the promise and terminate the engagement. Another common reason for termination was the man's inability to pay the advance portion of dowry (*mehr-i muaccel*), which was compulsory for the finalization of the marriage contract. It was also customary to send gifts to the girl's family or to determine the amount of the dowry to be paid when a couple got married. However, it should be noted that there were also rules about the value of gifts sent to the girl's family. These were sometimes expressed implicitly, and were something all parties were very well aware of. Such cases represent the material motivations of the parties to terminate engagement.

However, other cases specifically reveal women's feelings. For example, in a court record dating April 25, 1707,[26] Mehmed b. Şaban Beşe claimed that twenty years before, when Emine b. Ramamzan and himself were young, his mother, with the approval of Emine's father (who in the interim had deceased), had determined that they were to be engaged, but they had not legally married.[27] Mehmed wanted to marry Emine; however, Emine refused his request and Mehmed demanded that she be questioned.[28] In her reply, Emine declared that she would marry whomever she wanted to and she did not have *rıza* (contentment) to marry Mehmed.[29] The judge then gave Emine permission to marry whomsoever she wished.

In another court record, dating from April 29, 1661,[30] Alime bt. İbrahim refused to marry her *namzed* Hasan b. Mustafa because the engagement had been made by her sister's husband without her knowledge, and she did not

---

[26] Sak, "Osmanlı Toplumunda Namzedin (Nişanın) Bozulması," 504–5, quoted from Konya JCR 42: 218/1; "mahmiye-i Konya'da Sadırlar Mahallesi sakinlerinden İsmail nam şab tarafından husus-ı atiyyü'l-beyana vekil-i şerisi olan babası Halil bin Musa nam kimesne meclis-i şer'-i hatir-i lazımi't-tevkirde baisetü'l-kitab Fati nam bikr-i baliğanın babası ve velisi ve zikri ca'i hususa vekil-i şer'isi olan diğer el-Hac Halil bin Musa mahzarındaa üzerine bi'l-vekale dava ve takrir-i kelam idüb bundan akdem ben oğlum müvekkil-i mezbur İsmail için mezkurun kızı mezbure Fati'ye namzed itmişidim hala akd-ı nikah murad eylediğimde muhalefet üzeredir su'al olunsun didikde gıbbe's-sual merkum el-Hac Halil cevabında mukaddema mezbur Halil vech-i muharrer üzere namzed itmişidi likin tarih-i kitab gününe deign namzed helvasından gayri asla bir akça ve bir habbelik şey virmeyüb ve ila haze'l-an akd-ı nikah vaki olmamağla kızım mezbure bi'l-asale ve ben bi'l-velaye akd-i nikaha rıza virmeyüb müfarekat ve ahara tezvic murad iderin deyucek bade'l-istintak ila haze'l-an akd-i nikah olmayub ve helvadan gayri birşey virmediğini mezkur Halil ikrar itmeğin kızı mezbureyi dilediği kimesneye tezvice mezkur el-Hac Halil'e izin bir le ma-vaka'a bi't-taleb ketb olundu fi'l-yevmi'l-hamis ve'l-ışrin min şehr-i Rebi'ü'l-evvel li-sene erba'a ve mi eve elf (December 4, 1692)."

[27] "tarih-i kitabdan 20 sene mukaddem ben sagir iken validem Rahime bint-i Habib nam hatun mezbure Emine dahi sagire iken bundan akdem fevt olan babası Ramamzan bib el-Hac Abdurrahman izniyle benim için namzed idüp lakin akd-i nikah cari olmamış idi."

[28] "hala akd-i nikah murad eylediğimde mezbure Emine iba eder sual olsun."

[29] "ben nefsimi dilediğim kimesneye tezvic ve akd-i nikah ederim merkum Mehmed'e akd-i nikaha rızam yokdur."

[30] Sak, "Osmanlı Toplumunda Namzedin (Nişanın) Bozulması," 505, quoted from Konya JCR 11: 38/1.

feel contentment to marry her *namzed*. She further stated that she wanted to marry Satılmış b. Mevlud.[31]

A case from Adana represents another example of a non-Muslim refusing to marry the man she was engaged to. In this case,[32] a non-Muslim man, Nihabet veheled-i Merke, who was originally from the town of Malatya but was currently living in the Kırıtoğlu Lodge in Adana as a guest, made a claim in court against Varvar bint Artin. Varvar was a Christian girl who had reached puberty. Nihabet made the following allegation:

> Some time ago, I wanted to marry Varvar, and therefore I asked for her from her father Artin. Artin, who is now present in the court, one year before the date of this document, delegated the non-Muslim Acemoğlu to come to the church and make the betrothal prayer as per our ancient customs (*ayin-i atılamız üzere*) among our priests (*papaslarımız beyninde*) in our own church, and Acemoğlu accepted to be his proxy. Acemoğlu came to the church and prayers were held. I sent several goods to her through Acemoğlu, including a fabric of Karyağdı to make clothes, some Sakız velvet and some red silk fabric to make shirts, some İstanbuli fabric and two pieces of Egyptian gold. In addition to those, I sent five pieces of golden *müctemia*, twenty pieces of Egyptian gold on four occasions, four *çeki* cotton (1 çeki = 225,789 kg), two pieces of broom, ten *kıyye* wheat (1 kıyye = 1,282 kg), 200 *batman* grapes (1 batman = 7,697 kg), ten *yük* water melon and fifteen *yük* yellow melon (there is no standard for *yük*; for example, one yük of Bursa silk would weigh 155,86 kg) on our various special occasions. Her father Artin took the goods I had sent, showing his implicit approval, and we subsequently got engaged. Two days before the date of this document, and with the permission (*izinname*) that was given by the court, I demanded as per our ancient customs that we finalize our marriage and make a marriage contract. However, this Varvar refused to sign the marriage contract and marry me. Her father Artin confirmed his receipt of some of the goods that I had sent previously and the ones I had sent after our engagement, but denies having received some of them. Artin admitted that they had already eaten and consumed the watermelon, yellow melon, and the grapes, and that they had made *bulgur* from the wheat that I had sent, and sent back some of the wheat to me. Artin further stated that they could return the remaining goods, if I wanted them.

Then, Nihabet, the plaintiff, demanded that the legal requirements be implemented. The judge made his decision and warned the plaintiff that

---

[31] "ben akile ve baliğa olmam ile nefsimi hazırbi'l-meclis olan Satılmış bin Mevlud nam kimesneye tezvic murad ederin mezbur Hasan'a rızam yokdur."
[32] Adana JCR 14: 111/2.

the marriage contract would not be valid without the woman's *rıza*, and demanded that the remaining goods that had not yet been consumed be returned.

What is common in such cases is the use of the term *rıza*, referring to sense of pleasure, and I argue that it is the key concept to our understanding of the affective component of familial ties, linguistically expressed.[33] In most of these cases, the woman, even though engaged by family decision, refused to marry her *namzed* and rather chose to marry someone with whom she felt *rıza*. The term *rıza* in such court records implies the presence of a mutual understanding and an affective bond between those who chose to marry and establish a family. A man and woman who could not develop an emotional tie could thus refuse to marry even if their parents gave a significant amount of either money or goods/materials for their own benefit, or even if a significant amount of the advance portion of dowry had been determined to protect the woman by financial means.

The absence of any terms of endearment does not imply an absence of emotions and may be interpreted in a number of ways. Rather, emotions were embedded in the term *rıza*, which we have already seen while analyzing the relations between community members representing a mutual agreement. The word *rıza* infers being pleased, satisfied, or contented. *Rıza* in this sense was an overarching term denoting not only one's satisfaction and approval but also feelings of being pleased.

The period of engagement, if successful, would be followed by the marriage of man and woman, who were expected to become a family, entitling the members of their household to social and legal rights and obligations, with each member following an expected code of behavior towards the other. Defining the family in purely legal terms as a socially constructed unit, we may easily present it as follows: A family unit was established when a man and woman enter into a legal contract called *akd-i nikah*. This contract required the man to pay the bride an agreed amount of dowry (*mehr*). The dowry was made up of two parts; the first part was an advance payment (*mehr-i muaccel*), due at the time of the marriage, and the second part, a delayed portion (*mehr-i müeccel*), was due at the termination of the marriage or the death of the husband. Men were allowed to have more than one wife in Islamic law, although research shows that men usually tended to remain monogamous. There are records of marriage in

---

[33] For similar cases see Sak, "Osmanlı Toplumunda Namzedin (Nişanın) Bozulması ve Sonuçları," 505, quoted from Konya JCR 10: 165/2 and Konya JCR 47: 164/4.

court registers, which mostly record the financial terms of the marriage contract regarding the dowry.[34] Yet, the legal marriage records are silent about affective ties with only legal responsibilities recorded. However, divorce cases provide insights into affective ties between husbands and wives, as I will explore below.

Expressions of Emotions in Divorce

There were three types of divorce, all referred to with the term *talak*. In Islamic law, it was a husband's right to terminate a family union for any reason. Although women had the right to request a divorce, it always required her husband's approval. The first type of divorce was called *talak* in practice (although all three were basically called *talak*), in which the man repudiated his wife three times in the presence of witnesses. These words were sufficient to terminate the marriage and did not require the wife's approval. The second type of divorce was called *tefrik*: It could be initiated by either the wife or the husband, but only for special circumstances such as mental or sexual illness of one of the parties. It required the intervention of the *kadı*.[35]

The third type was called *hul* divorce, which was usually initiated by women. However, it was subject to the husband's approval, and the wife had to pay her husband compensation. This compensation took either the form of all or some of the dowry, her allowance for the three-month waiting period, an allowance for habitation, or an allowance that she had received for the children. The research produced so far shows that there were more divorce cases of *hul*-type recorded in court registers than other types. However, that does not mean that *hul*-type divorces were more common. The need for legal documentation was most probably due to the material compensation required for *hul* divorces.

The *hul*-type divorce cases are the ones that provide us with the most clues about the motivations or the emotions of married couples. Several valuable studies have examined divorce in general[36] and *hul*-type divorce in

---

[34] Sivas JCR 134: case no. 7; "Mehmed Bey karyesi sakinelerinden Saniye binti Şahaboğlu Veliüddin nam seyyibeyi Osman bin Hüseyin nam kimesne mahfil-i kazada 12.000 akçe mihr-i muaccel ve müeccele ile tesmiye-i mehr ile akd-i nikah olduğu bu mahalle kayd olundu. fi. 2 rebiiül ahir sene 1198."

[35] İsmail Kıvrım, "17. yüzyılda Osmanlı Toplumunda Boşanma Hadiseleri (Ayıntab Örneği: Talak, Muhalaa ve Tefrik)," *Gaziantep Üniversitesi Sosyal Bilimler Dergisi* 10, no. 1 (2011): 375.

[36] See for example Kıvrım, "17. yüzyılda Osmanlı Toplumunda Boşanma Hadiseleri," 371–400; Saadet Maydaer, "Klasik Dönem Osmanlı Toplumunda Boşanma (Bursa Şer'iyye Sicillerine Göre)," *Uludağ Üniversitesi İlahiyat Fakültesi Dergisi* 16, no. 1 (2007): 299–320.

particular[37] in Ottoman history, analyzing their legal dimensions. However, I will analyze the linguistic and textual analysis of the terms and the concepts used in the seemingly formulaic phrases recorded in *hul*-type divorce cases. First, I will explore the broader meaning of *hul* in Islamic jurisprudence.

The word *hul* in isolation encodes underlying emotional meanings. *Hul* is used in Islamic jurisprudence (*fıkıh*) as a term for dissolving material and nonmaterial ties. *Hul* or *nez'* also means taking off one's dress or the dissolution of power. Ömer Nasuhi Bilmen (1883–1971), a scholar of Islamic jurisprudence, described the close affective ties between husbands and wives as symbolized by an immaterial dress and defined *muhalaa* as the removal of that immaterial dress from one another's body. In other words, he defined marriage as a dress that the husband and wife put on one another. Divorce thus means taking this dress off. This symbolism is thus a tactile representation of marriage.[38]

The phrase *beynimizde hüsn-i zindegani ve musafaat* is the most commonly encountered expression used in *hul* divorce cases.[39] The parties who initiate divorce come to the court claiming that they do not have *hüsn-i zindegani* and *musafat* between them. Below, I explain these terms.

Zindegani is defined as life, a pleasant, joyous life, means of life, livelihood, and sustenance. *Hüsn*, on the other hand, means goodness, pleasantness, and politeness. The phrase *hüsn-i zindegani* denotes a good, prosperous, and pleasant life. One of its synonyms was *taayyüş*, "obtaining a living; a means of subsistence." Another synonym of *hüsn-i zindegani* was *musafat*, meaning to behave sincerely, act with pure affection towards another, and true friendship and sincerity. Drawing from this cluster of words and phrases, we may deduce that the expectations for a good marriage were perceived as achieving a good,

---

[37] See for example Madeline Zilfi, "We Don't Get Along: Women and the *Hul* Divorce in the Eighteenth Century," in *Women in the Ottoman Empire: Middle Eastern Women in the Early Modern Era*, ed. M. C. Zilfi (Leiden: Brill, 1997); İzzet Sak and Alaaddin Aköz, "Osmanlı Toplumunda Evliliğin Karşılıklı Anlaşma İle Sona Erdirilmesi: Muhala'a (18.Yüzyıl Konya Şer'iye Sicillerine Göre)," *Selçuk Üniversitesi Türkiyat Araştırmaları Enstitüsü Türkiyat Araştırmaları Dergisi* 15 (2004): 91–140.

[38] Ömer Nasuhi Bilmen, *Hukuki İslamiyye ve Islahatı Fıkhiyye Kamusu* (Istanbul: Bilmen Yayınevi, 1968), 2:268.

[39] Peirce, for example, argued that although the parallel terms *hüsn-i zindegani* and *hüsn-i muaşeret* were used in eighteenth-century İstanbul in records of women seeking divorce by making reference to Zilfi (1997), she further claimed that in sixteenth-century Aybtab, such language was limited to young girls in marriage on the grounds of a court record that she had encountered (AS2: 6b) in which a mother sued for the release of her daughter from a loveless marriage, pleading that "she has no pleasure in life and is utterly helpless" (*hüsn-i zindeganisi yok ve kız kendüden acizedir*). Leslie Peirce, *Morality Tales: Law and Gender in the Ottoman Court of Aintab* (Berkeley: University of California Press, 2003), 419. Based on my *sicil* readings, I think first that those terms were used not only by women but also men (albeit rarely) who were seeking divorce regardless of their age; and secondly, it seems quite questionable to claim that the phrase was limited to young girls in sixteenth-century Ayntab.

prosperous, and pleasant life, with affection and sincerity between husband and wife. There was, in other words, a reference, at least linguistically, not only to the material but also to the emotional well-being of husbands and wives. The presence of *hüsn-i zindegani* in a family demanded that the parties belonging to this social and legal unit would have rights and obligations towards one another that were determined by the law, traditions, and socially constructed practices. Practices and traditions were learned knowledge, which were transmitted from one generation to the next.

In a typical court case, dating from 1660 and recorded in the Konya registers, a woman named Hasene initiated a *hul* divorce case, claiming that "there is no *hüsn-i zindegani* and *musafat*" between her and her husband, and renounced her rights, including her delayed dowry of 400 akçe to be paid at the termination of a marriage or the death of her husband, her allowances for the three-month waiting period (*nafaka-i iddet*), and her conjugal rights (*zevciyete müteallika cem'i davamdan*). She also discharged her husband from all his liabilities. Her husband accepted the *hul* divorce. Various other cases also indicate that in *hul* divorces, in addition to renouncing their rights of *mehr-i müeccel* and *nafaka-i iddet*, women could also renounce their allowances for habitation (*meunet-i sükna*) or agree to give material compensation to their husbands such as cash, land, property, or other belongings.[40]

Among the many *hul*-type divorce cases recorded in the Ottoman court registers, there isn't anything unique about Hasene's *hul* divorce case. Her divorce looks much like any other *hul* divorce case in any other Ottoman city or town, recorded in a formulaic style, leaving out all the chances for any historical interpretation except about the practice of Islamic jurisprudence in the Ottoman Empire. All we know about the reason for the divorce is that there was no *hüsn-i zindegani* or *musafat* between the spouses. It is not possible to glean clues about either the emotions or the motivations of a couple from case records, which could easily be regarded as a template whose blanks had been filled by the scribes of the court, unless we make a lexicological and contextual analysis (as much as sources reveal) of the terms. If I use Ze'evi's terminology, records of *hul*

---

[40] Konya JCR 10: 160/6; "Mahmiye-i Konya'da merhum Pir Esad mahallesi sakinelerinden Hasene bint Mehmed nam hatun meclis-i şer'i hatir-i lazımü't-tevkirde zevci rafiü'l kitab Bayram ibn Yusuf mahzarında üzerine dava ve takrir-i kelam idüp, zevcim mezbur Bayram ile beynimizde hüsn-i zindegani ve musafat olmamağla zimmetinde mütekarrer olan 400 akçe mehr-i müecceldemden ve nafaka-i iddetimden ve zevciyete müteallika cem'i davamdan fariğa olub, zimmetini ibra eylediğimde ol dahi beni muhalaa idüb, kat'-ı alaka eyledi, min bad hak ve alakam kalmadı didikde gıbbe't-tasdik ma vakıa bi't-taleb ketb olundu."

divorce cases can be meaningful if each case is treated as a cultural artifact in itself. From a backward reading, divorce cases which always justified divorce due to an absence of "*hüsn-i zindegani* and *musafat*" indicate that an ideal marriage would necessitate a complementary relationship, based on affection, friendship, and sincerity.

Only some of the *hul*-type divorce cases, moreover, provide further insights and details for understanding the broader meaning of the terms *hüsn-i zindegani* and *musafat*. In such valuable records for historians, although scarce, emotions of husbands and wives who had decided to terminate their relationships were either intentionally or inadvertently recorded. Below I will give examples of individual *hul* divorce cases in which couples expressed their emotions.

The first case, dating from 1699, is a *hüccet* for a *hul*-type divorce issued on behalf of a woman named Saliha, the daughter of El-Hac Ebulkasım, who was a resident of Ahi Hacı Murat neighborhood in Ankara. Saliha delegated Seyyid Receb as her proxy (*vekil*) in her divorce case from her husband, Abdullah Çelebi, the son of Osman Efendi. The divorce proceedings were initiated by the proxy with two witnesses for the delegation: *hatip* Seyyid Yahya Efendi and Mustafa Çelebi. The titles of the parties involved indicate that both the wife's and the husband's families were from the religious class. Saliha Hatun, via her proxy in the court, stated that she had requested a *hul* divorce from her husband since there was *nüşuz* and *i'raz* between them, and she renounced her rights of her *mehr-i müeccel* amounting to 500 *guruş*, allowances for waiting period and habitation, and agreed to pay seventy *guruş* to her husband as a compensation for her demand of *hul* divorce. After the payment, they discharged one another from any further conjugal and legal liabilities.[41]

---

[41] Ankara JCR 78: 89; "Medine-i Ankara'da Ahi Hacı Murat Mahallesinde sakine Saliha bint El Hac Ebulkasım nam hatun tarafından hul'-i cai'i'z- zikri ikrara vekil olub, zat-ı mezbureyi marifet-i şer'iyye ile arifan olan fahrü'l-hüteba Es seyyid Yahya Efendi ibn Es Seyyid El Hac Abdürrahim efendi ve Mustafa Çelebi ibn El Hac Mehmed nam kimesneler şehadetleri ile şeran vekaleti sabite olan zahrü's-sadati'l-kiram Es Seyyid Recep Çelebi ibn Es Seyyid Mustafa nam kimesne meclis-i şer'-i hatir-i lazımü't-tevkirde müvekkile-i mezbure Saliha'nın zevc-i muhali'i işbu hafızü'l-vesika Abdullah Çelebi ibn Osman Efendi nam kimesne mahzarında bi'l-vekale ikrar ve takrir-i kelam idüb, müvekkile-i mezbure Saliha, zevcim mezbur Abdullah Çelebi ile nüşuz ve i'raz üzere olub, hul'a taliba olduğum eclden zimmetinde mütekarrır olan ve ma'kudun- aleyh olan 500 guruş mehr-i müeccel-i müsemmam ve nafaka-i iddet-i malume ve me'unet-i süknamdan farığa ve mal-i sarihimden dahi 70 guruş virmek üzere mezbur Abdullah Çelebi ile muhalaa-i sahiha-i ser'iyye ile hul" ve bedel-i hul' olan 70 guruşu mezbur Abdullah Çelebi'ye bad'-def' ve't-teslim her birimiz aherin zimmetini hukuk-ı zevciyyete müteallaka amme-i dava' ve mütalabat ve i'man-ı muhasematdan ve bedel-i hul' olan 70 guruşdan ibra-i amm-i kati'ü'n-niza' ile ibra eyledik. bade'l-yevm hukuk-ı zevciyyete müteallaka tarafeynden dava' ve niza sadır olursa lede'l-hükkami'l-kiram istima' olunmasın dedi didiği gıbbe't-tasdik ma vakıa bi't-taleb ketb olundu. fi'l-yevmi's-sani aşer min cemaziyü'l-ahere sene 1110."

If we try to interpret this legal document through its neutral tone, it may seem as if there is nothing that would make this case stand apart from various other *hul hüccets* registered, revealing nothing about the motivations or the emotions behind the scenes. The reason for the divorce, however, is stated as *nüşuz ve i'raz üzere olmak*. This expression was used in Islamic jurisprudence to refer to couples drifting apart from each other. A husband unwilling to continue the relationship was called *naşiz*, while a wife wanting to end the relationship was called *naşize*. What distinguishes this case from the other *hul* divorce cases are the phrases *nüşuz* and *i'raz*. In Islamic jurisprudence, *nüşuz* by the husband means treating his wide cruelly (*cefa*) and considering her disgusting, detestable, abominable (*kerih*). *Nüşuz* by the wife, on the other hand, denotes the wife's rebellion (*isyan*), opposition to her husband, and her disgust at him.[42] *İ'raz* means turning away (from a thing); a declining, shunning, avoiding. Lexicological analysis of the words *nüşuz* and *i'raz* thus gives us clues about the emotional tone of the relationship. In these two synonymous words, what is explained is a kind of turning away from one another grounded in hate and disgust. Both hate and disgust are emotions that do not suddenly occur, but evolve self-consciously and involve the application of past experience, which accumulate over time. The contextual analysis of words such as *nüşuz* and *i'raz* helps us discern the emotional states of the parties and their expressions of them.

In this document, we understand that they were in the termination period of a marriage; however, we do not know how long they had been experiencing problems, what was responsible for the divorce, which party had the deeper hate, or what led them to hate each other. However, we also understand from the *hüccet* that Saliha Hatun not only renounced her rights of *mehr-i müeccel* for 500 *guruş* and her allowances for the waiting period and habitation, but in addition, agreed to pay seventy *guruş* to her husband as compensation. This may indicate, together with her declaration indicating a degree of hate in her claim, that it was clearly she who demanded the termination of the marriage.

Another case from the Konya court records provides further clues about the broader meaning of the term *hüsn-i zindegani*. Fatma bint Ali claimed that there was no *hüsn-i zindegani* in their marriage on the grounds of the presence of *şikak* and absence of *vifak*. An absence of *vifak* means that they could not establish an emotional connection. *Vifak* means mutual agreement and peaceful coexistence, and *şikak* means incompatibility, quarreling, and contention. Her

---

[42] Bilmen, *Hukukı İslamiyye*, 2:269.

statement in court suggested that they had only recently wed. Furthermore, in her statement, she informed the court that she was unsure whether or not she was pregnant, but if she were, she would take full responsibility for the child with no obligation whatsoever from her former husband.[43] The term *vifak* in this case record shows that a requirement of marriage was a harmonious and peaceful relationship between the spouses, and the absence of such a relationship was considered grounds for divorce.

Concluding Remarks

In this chapter, I have examined what it *meant* and how it *felt* for wives to be protected in the hierarchical world of unequal power relations within marriages. Sources indicate that early modern familial relations were complementary, not based on equality. Contrary to the general assumption that marriages in the pre-modern era were grounded in purely practical considerations such as reproduction and material support, exploring the emotional norms of the familial relations in the book of ethics *Ahlak-i Ala'i* has clearly shown that, while husbands held superior legal and social status, they were expected to protect their wives not only materially, but also emotionally, by trying to gain their hearts and make them feel contented. Couples pursued their emotional well-being in their marriages in addition to pursuing their material or other goals. The emotion of *mahabbet* as a mutual love was expected to be felt among the couples. Yet there were constraints on its display; hence, husbands were not expected to be too generous in their displays of love. Women on the other hand were restrained from showing their emotions, particularly in public places. Display of emotions was to be moderated rather than suppressed, which also suited their emotion knowledge that I had explored in Chapter 1. Examining

---

[43] Konya JCR 58: 7/5; "Mahmiye-i Konya'da Dolab Ucu mahallesi sakinelerinden zatı muarefe olan Fatma bint Ali nam hatun meclis-i şer'-i enverde işbu rafiu'l-kitab zevc-i muhali'i Ahmed bin Emrullah mahzarında ikrar-ı tam ve takrir-i kelam idüb zevcim mezbur ile beynimizde şikak ve adem-i vifak vukuundan naşi hüsn-i zindeganimiz olmamağla zimmetinde mukarrer ma'kudun aleyh 13 guruş mihr-i müeccelim ve iddet nafaka ve meunet-i süknam kendi üzerime olub, hamlim dahi zuhur ider ise bir şey talebinde olmayıb, kendüm infak ve iksa itmek üzere cümlesinden fariğa olub, muhalaa-i sahih-i şer'i eylediğimde ol dahi ber minval-i muharrer hul' itmeğle, ibtida-i zevciyetden tarih-i kitaba gelince hukuk-ı zevciyete müteallika cüzzi ve külli amme-i deavi ve mutalabat ve kaffe-i muhasematdan zevcim mezburun zimmetini ibra-i amm ile ibra ve iskat-ı dava eyledim zimmetinde bir akçe ve bir habbe hak ve alakam kalmadı didikde gıbbe't-tasdik-i'ş-şeri ma vakıa bi't-taleb ketb olundu. fi 3 rebiü'l ahir 1177. musa efendi, hatib süleyman efendi, hüseyin bin ahmed, ibrahim bin mustafa, Anbdurrahman Beşe bin Ahmed."

judicial court records on engagement and *hul*-type divorce cases has also shown the emotional realities of marriages. Linguistic and contextual analysis of the frequently used terms *hüsn-i zindegani and musafat* also showed that a good marriage meant achieving a good, prosperous, and pleasant life, with affection and sincerity between husband and wife, indicating absence of affective ties as the motivations for divorce.

6

Changing Meanings of Protection and Transformation of Emotions

In the preceding chapters, I have first explored the emotion knowledge of Ottoman society and then explored what it *meant* and how it *felt* like to be protected in the political, social, and familial ties in the early modern era, roughly covering the period from the sixteenth century to the beginning of the nineteenth century, and I have shown how the frequently used emotion concepts in all three scales provided the various meanings of protection at each level. On the political scale, it was the emotions of compassion (*merhamet*) and love (*mahabbet*) that made the concept of protection plausible. On the social level, it was the feelings of contentment and gratitude (*rıza* and *şükran*) rather than their secondary identities that helped them to draw boundaries of their sub-communities. On the familial level, it was the feelings of love (*mahabbet*), pure affection and sincerity (*musafat*) and contentment (*rıza*) that provided the meaning of protection of wives by their husbands. In this chapter I focus on the nineteenth century and particularly the *Tanzimat* (literally "giving order") era (1839–76), which has long been researched by Ottoman historians, who have explored the political and social transformations, adding much to our understanding of the era.[1] However, none of the research produced so far has focused on the changing notions of protection and emotions associated with it. It was a period of political revolutions, separatist movements, change in communication and

---

[1] It is not possible to cite all the research, but for reference studies please see Halil İnalcık and Mehmet Seyitdanlıoğlu, eds, *Tanzimat/Değişim Sürecinde Osmanlı İmparatorluğu* (İstanbul: Phoenix Yayınları, 2006); Carter Vaughn Findley, *Turkey, Islam, Nationalism, and Modernity* (New Haven: Yale University Press, 2010); Roderic H. Davison, *Reform in the Ottoman Empire 1856–1876* (Princeton: Princeton University Press, 1963); Halil İnalcık, "Application of the Tanzimat," *Archivum Ottomanicum* 5 (1973): 97–128; Butrus Abu-Manneh, "The Islamic Roots of the Gülhane Rescript," *Die Welt des Islams* 34, no. 2 (1994): 173–203; Şükrü Hanioğlu, *A Brief History of the Late Ottoman Empire* (Princeton: Princeton University Press, 2008).

transportation technologies, with emerging new fields of knowledge, new military technologies, interwoven with global trends of nationality, empire-wide educational reforms going hand in hand with secular understanding of knowledge, and each had a transformative effect on politics, society and the individual.[2]

But it was a gradual process, the consequences of which were more apparent and more prompt at some levels, while unclear and slow in others. Rather, there was a continuity of previous centuries' understanding of protection and thus its associated emotions. The most apparent change started in the political sphere, since *Tanzimat* reforms represented a change from subjects of an empire to citizens, which demanded immediate enactments defining the obligations on the part of the citizens. There was also a continuity in the emotions on the societal level, but change started to show up, at least in some parts of the empire, particularly in the cities, which had high rates of population increase because of migrations. Unsurprisingly, the least impact occurred at the familial level, between husbands and wives. In terms of their understanding of protection, almost nothing changed during the nineteenth century, except some women's activism, mostly in the capital, and which would not turn out to be a widespread movement.

Modernization Efforts in the 19th Century

In this section, instead of giving a detailed analysis of the reforms launched during this period, I will consider those that were closely related to the changing meaning of protection. The Tanzimat era, for historians of the Ottoman Empire, represents a turning point towards modernization. Although modernity is an elusive concept, it was definitely a time of change and transformation at all levels, political, social, and individual. Findley rightly defines modernity as understood by the Ottomans as "an epoch turned toward the future, characterized by the expectation that the world of the future will be better, including not just forward spatial motion, but qualitative improvement through reason and scientific experimentation."[3] Ottoman bureaucracy and the intelligentsia were determined to build a "better" world for the state and society, as evidenced by a recurrent use of the term "new" (*cedid*).

---

[2] Findley, *Turkey, Islam, Nationalism, and Modernity*, 15.
[3] Ibid.

Indeed, the modernization efforts had already started in the late eighteenth century, during the reign of Sultan Selim III (r. 1789–1807), when the Ottomans first realized their military incompetency against the Western powers. Several improvements were made, particularly in military forces, including gunpowder production, artillery, and navy. The Army Engineering School (*Mühendishane-i Berri i Hümayun*) was founded in 1795. The major military initiative was the new infantry (*Nizam-ı Cedid*, "new order"), supported by its own treasury (*İrad-ı Cedid*, "new revenue").[4] Indeed, *Nizam-ı Cedid* also became the name of his whole reign of reforms. However, the program of military reorganization and reforms ended with the collapse of the "New Order" when Selim III was deposed in 1807 by a Janissary revolt.[5] Although his reforms were restricted to the military sphere only, its scope would soon be expanded to the social sphere as well, by his successors.

Modernization efforts continued through the reign of Mahmud II (r. 1808–39). After the dissolution of the Janissary corps in 1826 by Mahmud II, the regulations of Selim III continued with revisions and recruitment, and training began for the new army, the Trained Victorious Soldiers of Muhammad (*Muallem Asakir-i Mansure-i Muhammediye*). During the reign of Mahmud II, the empire launched new educational institutions such as military engineering schools, a new Military Medical School (1827) and Military Academy (Harbiye, 1834), and hired foreign experts (primarily from France) and started sending students to Europe.[6] Apart from the schools for educating military officers, the Translation Office of the Sublime Porte (*Tercüme Ofisi*) was also established during his reign, which is regarded as the first Ottoman educational body for bureaucrats.[7] It was also Mahmud II who laid the grounds for a modern system of education, evidenced by starting a new type of school, *rüşdiye* (the higher elementary school). Moreover, the first Ottoman official gazette *Takvim-i*

---

[4] Ibid., 33.
[5] Ali Yaycıoğlu, "Guarding Traditions and Law—Disciplining Bodies and Souls: Tradition, Science and Religion in the Age of Ottoman Reform," *Modern Asian Studies* 52, no. 5 (2018): 1542–603. Although the "New Order" has usually been examined within the framework of the Westernization of Ottoman military and administrative forces, and the Janissary-led opposition to it understood as a conservative resistance, Yaycıoğlu challenges this assumption. Instead, he argues that there were two trans-imperial movements that formed a discursive alliance against established norms, local conventions and vested privileges. On the one hand, it was a Europeanist movement carried out by bureaucrats, and Ottoman and European military engineers representing a global trend in military and fiscal reorganization. On the other hand, it also represented a "Muslim New Order" advocated by Nakşibendi-Müceddidi dervishes.
[6] For educational reforms during the Tanzimat era see Berrak Burçak, "Science, a Remedy for All Ills. Healing the 'Sick Man of Europe': A Case for Ottoman Scientism" (unpublished PhD diss., Princeton University, 2005).
[7] Findley, *Turkey, Islam, Nationalism, and Modernity*, 41.

Vekayi was published in 1831, representing a new channel for dissemination of knowledge. Journalism would increase unprecedently in the following decades, in which several new periodicals and papers appeared, including but not limited to *Ceride-i Havadis* (Newspaper of Events), *Tercümân-ı Ahvâl* (Interpreter of Situations), *Tasvir-i Efkâr* (Representation of Opinions), *Tercümân-ı Hakikat* (Interpreter of Truth).[8] On the political level, complete autonomy of Serbia under Ottoman suzerainty which was formalized in the Treaty of Edirne (1829) and the Greek War of Independence (1821–30) also coincided with the period of Mahmud II's modernization efforts, which would later have larger implications for the non-Muslim subjects of the empire in the following decades.[9] The reigns of Selim III and Mahmud II represent the initial steps of reform acts soon to be implemented.

Abdülmecid (r. 1839–61) was enthroned in July 1839 at the age of sixteen and continued the reforms that his father Mahmud II had already started. On November 3, 1839, an edict *Gülhane Hatt-ı Hümayunu* (Gülhane imperial rescript) was proclaimed, also known as *Tanzimat Fermanı*. The Tanzimat era, starting with the Gülhane imperial rescript in 1839, continuing with *Islahat Fermanı* (the Reform decree) in 1856 until the constitution of 1876, was a period in which transformation had started on political, social, and individual levels. The main themes of *Tanzimat* included but were not limited to civil bureaucratic hegemony; elite formation; legislation; governmental expansion; changes in intercommunal relations; and transformation of the political process.[10] Whether Tanzimat reforms were undertaken under the influence of the West or not has been long debated by historians. The rescript itself showed no evidence of ideas or ideals borrowed from Western political theory, but rather represented a reconfirmation of traditional state philosophy.[11] Traditional state philosophy was still formulated with the concept of "circle of justice" and an understanding of protection according to which all the subjects of the empire were protected subjects of the ruler, entrusted to him by God. As per Islamic law, still, legal status of a subject was determined by faith, gender, and whether or not they were a slave or free person. The Tanzimat edict was thus not any different from the previous rescripts of justice, with non-Muslim subjects ruled within the

---

[8] Burçak, "Science, a Remedy for All Ills," 65.
[9] Stanford Shaw, *History of the Ottoman Empire and Modern Turkey Volume II: Reform, Revolution, and Republic: The Rise of Modern Turkey, 1808–1975* (Cambridge: Cambridge University Press, 1977), 15.
[10] Findley, *Turkey, Islam, Nationalism, and Modernity*, 88.
[11] Butrus Abu-Manneh, "The Islamic Roots of the Gülhane Rescript," *Die Welt des Islams* 34, no. 2 (1994): 173–203.

framework of *zimmi* law (hence, the word *zimmi* originates from *zimmet* which literally means "protection") and the laws and regulations applied equally to all subjects. This time, however, the edict started with the opening "the last 150 years... the sacred sharia was not obeyed nor were the beneficent regulations [of sultans] followed. Consequently, the former strength and prosperity have changed into weakness and poverty," which evidences that abiding to sharia and law was prescribed as a remedy to restore the state in its strength and prosperity.[12]

Indeed, Sultan Abdülmecid issued an *irade* (edict) on July 17, 1839, shortly before the Gülhane Script, to be read to ministers in which he exhorted them "to follow the laws of justice and equity in all matters" and "to observe constantly the application of the honored sharia in all the affairs of the exalted sultanate." Butrus Abu-Manneh, basing his argument on this previously issued edict, suggests that it was a prelude to the Gülhane Script, evidencing that the Gülhane Script had its roots in Muslim thought and political concepts.[13] The Gülhane Script was not, according to Abu-Manneh, a "bill of rights," but a declaration of the need to abide by a just government according to sharia, which stands as the basic duty of any Muslim leader in Islam.[14] Disparities between Muslim/non-Muslim, man/woman, slave/free person in terms of legal status were still a fact of life and immutable.

Thus, the Tanzimat edict did not imply civil or political equality among the subjects, and the subordinate legal status of non-Muslims did not change. Although the government made an effort to promote it as the beginning of a new era, it did not aim to offer an equal legal or social status to non-Muslims. Still, the subjects, Muslim and non-Muslim were under the protection of their sultan, representing the state as well, and all were entitled to his compassion and fatherly love without exception. Ottoman bureaucrats still thought restoration of justice, understood as a traditional Muslim political concept, would be enough to prevent separatist tendencies of non-Muslims and unite all the subjects of the empire with feelings of *mahabbet* to their protector. Indeed, the main topic of discussion in the Tanzimat era among the Ottoman modernist intelligentsia was on a remedy that would cement unity for all the citizens of the empire, expressed with the term "*ittihad-ı anasır*," meaning uniting different elements.

The Reform decree (*Islahat Fermanı*) of 1856 confirmed the issue of equality decidedly. It was a decree about reforms to be enacted, "as required by the imperial

---

[12] Abu-Manneh, "The Islamic Roots of the Gülhane," 195.
[13] Ibid., 201.
[14] Ibid.

decree read at Gülhane and by my auspicious Tanzimat" for the benefit "without exception, of all my imperial subjects of every religion and sect."[15] The different religious communities were to form assemblies to reorganize their affairs. As a result, non-Muslim communities acquired communal "constitutions" and new quasi-parliamentary bodies by the early 1860s. The decree liberalized the conditions for building and repairing non-Muslim religious buildings. It forbade language or practices that "held some communities lower than others." It proclaimed Ottoman subjects of all religions eligible for official appointment depending on their ability, and opened both civil and military schools to all. It extended the obligation of military service to non-Muslims but allowed exemption on payment of a substitution fee.[16] It was also a time when the concept of "protection" started to be debated and negotiated. Every group had different interpretations of the reform decree of 1856 in terms of the concept of "protection."

From *Mahabbet* to Love of Fatherland

In the political sphere, Tanzimat reforms represented an attempt to reconfigure ruler–subject relations. They mainly consisted of the de-personification of the state and its transformation to an abstract entity, thus leading also to a change in commonly shared emotion codes associated with protection. Protection of the subjects with compassion (*merhamet*) and affection (*mahabbet*), and subjects' feelings of *mahabbet* for their protector, for example, were culturally and historically significant during the period between the sixteenth and the eighteenth centuries, when it was compatible with the personification of the state in the body of the ruler. Although it was a gradual process, throughout the nineteenth century, the expectations of being protected by compassion and love slowly started to disappear. Now, it was the law of the rule that granted the protection of the subjects as individuals. Protection, for the subjects, started to mean being entitled to equal rights and obligations, with equal treatments before the law. It was no longer their wish to be personally protected by the sultan by *merhamet* (compassion) or *mahabbet* (love), but rather to be protected by the laws of the state, which were expected to be void of emotions. It was a time to transform the subjects of an empire (*teb'a*) to dutiful citizens (*vatandaş*). The

[15] Findley, *Turkey, Islam, Nationalism, and Modernity*, 92.
[16] Ibid.

phrase "bonding with the hearts of citizens" (*revabıt-ı kalbiyye-i vatandaşi*) used in the Reform decree (*Islahat Fermanı*) of 1856 is particularly revealing. On the one hand, it resembles the metaphoric expression of "uniting with the hearts" of the subjects (*te'lif-i kulûb-ı reaya*), with its several synonyms such as prospering,[17] calming,[18] attracting,[19] and consoling,[20] that we have already seen in Chapter 3. On the other hand, this time it refers to *vatandaş* (meaning citizens sharing the same fatherland), instead of *reaya* (subjects of an empire). It was also during this period when the meaning of "*vatan*" changed, too. Previously, it referred to a place of birth or residence, but in this era it started to mean "fatherland." Sometimes it was phrased as "*mahabbet-i vataniyye*" (love of fatherland). While it was the feelings of *mahabbet* of the subjects for their protector that could cement unity in the early modern period, now, thought the Ottoman bureaucrats, the patriotic feelings of dutiful citizens for their fatherland would provide the necessary factor for unity. However, the feelings of *mahabbet* which was expected to be felt by the citizens of an abstract entity of state, providing protection due to its promise to abide the new law and regulations, would not be the same feelings of *mahabbet* as had been felt by the subjects of the empire to their protector.

The period of Tanzimat can be viewed as a flood of legislations, regulations, orders, and laws enacted with recurrent reference to "rationality." Volumes of new legislations and regulations had been published in this transformative era. Apart from the reform acts of 1839, 1856, and 1876, an initial penal code (*Ceza Kanunnamesi*, 1840), asserting the equality of all subjects before the law without deference to rank, was revised in 1851 and replaced with a code of French origin in 1858.[21] Several laws, regulations, and orders were issued during the Tanzimat era, confirming that the Ottoman bureaucracy was determined more than ever to give "order" to Ottoman society. These included (but were not limited to) the codes of commerce (1850) and maritime commerce (1863), the agrarian code (*Arazi Kanunnamesi*, 1858), and a codification of sharia law under the direction of Ahmed Cevdet Paşa and published as the *Mecelle* (1870–77).[22]

However, the persistence of the value and meaning of the emotion codes of the preceding era was still apparent and is best reflected in the verses of an

---

[17] "terfih-i kulub-ı reaya."
[18] "tatmin-i kulub-ı reaya."
[19] "celb-i kulub-ı reaya."
[20] "tatyib-i kulub-ı reaya."
[21] Findley, *Turkey, Islam, Nationalism, and Modernity*, 93.
[22] Ibid.

Ottoman intellectual, Ziya Paşa (1825–80), who lived in a period when most of the traditional Ottoman institutions were being renewed and restructured. His famous poem "*terkib-i bend*" implicitly bears a criticism of modernity, a part of which is quoted below:

Evrâk ile i'lân olunur cümle nizâmât
Elfâz ile terfîh-i ra'iyyet yeni çıkdı

This can be roughly translated as: "Regulations are enacted by written orders / For prospering the subjects literally, that's new!" The term *evrak* (pl. of *varak*: sheet of paper) in this couplet denotes the new statutes, written rules or regulations, enacted during the Tanzimat era and publicized in their written forms as a requisite of modernity, in an attempt to give order to society that had long, in their view, been neglected. *Elfaz* (pl. of *lafz*: word, letter), on the other hand, denotes literal understanding of law. The second line indicates his criticism of the new regulations. The couplet resonates different interpretations of law, some of which are still under debate. One rule for interpretation of law is the "literal rule," according to which the words and terms used in the statutes are construed in their plain sense with the presupposition that they are precise enough not to need consideration of the function, the "sense", or the "spirit" of law. Ziya Paşa criticizes the Tanzimat regulations for lacking "sense" of law, while aiming for the prosperity and welfare of the subjects. The new regulations and laws enacted were, according to Ziya Paşa, all void of emotions with no reference to emotional codes that provide the meaning of the concept of "protection." The new codification of law was based solely on reason, without any embedded or accompanying emotion codes. In other words, he criticizes the separation of reason and emotions in political thought. Modernity, for Ziya Paşa, denotes a purely rational political ideology void of emotions. The regulations were so precisely defined that there was no room left for negotiation, which is in contrast with the previous practices of legislation. It seems that Ziya Paşa stands as the last representative of the classical period.

Change in the Domain of Medical Knowledge

Tanzimat was also an era for new fields of knowledge, the most important of which constituted the modern positivist science. Its transformative impact on society was important on two grounds. On the one hand it would transform the relationship that people had created with the world. On the other hand, as

Berrak Burçak persuasively showed in her thesis, "scientific" writings during the Tanzimat era (encompassing a wide variety of topics on astronomy, geology, formation of the earth, chemistry, physics, metallurgy, concept of atom, volcanoes, earthquakes, magnetism) were a perfect tool with which to instill loyalty to the sultan and the state, and to ensure that educated people would become obedient and dutiful Ottoman citizens.[23] Journalism, in that sense, provided the most effective new channel to disseminate science as a new field of knowledge. Moreover, it laid the grounds for the dichotomy between reason and emotion.

As a new field of knowledge, psychology also had its repercussions in the opposition between reason and emotion, although its thorough establishment would occur after the Tanzimat era. The years between the 1870s and 1920s have been considered a period of transformation for psychology, during which it prepared to leave the house of metaphysics, religious thought, and moral sciences to join the team of sciences, according to Afacan.[24] It was quite late, however (only in the first decades of the twentieth century), that psychology would become a new field of science and take its place in the curricula of the university, *Darülfünun*. The first known dedicated psychology textbook taught at the *Darülfünun* was written by Filibeli Ahmed Hilmi in 1911 based on a French textbook, *Cours Élémentaire de Philosophie* (Elementary courses of philosophy) written by Émile Boirac, which Afacan sees as a turning point in psychological education.[25] For a long time, up until the twentieth century, the Ottoman intelligentsia tried to integrate psychology as a new field of knowledge into the long-established tradition of *İlm-i Ahlak*, that we have already covered in Chapter 1. It was only in the twentieth century during which emotions were no longer considered as either vices or virtues, expressed in actions, relations, practices, but rather were moved inside the bodies, into inner space, waiting to be explored, evaluated and expressed by self-reflection. Morality no longer provided the philosophical framework in which emotions were situated. Refutation of the Galenic understanding of medicine by the new medical knowledge based on evidence and experiments also went hand in hand with a change in the place of emotions in the philosophical knowledge. Emotions were no longer to be sought in moral behaviors. I would argue that this is the reason

---

[23] Burçak, "Science, a Remedy for All Ills," 103.
[24] Şeyma Afacan, "Of the Soul and Emotions: Conceptualizing 'the Ottoman Individual' Through Psychology" (unpublished PhD diss., University of Oxford, 2016): 66.
[25] Afacan, "Of the Soul and Emotions," 89.

why people more frequently started writing self-narratives, their inner thoughts and feelings, hidden but only sought by self-reflection. Adaptation of psychology as a new field of science gradually paved the way to perceive emotions as obstacles to reason, which should be suppressed. Previously, however, it was the idea of "moderation," "equilibrium," and "justice" (*adl*) of faculties that provided the basis for virtuous emotions, both the excess and the deficiency of which would be regarded as emotion-vices.

Transformation of Emotions in Societal and Familial Relations

Transformations, however, were not limited by the political relations established between the rulers and the ruled. Reforms of the era also paved the way to a different understanding of protection of and by the community members. In the early modern period, it was the emotions of "*rıza*" and "*şükran*" that provided the meaning to whom to protect and how, and how to define the borders of their communities in which relations were usually conducted face-to-face and with people acting as guarantors of their fellows, as we have already seen in the preceding chapters. In the early modern period, subjects of the Ottoman state having different religious, ethnic, spatial, occupational, or otherwise subsidiary identities, were termed as either *taife* or *cemaat*. Some of them were spatially defined, like residents of neighborhoods (*mahalle cemaati*) or of villages (*köy cemaati*); some were religiously defined, like Armenian *taife*, Rum (Orthodox Christian) *taife*; and still others were occupationally defined, like bread-maker *taifesi* or blacksmith *taifesi*. Although the general terms used for all of the communities were either *cemaat* or *taife*, the terms *millet* or *fırka* were also used when referring to the subjects' religious identities. However, the term *taife* was very revealing in representing the sub-communities in terms of occupation, faith, and ethnicity. During the Tanzimat era, however, the term *millet* started to be used exclusively for non-Muslims. *Taife* lost its neutral meaning as a term.

The new rules and regulations implemented the concept of equality between Muslim and non-Muslim citizens of the empire, and the continuing separatist movements from the Ottoman Empire also had consequences on the societal level. Moreover, increased spatial mobility in the empire during the Tanzimat era had repercussions. There was an unprecedented movement of populations, which also went hand in hand with movement of ideas and cultural practices. According to Findley, between 1840 and 1890, urban populations grew from 400,000 to about 900,000 in Istanbul, from 110,000 to 200,000 in Izmir, and from about 10,000 to more than 100,000 in Beirut.[26] As of 1860, Cairo had a population of 300,000, Damascus 100,000, and Baghdad 60,000; the populations of those three cities more than doubled by 1914.[27] Economic growth, rural-to-urban migration in search of opportunity, and the benefits of early improvements in public hygiene and infrastructure stimulated urban growth. Rural populations were in flux, too, and not only because of rebellions and intercommunal disturbances. Each stage of Russian expansion in the Black Sea region and the Caucasus led to expulsions of Muslims, starting with the Crimean and other Tatars after 1783, and continuing with non-Turkish Caucasian Muslims (Circassians, Abkhazians, Daghestanis) in the 1860s. The refugee flows numbered in the hundreds of thousands from 1854 on, rising to 400,000 in 1864.[28] Settlement of new populations in the domains of Ottoman land, however, was not an easy process. Newcomers from foreign lands, and the new rural populations in the urban sites still sought their old communities, and believed that instead of a state as an abstract entity, they would be better protected by their fellows to whom they felt *rıza* and *şükran*.

It seems that it was no longer the feelings of *rıza* and *şükran* that bonded the subcommunities, but rather it was laws and regulations, with a literal approach to law that Ziya Paşa had criticized, according to which the citizens of the empire would be protected by the state on an individual basis. The moving out of the domain of gratitude was a long process as we have seen, starting with counseling, warning, keeping under watch, and only in some cases, continuing with legal action. In the Tanzimat era and the succeeding periods of reform, however, it was now the state that would interfere with the intracommunal affairs, dispelling the long process of counseling, warning, and watching of fellow members by the community. While it was the neighborhoods to which one belonged that were the main determinant of subsidiary identities, in time, throughout the nineteenth century, people started moving to cities due to changing transportation technology in search of better opportunities, and now, started identifying themselves with the places where they were born. *Rıza* and *şükran* started to transform into feelings of belonging to the same place of birth, to a place where one had come from, which was termed as "*hemşehri*." Although the term literally means "from the same city," it was rather used as "sharing the

---

[26] Findley, *Turkey, Islam, Nationalism, and Modernity*, 116.
[27] Ibid.
[28] Ibid.

same birth place." That was why the newcomers to the cities usually settled in close proximity to those who had earlier come from the same place of birth.

The least, or perhaps better put almost invisible, impact of reforms was on familial ties and the understanding of women's protection by either husbands or male members of the family. Marriage still occurred largely by arrangement among families, for most girls in their later teenage years. As Findley rightly argues, in Islamic law, the relationship of husband and wife was "one of complementarity, not equality" and "spousal rights and obligations included important safeguards for the woman."[29] As we have seen in the preceding chapter on family, in the engagement period, or if engaged by their parents at an early age, women had the right to refuse a candidate or appoint their own agent to arrange a marriage for them. Although the women had their rights to property ownership after marriage, they were still under the protection of their husbands, with entitlement not only to material support but also emotional support, with mutual feelings of love (*mahabbet*) and affection (*musafat*). Although the Ottoman women's movement dates back as far as 1868, it did not lead to a widespread understanding of anything new in complementary obligations of husbands and wives, at least for the period under discussion. Although there was a flood of reform edicts in the Tanzimat era, nothing much changed in terms of legal and social status of women in general and wives in particular, and family law remained outside the scope of the reform movements. The first family law was enacted in 1917 and after a short period of time it was abolished in 1919. Before 1917, there had been some new regulations, but they were limited to some administrative changes such as identification of the minimum and maximum values of *mehr* (dowry) in 1874, registration of marriages in 1881, extensions for the time allowance of registration in 1900, and specifications of fines for any case of non-registration of marriage in 1913.

Concluding Remarks

In this chapter I have analyzed the reform period of the nineteenth century and its impact on the changing understanding of what it meant and how it felt to protect and be protected. Although transformation was gradual and not equally apparent for all the subjects of the empire, the political sphere was the first where

---

[29] Ibid., 67.

a change on understanding of protection started to show up, particularly in the transformation from subjects to citizens. They were no longer subjects to be protected by their sultan with associated emotions of *merhamet* and *mahabbet*, but they were instead transformed into equal citizens of a state as an abstract political entity. The subjects' mutual love of *mahabbet* to their protectors was beginning to turn into a love of fatherland. The first and foremost concern of the state was trying to cement unity among the differences that had already started with separatist movements, and reforms on the political level perhaps seemed easier to implement for the Ottoman intellectuals.

On the societal level, non-Muslims' changing understanding of protection and the changing rights to protection followed the changes in the political sphere. As we have seen, there was an unprecedented increase in spatial mobility in this period. On the one hand, the empire started to lose its non-Muslim subjects along with separatist movements. On the other hand, there were many Muslim refugees incoming from the lost territories of the empire and an increase in rural to urban migration in search of new opportunities. Population movements also had consequences for the meaning of protection and its associated emotions. While it had always been the communities themselves that regulated and sustained the politics of difference among their fellows for the early modern period, as we have seen in the previous chapters, the state started to intervene in communities at an individual level, particularly with the aid of new rules and regulations in its attempt to give order to chaos in the society. The change in emotions of contentment and gratitude (*rıza ve şükran*) started to show itself, although as a slow and gradual process. Moreover, it was not the same for subjects of every part of the empire. Even among the Muslims too, there were different opinions and debates regarding the new and equal legal status of non-Muslim subjects of the empire. The feelings of *rıza ve şükran* started to transform into feelings of belonging to the same place of birth, seeking the comfort and protection of their previous communities in the new places to which they had moved.

Change in the domain of medical knowledge, along with the modern positivist understanding of science, also started during this period, and had an impact on emotions. Emotions were no longer perceived as vices or virtues, based on the concept of moderation (*adl*) to be expressed in their moral behaviors. Rather, they were moved into individuals' bodies with a new understanding of emotions as obstacles to rationality.

While the impact of reforms on the societal level was less than on the political, not surprisingly, the least impact was on the superior–subordinate relations between husbands and wives, which remained as a complementary relation rather than an equal one during the nineteenth century. This could only be possible after the dissolution of the empire and the ultimate change from *rıza* and *musafat* to a romantic love, which would need to wait for the emergence of the Turkish Republic.

Conclusion

As a citizen of a nation-state with equal rights for all, including equal rights for husbands and wives and intracommunal relations set and defined by civil law, I initially found it challenging to answer the question of what it *meant* and how it *felt* to protect and be protected, and to understand the meaning-making mechanisms underlying the concept of protection, in early modern Ottoman society. This was challenging in part because this was a world of inequalities, with strict hierarchical distinctions between the rulers and the ruled, Muslims and non-Muslims, men and women, and tax-paying and tax-exempt subjects. Differences in faith, ethnicity, gender, economic, social and legal status were indeed a fact of life. On the other hand, like every other durable empire, the Ottoman Empire had its own policies for accommodating differences within its domain. The state and communities themselves could support diversity and sustain a relatively harmonious society.

Previous scholarship has attempted to interpret the reality of political, interpersonal, and domestic relationships in the Ottoman Empire in terms of the protection of subordinates by their superiors. In the political realm, for example, the metaphor of a shepherd acting as the protector of his flock, drawn from scholarship based on ancient Indo-Persian theories of governance, seemed to Ottoman historians to give explanatory power to the strictly hierarchical superior–subordinate political relationship between rulers and subjects.

The Ottoman Empire's ability to peaceably incorporate diverse populations—and the relationships among these populations—has also been a subject of interest among historians. Some historians have tried to explain these complex relationships in terms of the Ottoman state's carrot/stick policy of concessions and material benefits, which enabled diverse subjects to be incorporated into the Ottoman polity. However, it had also long been thought that members of communities from diverse populations—such as residents of a community with different faiths, for example—lived parallel lives, without much interaction with one another. Members of lower-status groups accepted and internalized their inferior positions, yet were always ready to revolt, waiting for a suitable occasion to do so.

In familial relations, husbands were the all-powerful heads of the family, with the obligation to discipline their wives, who as women were perceived to be flawed versions of men, according to the single sex paradigm. Indeed, this mirrors the metaphoric image of a shepherd and his flock in political relationships. Just as the shepherd takes his flock to rich pastures and protects it from beasts, the husband, as the head of the household, has to support his household. This meant that wives, being under the control and governance of their husbands, held an inferior status both socially and legally to their husbands.

These approaches, in all three spheres, however, had two basic and implicit assumptions. One is the assumption that subordinate parties in these inequal relationships acted only to protect their material interests. The second assumption is that historical actors' interests and motivations were purely rational rather than emotional, and if emotions were to be considered at all, they were perceived as obstacles to rationality.

Yet, acknowledging the historic nature and role of emotions has offered a new lens for understanding Ottoman history and capturing what protection as a culturally specific and historically contingent concept *meant* and how it *felt*. In the preceding chapters, I argued that emotions need to be historicized, because they are neither brute reflexes nor are they universal or incompatible with rationality. Rather, they are mental concepts voluntarily enacted by a mindful body and manifest themselves in cultural practices.

Such an approach poses another challenge, however: Even if historical texts contain linguistic expressions for emotions, once one acknowledges that emotion terms and concepts change across time and space and thus should be historicized, the meanings of emotions described in texts become less apparent, as do the values attributed to them and their functioning as tools for social communication. Yet, a fresh look at already familiar Ottoman sources incorporating a lexicographic, contextual, and conceptual analysis of emotion terms revealed the meaning-making mechanisms underlying the concept of protection.

In state–subject relations, the first and top obligation of a sultan seeking to be a just and legitimate ruler was to protect his subjects, regardless of their faith, ethnicity, occupation, settlement practice, wealth, or social or legal status. For subjects, the concept of protection, which included an understanding that the state was physically embodied in the sultan himself, was understood through a cluster of emotions related to compassion (*merhamet*) and love (*mahabbet*). Compassion was a hierarchical emotion only expressed by superiors towards subordinates. But it was not only a normative linguistic expression: Feelings were realized only if acted upon according to the early modern philosophical knowledge framework. Thus, compassion was not merely a term of political rhetoric manifested in the political language of the state to deceive subjects, but was regularly enacted through actions, as we have seen from the archival material. Acts of compassion were acts of mindful bodies done for the good of the society; this conception of compassion served to explain the seemingly arbitrary decisions emanating from the will of the sultan. Conversely, subjects' understanding of protection demanded their complete deference to their sultan as their protector. The emotion of love (*mahabbet*) provided the meaning-making mechanism for the concept of protection and mirrored their love of God, reaching a different and deeper level of love (*meveddet*), if it denoted feelings of love of God as a servant.

Indeed, the same understanding of protection was also apparent in familial relations. The emotions of love (*mahabbet*), contentment (*rıza*), and affection and sincerity (*musafat*) provided the specific meaning of protection in familial relationships. Protection, in their understanding, did not mean only providing for the material needs but also the emotional needs of the protected in an unequal but complementary relationship. It is thus unsurprising that Kınalızade identified "home" as "house of companionship and love" (*hane-i ülfet ve mahabbet*), representing a very different experience of love than our contemporary understanding.

In communal relations, protection was crucial for one's survival. Neighborhood and guild communities provided protection for their members. If not protected by their communities, members could be subject to false allegations and face severe penalties including expulsion, dismissal from leadership positions, loss of community support in the event of oppression by government officials, or loss of the personal support and endorsement of their neighbors. The emotions of contentment, pleasure, and gratitude (*rıza, hoşnud, şükran*) provided meaning to the concept of who to protect, and the presence or absence of these emotions, realized as physical and moral sensations of discomfort or satisfaction, determined how to draw boundaries of their communities. I therefore called neighborhoods and guilds "domains of gratitude": Being a member of an emotional community and showing careful consideration to remain a member in good standing acted as a shield of protection and a tool for social communication. However, emotions were also realized as performatives, practices, and deeds manifested, for instance in assuming the tax burden of those who could not afford to pay or acting as guarantors both materially and morally for their neighbors of a different faith.

At first glance, it may seem ambitious to explore what it meant and how it felt like to protect and be protected at all three relationship levels—the political, social, and familial. But as we have seen, the same model essentially holds true for all levels, with familial, social, and political relations intertwined and interconnected in a common understanding of a harmonious and virtuous society.

Like any other concept in history, the contested concept of protection, whom to protect, and how to offer protection would change. The reforms of the nineteenth century would set the stage for a gradual shift in the meaning of protection. Following the legal transformation of subjects into dutiful citizens, the meaning of protection shifted to mean equality before the law, regardless of one's faith. Political change also transformed emotions of compassion (*merhamet*) and love (*mahabbet*) embodied in the sultan as their protector into a citizen's love of fatherland (*vatan sevgisi*). Moreover, migration from the lost dominions of the empire into Anatolia and from rural to urban cities started to change both the meaning of protection and to whom and how to offer protection, as well as the nature of feelings of contentment, pleasure, and gratitude towards fellow community members. Feelings of community based on being from the same birth place (*hemşehri*) started to replace feelings of community based on contentment, pleasure, and gratitude: Newcomers to cities preferred to settle near others from their community of origin and placed more trust in them to provide a safe and secure environment than they did the state, which they saw as an abstract political entity. Indeed, this still holds true for neighborhoods of some cities, reflecting the continuity and legacy of the past traditions and cultural values. In contrast, the traditional complementary relation between husbands and wives continued until the end of the empire. It was only during the time of the Turkish Republic that equality became a feature of familial relations, transforming the feelings of *mahabbet* into different experiences of love.

Today, the concept of protection means equality under the law for every citizen of the Turkish Republic, regardless of faith, ethnicity, wealth, status, or gender. Equality means equal access to education, health, and property, and the Turkish Republic has the obligation to protect subjects' political, social, and economic rights. Yet, acknowledging that emotions provide meaning to the concept of protection can offer a better understanding of political undertakings. As an example, I will examine a recent and important development in modern Turkey.

Hagia Sophia, a UNESCO World Heritage Site, was built in the sixth century as a Byzantine church, converted into a mosque in 1453 by Mehmed II, extensively restored by Mimar Sinan between 1566 and 1574, and turned into a museum by Mustafa Kemal Atatürk in 1931, symbolizing the secular Republic of Turkey.[1] It has very recently been reconverted into a mosque, a move that provoked heated debate among intellectuals, religious and political leaders, and scholars of Ottoman history and art history.[2] Nobody could deny the fact that it is one of the most glorious aesthetic achievements in the world, owing much not only to those who built it, but also to those who protected and strengthened it throughout its centuries-long life. If the protection of its citizens by the Turkish Republic were to mean equal access to aesthetic beauty, it would have remained a museum.

Yet, something else makes this structure unique. As a material reality, Hagia Sophia had several religious, cultural, and political associations and has symbolized a variety of concepts over time. A decade-long study conducted by a team of scholars from Stanford University led by Bissera Pentcheva, a professor of art history and an expert in the field of acoustic archaeology, combined literary analysis, philological inquiry, and scientific work, and persuasively showed that the effect of polymorphy on the viewer was culturally and religiously conditioned. Hagia Sophia was indeed designed, she argued, to afford the worshipper a multisensory aesthetic experience. She showed how the appearance of marble and gold changed at specific times of the day and recorded how light affects its reflective surfaces. She also claimed that its interior was meant to be experienced during eucharistic liturgy, which coincided with the Byzantine third hour of the

---

[1] In the early republican period, turning the Hagia Sophia into a museum symbolized a move to a secular state ideology. According to the commission responsible for the presentation of the monument as a museum, the reason behind its conversion was its significance not only as an Ottoman mosque but also as a Byzantine church: "Hagia Sophia is an architectural masterpiece as a Byzantine church as well as an Ottoman Mosque... The interventions by Turks are so thorough and so integrated with the identity of the building that, just like people defining it as a church, there are even more people that define the building as a mosque. Therefore, the Republic of Turkey converted the building into a museum to present it to whole humanity" (Museologists Commission, May 13, 1939, IHMDA). Pınar Aykaç, "Contesting the Byzantine Past: Four Hagia Sophias as Ideological Battlegrounds of Architectural Conservation in Turkey," Heritage & Society 11, no. 2 (2018): 156–7.

[2] For example, Ali Yaycıoğlu, an Ottomanist, argued in Stanford News that the building itself served as a kind of link between cultures. It was the symbol of the Roman political tradition. The Ottoman sultans, he pointed out, claimed to be not just sultans but also caesars—a Roman emperor—and Hagia Sophia symbolized this Roman–Ottoman universal sovereignty. In other words, the Ottomans redefined it for their own spiritual tradition, and their spiritual tradition was redefined by Hagia Sophia. While the Ottomans transformed Hagia Sophia into a mosque and changed it, they were also changed by it, since their entire notion of imperial architecture was shaped by the Hagia Sophia. Yaycıoğlu added that he would have preferred Hagia Sophia to have remained as a museum. Ali Yaycıoğlu, Stanford News, Aug. 7, 2020.

day (approximately between sunrise and mid-morning). The team also created a program by which the acoustics of Hagia Sophia could be imposed on any sound one desires. They could, for example, recreate what a Byzantine chant might have sounded in the thirteenth-century Hagia Sophia, which would be very different from the same chant sung by a contemporary choir.[3]

This study showed that the intended multisensorial experience facilitated by the interior architecture of Hagia Sophia was (and is) culturally and religiously significant for believers of the Orthodox Christian faith. But this argument misses something important. If we acknowledge that all reality, from the moment it is perceived by humans, is socially framed and built on incorporated memories of previous experiences, and on one's own cultural and traditional values, then we can understand that people of different faiths would impose different meanings on Hagia Sophia, even if it was designed to provide a specific multisensorial experience for Orthodox Christians. The Friday prayers of Muslims would thus sound different for people of different faiths, its unique architecture and the shifting appearance of its marble and gold would perhaps evoke a visual image of heavenly rivers for Muslims but something else for Jews and Christians. Even one's knowledge of Ottoman or Byzantine history would impose different meanings on one's sensations.

With this understanding of emotions, even turning Hagia Sophia back into a museum would not be enough to capture the full significance of Hagia Sophia to the many communities that have used it. One cannot but agree with Sahak Maşalyan, the patriarch of the Armenian Church of Turkey, who suggested, "Why not keep it as a museum for part of the week, and open it for an Alevi semah ritual Thursday night, for Sunni prayers on Fridays, for the Jewish community on Saturdays, and for Christian congregations on Sundays?"[4] Knowing that they have equal rights to experience its aesthetic beauty, perform the rituals of their own faith, and enjoy the physical sensations offered by Hagia Sophia would provide different meanings to each community. More importantly, such

---

[3] Bissera V. Pentcheva, "Hagia Sophia and Multisensory Aesthetics," *Gesta* 50, no. 2 (2011): 93–111. Utilizing literary analysis, philological inquiry, and scientific work, she focused on the effect of polymorphy on the viewer and how it was culturally and religiously conditioned. She investigated Hagia Sophia as an integrated work in which sight and sound work together, and argued that Hagia Sophia was designed to afford the worshipper a multisensory aesthetic experience. Her existing work culminated in the release of an album entitled *The Lost Voices of Hagia Sophia*.

[4] Baki Tezcan, a scholar of Ottoman history at UC Davis, relying on the opinion of Sahak Maşalyan, claimed that such a move would keep Hagia Sophia alive and better serve its long-term preservation as a cultural heritage site, offer an alternative to Islamist political hegemony, recognize Turkey's diversity, and set an exemplary international precedent for other similar sites globally. Baki Tezcan, *Jadaliyya*, July 20, 2020.

a move would also make real the concept of equal rights and protection for all citizens of the Turkish Republic. As we have seen in this book, the people of early modern Ottoman society accepted both diversity and inherent inequality in their communities, building their relationships with each other on the shared concepts of *rıza* and *şükran*. We now live in a different world, and neither the meaning of being a protected member of a community, nor the feelings and emotions associated with this, are the same. But the past offers the necessary tools, such as the shared concepts of *rıza* and *şükran*, for embracing diversity, and can still give meaning (albeit different) to what it means to be an equal and respected citizen of the Turkish Republic. What one feels now depends on one's previous experience and the traditional values that one's culture provides.

Similarly, what we now feel shapes our tomorrow, as the present slides into the past and our minds use our past experience to better process future external physical sensations. I am a proud citizen of the Turkish Republic, yet exploring what the subjects of the Ottoman Empire may have felt when giving and accepting protection opens up an avenue to building a better future by again embracing diversity and heterogeneity complemented by feelings of solidarity, unity, and belonging to the same fatherland with a long-shared past. I strongly believe that whatever we feel today will have an impact on how we will feel and act tomorrow.

It is my hope that this book will help fill the still-widening geographical gap in historical research on emotions resulting from the relative scarcity of non-European research. But more importantly, I hope I have been able to show in this book how the theoretical and methodological approaches offered so far can be utilized (or not) given the constraints imposed by the Ottoman primary sources. It is also my will—or better put, my humble call—to Ottoman historians to search in their future studies for ways in which emotions provided meaning to other contested concepts.

Bibliography

Abacı, Nurcan. *Bursa Şehrinde Osmanlı Hukukunun Uygulanması (17. Yüzyıl)*. Ankara: Kültür Bakanlığı Yayınları, 2001.

Abacı, Nurcan. *The Ottoman Judges and Their Registers: The Bursa Court Register B-90/295 (dated AH 1081/AD 1670-71)*. Cambridge, MA: Harvard University Press, 2007.

Abdal-Rehim, Abdal Rahman. "The Family and Gender Laws in Egypt During the Ottoman Period." In *Women, the Family, and Divorce Laws in Islamic History*, edited by A. E. Sonbol, 96–112. Syracuse, NY: Syracuse University Press, 1996.

Abou-El-Haj, Rifa'at 'Ali. *Formation of the Modern State: The Ottoman Empire, Sixteenth to Eighteenth Centuries*. Syracuse, NY: Syracuse University Press, 2005.

Abu-Lughod, L. *Veiled Sentiments: Honor and Poetry in a Bedouin Society*. Berkeley: University of California Press, 1986.

Abu-Manneh, Butrus. "The Islamic Roots of the Gülhane Rescript." *Die Welt des Islams* 34, no. 2 (1994): 173–203.

Afacan, Şeyma. "Of the Soul and Emotions: Conceptualizing 'the Ottoman Individual' Through Psychology." Unpublished PhD diss., University of Oxford, 2016.

Ahmed, Shahab. *What Is Islam? The Importance of Being Islamic*. Princeton: Princeton University Press, 2015.

Akyıldırım, Taylan. "259 Numaralı Şeriyye icili Defterine göre Galata (Metin ve Değerlendirme)." MA diss., Mimar Sinan Güzel Sanatlar Üniversitesi, 2010.

Al Jallad, Nader. "The Concept of *'Shame'* in Arabic: Bilingual Dictionaries and the Challenge of Defining Culture-Based Emotions." *Language Design* 12 (2010): 31–57.

Alam, Muzaffar. *The Languages of Political Islam: India, 1200–1800*. Chicago: University of Chicago Press, 2004.

Andrews, Walter. "Ottoman Love: Preface to a Theory of Emotional Ecology." In *A History of Emotions, 1200–1800*, edited by Jonas Liliequist, 21–47. London: Pickering & Chatto, 2012.

Andrews, Walter and Ayşe Dalyan. "Poetry, Culture, Neuroscience, Emotions and the Case of Bonding, Separation, and Separation Anxiety in Sixteenth Century Ottoman Culture: A Theoretical Preface." *JOTSA* 7, no. 2 (2020): 147–74, https://doi.org/10.2979/jottturstuass.7.2.10.

Asceric-Todd, Ines. "The Noble Traders: The Islamic Tradition of 'Spiritual Chivalry' (*futuwwa*) in Bosnian Trade-guilds (16th–19th centuries)." *The Muslim World* 97 (2007): 159–73.

Ayar, Ali Rıza and Recep Orhan Özel, eds. *Amasya Fetvâları ve İlk Amasya Şehir Tarihi (Belâbilü'r-Râsiye Fî Riyâz-ı Mesâili'l- Amâsiyye. Mustafa Vazıh Efendi (1764–1831)*. Amasya: Amasya Belediyesi, 2011.

Aykaç, Pınar. "Contesting the Byzantine Past: Four Hagia Sophias as Ideological Battlegrounds of Architectural Conservation in Turkey." *Heritage & Society* 11, no. 2 (2018): 151–78.

Baldwin, James E. "Prostitution, Islamic Law and Ottoman Societies." *Journal of the Economic and Social History of the Orient* 55 (2012): 117–52.

Barkan, Ömer Lütfi. "Avarız." *İA* 2 (1979): 13–19.

Barkey, Karen. *Empire of Difference: The Ottomans in Comparative Perspective.* Cambridge: Cambridge University Press, 2008.

Barrett, Lisa Feldman. *How Emotions Are Made: The Secret Life of the Brain.* New York: Mariner Books, 2017.

Bauer, Karen. "Emotion in the Quran: An Overview." *Journal of Quranic Studies* 19, no. 2 (2017): 1–30, http://doi.org.10.3366/jqs.2017.0282.

Ben-Ami, Ido. "Wonder in Early Modern Ottoman Society: A Case Study in the History of Emotions." *History Compass*, no. 17 (2019): 1–12, http://doi.org.10.1111/hic3.12578.

Bilmen, Ömer Nasuhi. *Hukukı İslamiyye ve Islahatı Fıkhiyye Kamusu.* Istanbul: Bilmen Yayınevi, 1968.

Binbaş, İlker Evrim. "Autobiographies and Weak Ties: Sa'in al-Din Turka's Self-Narratives." *International Journal of Middle East Studies* 53 (2021): 309–13.

Boddice, Rob. *The History of Emotions.* Manchester: Manchester University Press, 2018.

Boddice, Rob. *A History of Feelings.* London: Reaktion Books, 2019.

Boddice, Rob. "History Looks Forward: Interdisciplinarity and Critical Emotion Research." *Emotion Review* 12, no. 3 (2020): 131–4.

Burbank, Jane and Frederick Cooper. *Empires in World History: Power and the Politics of Difference.* Princeton: Princeton University Press, 2011.

Burçak, Berrak. "Science, a Remedy for All Ills. Healing the 'Sick Man of Europe': A Case for Ottoman Scientism." Unpublished PhD diss., Princeton University, 2005.

Çetin, Cemal. "Anadolu'da Kapıya Katran Sürme Vak'alari: Konya Şeriyye sicilleri Işığında Hukuki, Kültürel, Toplumsal Boyutları 1645–1750." *Turkish Studies* 9, no. 1 (2014): 133–56.

Çörekçi, Semra. "The Dream Diary of an Ottoman Governor: Kulakzade Mahmud Pasha's Düşnama." *International Journal of Middle East Studies* 53, no. 2 (2021): 331–5.

Czygan, Christiane. "Depicting Imperial Love: Songs and Letters Between Sultan Süleyman (Muhibbi) and Hürrem." In *Kanûnî Sultan Süleyman ve Dönemi. Yeni Kaynaklar, Yeni Yaklaşlaşımlar*, edited by Muhammed Fatih Çalışır, Suraiya Roschan Faroqhi and Mehmet Şakir Yılmaz, 247–65. İstanbul: İbn Haldun Yayınları, 2020.

Czygan, Christiane. "Power and Poetry: Kanuni Sultan Suleyman's Third Divan." In *Contemporary Turkey at a Glance II, Turkey Transformed? Power, History, Culture*, edited by Meltem Ersoy and Esra Ozyurek, 101–13. Weisbaden: Springer VS, 2017.

Dankoff, Robert. "Ayıp Değil! (No Disgrace)." *Journal of Turkish Literature* 5 (2008): 77–90.

Dankoff, Robert. "Ayıp Değil!" In *Çağının Sıradışı Yazarı Evliya Çelebi*, edited by Nuran Tezcan, 109–22. Istanbul: YKY, 2009.

Darling, Linda. *A History of Social Justice and Political Power in the Middle East: The Circle of Justice from Mesopotamia to Globalization*. New York: Routledge, 2013.

Darling, Linda. *Revenue-Raising and Legitimacy: Tax Collection and Financial Administration in the Ottoman Empire, 1560–1660*. Leiden: Brill, 1996.

Davison, Roderic H. *Reform in the Ottoman Empire 1856–1876*. Princeton: Princeton University Press, 1963.

Demirci, Süleyman. "Demography and History: The Value of the Avarızhane Registers for Demographic Research. A Case Study of the Ottoman Sub-Provinces of Konya, Kayseri and Niğde, c. 1620s–1700." *Turcica* 38 (2006): 181–211.

Demirel, Ömer. "1700–1730 Tarihlerinde Ankara'da Ailenin Niceliksel Yapısı." *Belleten* 64, no. 211 (1990): 945–61.

Dixon, Thomas. "What Is the History of Anger a History Of?" *Emotions: History, Culture, Society* 4 (2020): 1–34.

Duben, Alan and Cem Bahar. *Istanbul Households: Marriage, Family and Fertility 1880–1940*. Cambridge: Cambridge University Press, 1991.

Düzenli, Pehlul. "Osmanlı Hukukçusu Şeyhülislâm Ebussuûd Efendi ve Fetvâları." PhD diss., Selçuk Üniversitesi, 2007.

Ergenç, Özer. "Osmanlı Şehrindeki Mahallenin İşlevleri ve Nitelikleri Üzerine." In *Osmanlı Tarihi Yazıları Şehir, Toplum, Devlet*, 75–85, edited by Derya Önder. İstanbul: Tarih Vakfı Yurt Yayınları, 2012.

Ergenç, Özer. *Osmanlı Tarihi Yazıları Şehir, Toplum, Devlet*. İstanbul: Tarih Vakfı Yurt Yayınları, 2012.

Ergenç, Özer. *XVI. Yüzyılda Ankara ve Konya* (2nd edn). Istanbul: Tarih Vakfı Yurt Yayınları, 2012.

Ergene, Boğaç. 2001. "On Ottoman Justice: Interpretations in Conflict (1600–1800)." *Islamic Law and Society* 8, no. 1 (2001): 52–87.

Ermiş, Fatih, *A History of Ottoman Economic Thought: Developments Before the Nineteenth Century*. New York: Routledge, 2014.

Eustace, Nicole, Eugenia Lean, Julie Livingston, Jan Plamper, William M. Reddy and Barbara H. Rosenwein. "AHR Conversation: The Historical Study of Emotions." *American Historical Review* 117, no. 5 (December 2012): 1487–531.

Faroqhi, Suraiya. *Men of Modest Substance: House Owners and House Property in Seventeenth Century Ankara and Kayseri*. Cambridge: Cambridge University Press, 1987.

Fay, Mary Ann. "The Ties That Bound: Women and Households in Eighteenth-Century Egypt." In *Women, the Family, and Divorce Laws in Islamic History*, edited by A. E. A. Sonbol, 155–73. Syracuse, NY: Syracuse University Press, 1996.

Findley, Carter Vaughn. *Turkey, Islam, Nationalism, and Modernity*. New Haven: Yale University Press, 2010.

Frevert, Ute. *Emotions in History: Lost and Found*. Budapest: Central European University Press, 2011.

Gade, Anna. "Islam." In *The Oxford Handbook of Religion and Emotion*, edited by John Corrigan, 35–50. Oxford: Oxford University Press, 2008.

Gara, Eleni. "Conceptualizing Interreligious Relations in the Ottoman Empire: The Early Modern Centuries." *Acta Poloniae Historica* 116 (2017): 57–93. https://doi.org/10.12775/APH.2017.116.03.

Giorgi, Kyra. *Emotions, Language and Identity in the Margins of Europe*. Basingstoke: Palgrave Macmillan, 2014.

Hambly, G., ed. *Woman in the Medieval Islamic World: Power, Patronage, Piety*. Cambridge: Garland Publishing, 1997.

Hanioğlu, Şükrü. *A Brief History of the Late Ottoman Empire*. Princeton: Princeton University Press, 2008.

Hanna, Nelly. "Sources for the Study of Slave Women and Concubines." In *Beyond the Exotic: Women's Histories in Islamic Societies*, edited by A. E. A. Sonbol, 119–30. Syracuse, NY: Syracuse University Press, 2005.

Hoca Saadettin Efendi. *Tacü't-Tevarih*, vol. 2. İstanbul: Matba'a-i Amire, h.1279/1862.

Ilgürel, Mücteba. "istimalet." *Türkiye Diyanet Vakfı İslam Ansiklopedisi*, 362–3. İstanbul: Diyanet Vakfı, 2001.

İnalcık, Halil. "Adaletnameler." In *Osmanlı'da Devlet, Hukuk, Adalet, 75–191*, edited by Muhittin Salih Eren. İstanbul: Eren, 2005.

İnalcık, Halil. "Application of the Tanzimat." *Archivum Ottomanicum* 5 (1973): 97–128.

İnalcık, Halil. *The Ottoman Empire: The Classical Age, 1300–1600*. London: Weidenfeld and Nicolson, 1973.

İnalcık, Halil. "State and Ideology under Sultan Süleyman I." In *The Middle East and the Balkans under the Ottoman Empire*, edited by İlhan Başgöz, 70–94. Bloomington: Indiana University Press, 1993.

İnalcık, Halil. "Türkler ve Balkanlar." In *Balkanlar*, edited by Ortadoğu ve Balkan İncelemeleri Vakfı (OBİV), 9–32. İstanbul: Eren Yayınları, 1993.

İnalcık, Halil and Mehmet Seyitdanlıoğlu, eds. *Tanzimat/Değişim Sürecinde Osmanlı İmparatorluğu*. İstanbul: Phoenix Yayınları, 2006.

Ivanova, Svetlana. "The Divorce Between Zubaida Hatun and Esseid Osman Aga." In *Women, the Family, and Divorce Laws in Islamic History*, edited by A. E. A. Sonbol, 112–25. Syracuse, NY: Syracuse University Press, 1996.

Ivanova, Svetlana. "The Ottoman Decrees 'Up' in Istanbul and What the Rumelia Subject Perceived at the 'Bottom' (Seventeenth–Eighteenth Centuries)." In *Political Initiatives "From the Bottom Up" in the Ottoman Empire*, edited by Antonis Anastasopoulos, 345–78. Rethymno: Crete University Press, 2012.

Kafadar, Cemal. "A Rome of One's Own: Reflections on Cultural Geography and Identity in the Lands of Rum." *Muqarnas* 24, no. 1 (2007): 7–25, https://doi.org/10.1163/22118993_02401003.

Kafadar, Cemal. *Between Two Worlds: The Construction of the Ottoman State*. Berkeley: University of California Press, 1995.

Kafadar, Cemal. "Self and Other: The Diary of a Dervish in Seventeenth-Century Istanbul and First-Person Narratives in Classical Ottoman Literature." *Studia Islamica* 69 (1989): 121–50.

Kalpaklı, Mehmet and Water G. Andrews. *The Age of Beloveds*. Durham; London: Duke University Press, 2005.

Kankal, Ahmet and Kenan Z. Taş, eds. *252 Nolu Mardin Şer'iye Sicili Belge Özetleri Ve Mardin*. İstanbul: Mardin Tarihi İhtisas Kütüphanesi, 2006.

Karadöl, Bünyamin. "Şeyhülsilam Minkarizade Yahya Efendi'nin Nikah Akdi/Evlilik ile İlgili Fetvaları." MA diss., Çukurova University, 2006.

Karahasanoğlu, Selim. *Kadı ve Günlüğü Sadreddinzade Telhisi Mustafa Efendi Günlüğü (1711-1735) Üstüne Bir İnceleme*. Istanbul: Türkiye İş Bankası Kültür Yayınları, 2013.

Karahasanoğlu, Selim. "Ottoman Ego-Documents: State of the Art." *International Journal of Middle East Studies* 53 (2021): 301–8.

Karateke, Hakan T. "Legitimizing the Ottoman Sultanate." In *Legitimizing the Order: The Ottoman Rhetoric of State Power*, edited by Hakan Karateke and Maurus Reinkowski, 13–52. Leiden: Brill, 2005.

Karateke, Hakan T., H. Erdem Çıpa and Helga Anetshofer, eds. *Disliking Others: Loathing, Hostility, and Distrust in Premodern Ottoman Lands*. Boston: Academic Studies Press, 2018.

Karateke, Hakan T. and Maurus Reinkowski, eds. *Legitimizing the Order: The Ottoman Rhetoric of State Power*. Leiden: Brill, 2005.

Katz, Marion Holmes. "Shame (Haya) as an Affective Disposition in Islamic Legal Thought." *Journal of Law, Religion and State* 3, no. 2 (2014): 139–69.

Kayyal, Mary H. and James A. Russell. "Language and Emotion: Certain English–Arabic Translations Are Not Equivalent." *Journal of Language and Social Psychology* 32 (2013): 261–71.

Khan, Razak. "The Social Production of Space and Emotions." *Journal of the Economic and Social History of the Orient* 58 (2015): 611–33.

Kıvrım, İsmail. "17. yüzyılda Osmanlı Toplumunda Boşanma Hadiseleri (Ayıntab Örneği: Talak, Muhalaa ve Tefrik)." *Gaziantep Üniversitesi Sosyal Bilimler Dergisi* 10, no. 1 (2011): 371–400.

Koç, Mustafa, ed. *Kınalızade Ali Çelebi: Ahlak-ı Alâ'î*. İstanbul: Klasik, 2007.

Kolovos, Elias. "İstimalet: What Do We Actually Know About It?" In *Political Thought and Practice in the Ottoman Empire*, edited by Marinos Sariyannis, 59–70. Rethymno: Crete University Press, 2019.

Kumin, Beat and Cornelie Usbor. "At Home and in the Workplace: A Historical Introduction to the 'Spatial Turn'." *History and Theory* 52 (2013): 305–18.

Kuran, Timur, ed. *Mahkeme Kayıtları Işığında 17. Yüzyıl İstanbul'unda Sosyo-Ekonomik Yaşam*. V:1. *Esnaf ve Loncalar, Hıristiyan ve Yahudi Cemaat İşleri, Yabancılar*. İstanbul: İş Bankası Kültür Yayınları, 2010.

Kurat, Akdes Nimet. *Rusya Tarihi: Başlangıcından 1917'ye kadar*. Ankara: TTK, 2014.

Kurt, Abdurrahman. *Bursa Sicillerine Göre Osmanlı Ailesi (1839–1876)*. Bursa: Uludağ Üniversitesi, 1998.

Kurt, Zeynep. "13 Numaralı ve 1727–1730 Tarihli Mühimme Zeyli Defteri (Değerlendirme-Transkripsiyon-Dizin)." MA diss., Fırat Üniversitesi, 2005.

Kurz, Marlene. "Gracious Sultan, Grateful Subjects: Spreading Ottoman Imperial 'Ideology' Throughout the Empire." *Studia Islamica* 107 (2012): 96–121.

Liliquest, Jonas, ed. *A History of Emotions, 1200–1800*. London: Pickering & Chatto, 2012.

Loseke, Donileen R. "Examining Emotion as Discourse: Emotion Codes and Presidential Speeches Justifying War." *The Sociological Quarterly* 50, no. 3 (2009): 497–524.

Lütfi Paşa. *Tevarih-i Ali Osman Li-Lütfi Paşa*. İstanbul: Matba'a-i Amire, 1341/1925.

Lutz, Catherine. "Emotion, Thought and Estrangement: Emotion as a Cultural Category." *Cultural Anthropology* 1, no. 3 (1986): 287–309.

Lutz, Catherine. *Unnatural Emotions: Everyday Sentiments on a Micronesian Atoll and Their Challenge to Western Theory*. Chicago: University of Chicago Press, 1988.

Maydaer, Saadet. "Klâsik Dönem Osmanlı Toplumunda Boşanma (Bursa Şer'iyye Sicillerine Göre)." *Uludağ Üniversitesi İlahiyat Fakültesi Dergisi* 16, no. 1 (2007): 299–320.

Meriwether, Margaret Lee. *The Kin Who Count: Family and Society in Ottoman Aleppo, 1770–1840*. Austin: University of Texas Press, 1999.

Meriwether, Margaret Lee. "The Rights of Children and the Responsibilities of Women: Women as Wasis in Ottoman Aleppo." In *Women, the Family, and Divorce Laws in Islamic History*, edited by A. E. A. Sonbol, 219–35. Syracuse, NY: Syracuse University Press, 1996.

Messner, Angelika C. "Aspects of Emotion in Late Imperial China: Editor's Introduction to the Thematic Section." *Asiatische Studien Études Asiatiques* 66, no. 4 (2012): 893–913.

Morris, Michael W., Kwok Leung, Daniel Ames and Brian Lickel. "Views From Inside and Outside: Integrating Emic and Etic Insights About Culture and Justice Judgment." *Academy of Management Review* 24, no. 4 (1999): 781–96.

Morsbach, H. and W. J. Tyler. "A Japaneese Emotion: Amae." In *The Social Construction of Emotions*, edited by Rom Harre, 289–308. New York: Basil Blackwell, 1986.

Mutaf, Abdulmecid. "Osmanlı'da Zina ve Fuhuş Olaylarına Karşı Toplumsal Bir Tepki: Kapıya Katran Sürmek ve Boynuz Asmak." In *Osmanlı'dan Cumhuriyete Balıkesir*, edited by Bülent Özdemir and Zübeyde Güneş Yağcı, 93–104. Istanbul: Yeditepe Yayınevi, 2007.

Okyay, Ayşe Sıdıka. *Kınalızade Ali Efendi ve Ahlak-i Ala'i*. Istanbul: İz Yayıncılık, 2011.

Ortaylı, İlber. "Osmanlı Toplumunda Ailenin Yeri." In *Türk Aile Ansiklopedisi*, edited by T. C. Başbakanlık Aile Araştırma Kurumu Başkanlığı, 74–81. Ankara: T.C. Başbakanlık Aile Araştırma Kurumu Yayınları, 1991.

Ortaylı, İlber. *Osmanlı Toplumunda Aile*. İstanbul: Pan Yayıncılık, 2002.

Öz, Mehmet. "Klasik Dönem Osmanlı Siyasi Düşüncesi: Tarihi Temeller ve Ana İlkeler." *İslami Araştırmalar* 12, no. 1 (1999): 27–39.

Özbay, Kadir. "177 Numaralı Mühimme Defterinin Transkripsiyon ve Tahlili (H.1192–1193/M.1777–1778)." MA diss., Yüzüncü Yıl Üniversitesi, 2008.

Özcan, Abdülkadir, et al. *Tarih-i Raşid ve Zeyli Raşid Mehmed Efendi ve Çelebizade İsmail Asım Efendi (1071–1141 /1660–1729) Cilt I-III*. İstanbul: Klasik, 2013.

Özel, Oktay. "Population Changes in Ottoman Anatolia during the 16th and 17th Centuries: The 'Demographic Crisis' Reconsidered." *International Journal of Middle East Studies* 36 (2004): 183–205.

Özizmirli, Görkem. "Fear in Evliya Çelebi's Seyahatname: Politics and Historiography in a Seventeenth Century Ottoman Travelogue." MA diss., Koç Üniversitesi, 2014.

Öztürk, Hüseyin. *Kınalızâde Ali Çelebi'de Aile*. Ankara: Aile Araştırma Kurumu Başkanlığı, 1990.

Peirce, Leslie. *Harem-i Hümayn, Osmanlı İmparatorluğu'nda Hükümranlık ve Kadınlar*. İstanbul: Tarih Vakfı Yurt Yayınları, 2002.

Peirce, Leslie. *Morality Tales: Law and Gender in the Ottoman Court of Aintab*. Berkeley: University of California Press, 2003.

Pentcheva, Bissera V. "Hagia Sophia and Multisensory Aesthetics." *Gesta* 50, no. 2 (2011): 93–111.

Pernau, Margrit. "Feeling Communities: Introduction." *The Indian Economic and Social History Review* 54, no. 1 (2017): 1–20.

Pernau, Margrit. "From Morality to Psychology: Emotion Concepts in Urdu, 1870–1920." *Contributions to the History of Concepts* 11, no. 1 (2016): 38–57.

Pernau, Margrit. "The Indian Body and Unani Medicine: Body History as Entangled History." *Paragrana* 18, no. 1 (2009): 107–18.

Pernau, Margrit. "Love and Compassion for the Community: Emotions and Practices Among North Indian Muslims, c. 1870–1930." *The Indian Economic and Social History Review* 54, no. 1 (2017): 21–42.

Pernau, Margrit. "Male Anger and Female Malice: Emotions in Indo-Muslim Advice Literature." *History Compass* 10, no. 2 (2012): 119–28.

Pernau, Margrit. "Mapping Emotions, Constructing Feelings: Delhi in the 1840s." *Journal of the Economic and Social History of the Orient* 58 (2015): 634–67.

Pernau, Margrit and Helga Jordheim, eds. et al. *Civilizing Emotions: Concepts in Nineteenth-Century Asia and Europe*. Oxford: Oxford University Press, 2015.

Pernau, Margrit and Imke Rajamani. "Emotional Translations: Conceptual History Beyond Language." *History and Theory* 55 (2016): 46–65.

Plamper, Jan. "Emotional Turn? Feelings in Russian History and Culture (Special Section)." *Slavic Review* 68, no. 2 (2009): 229–37.

Plamper, Jan. "The History of Emotions: An Interview with William Reddy, Barbara Rosenwein, and Peter Stearns." *History and Theory* 49, no. 2 (2010): 237–65.

Plamper, Jan. *The History of Emotions: An Introduction*. Translated by Keith Tribe. Oxford: Oxford University Press, 2015.

Raşid Efendi. *Tarih-i Raşid*. İstanbul: Matbaa-i Amire, 1282.
Raymond, Andre. *Osmanlı Döneminde Arap Kentleri*. Translated by Ali Berktay. İstanbul: Tarih Vakfı Yurt Yayınları, 1995.
Reddy, William. *The Making of Romantic Love: Longing and Sexuality in Europe, South Asia and Japan, 900-1200 CE*. Chicago: University of Chicago Press, 2012.
Reddy, William. *The Navigation of Feeling: A Framework for the History of Emotions*. Cambridge: Cambridge University Press, 2001.
Reddy, William. "The Unavoidable Intentionality of Affect." *Emotion Review* 12, no. 3 (2020): 168-78.
Reinkowski, Maurus. "The State's Security and the Subjects' Prosperity: Notions of Order in Ottoman Bureaucratic Correspondence (19th Century)." In *Legitimizing the Order: The Ottoman Rhetoric of State Power*, edited by Hakan Karateke and Maurus Reinkowski, 196-212. Leiden: Brill, 2005.
Rosenwein, Barbara. "AHR Conversation: The Historical Study of Emotions." *American Historical Review* 117, no. 5 (December 2012): 1487-531.
Rosenwein, Barbara. *Emotional Communities in the Early Middle Ages*. Ithaca, NY: Cornell University Press, 2006.
Rosenwein, Barbara. "Problems and Methods in the History of Emotions." *Passions in Context* 1 (2010): 1-32.
Rosenwein, Barbara. "Worrying About Emotions in History." *American Historical Review* 107, no. 3 (2002): 821-45.
Rosenwein, Barbara H. and Riccardo Cristiani. *What Is the History of Emotions?* Cambridge: Polity Press, 2018.
Sak, İzzet. "Osmanlı Toplumunda Namzedin (Nişanın) Bozulması ve Sonuçları: Konya Örneği (18. Yüzyılın İlk Çeyreğine Ait Konya Şeriyye Sicillerine Göre)." *Selçuk Üniversitesi Sosyal Bilimler Enstitüsü Dergisi* 16 (2006): 493-523.
Sak, İzzet and Alaaddin Aköz. "Osmanlı Toplumunda Evliliğin Karşılıklı Anlaşma İle Sona Erdirilmesi: Muhâla`a (18.Yüzyıl Konya Şer'iye Sicillerine Göre)." *Selçuk Üniversitesi Türkiyat Araştırmaları Enstitüsü Türkiyat Araştırmaları Dergisi* 15 (2004): 91-140.
Sak, İzzet and İbrahim Solak. *38 Numaralı Konya Şer'iye Sicili (1103-1104/1692-1693) Transkripsiyon ve Dizin*. Konya: Selçuk Ünviversitesi, 2014.
Sak, İzzet and İbrahim Solak. *53 Numaralı Konya Şer'iye Sicili (1148-1149/1736-1737) Transkripsiyon ve Dizin*, Konya: Selçuk Üniversitesi, 2014.
Samıkıran, Oğuzhan. "138 Numaralı Edirne Şer'iyye Sicili H.1119-1161/M.1707-1748." MA. diss., Fırat Üniversity, 2006.
Sardelic, Mirco. "John of Plano Carpini vs Simon of Saint-Quentin: 13th Century Emotions in the Eurosian Steppe." *Golden Horde Review* 5, no. 3 (2017): 494-508.
Sariyannis, Marinos, ed. *Ottoman Political Thought up to the Tanzimat: A Concise History*. Rethymno, Crete: Institute for Mediterranean Studies, 2015.
Schacht, Joseph. *An Introduction to Islamic Law*. Oxford: Oxford University Press, 1986.

Scheer, Monique. "Are Emotions a Kind of Practice (and Is That What Makes Them Have a History)? A Bourdieuian Approach to Understanding Emotion." *History and Theory* 51, no. 2 (2012): 193–220.

Şen, A. Tunç. "The Emotional Universe of Insecure Scholars in the Early Modern Hierarchy of Learning." *International Journal of Middle East Studies* 53 (2021): 315–21.

Şenışık, Pınar. "Politics of Emotions in the Late Ottoman Empire: Our Beloved Crete." *Journal of Balkan and Near Eastern Studies* (2021): 1–22, http://doi.org.10.1080/19448953.2021.2006003.

Shaw, Stanford. *History of the Ottoman Empire and Modern Turkey Volume II: Reform, Revolution, and Republic: The Rise of Modern Turkey, 1808–1975*. Cambridge: Cambridge University Press, 1977.

Sheridan, R. Aslıhan Aksoy. "Nostalgia of a Frustrated Ottoman Subject: Reading Osman Agha of Timişoara's Memoirs as Self Narrative." *International Journal of Middle East Studies* 53 (2021): 323–30.

Sonbol, A. E. A., ed. *Beyond the Exotic: Women's Histories in Islamic Societies*. Syracuse, NY: Syracuse University Press, 2005.

Stearns, Peter N. *Shame: A Brief History*. Urbana: University of Illinois Press, 2017.

Stearns, Peters N. and Carol Z. Stearns. "Emotionlogy: Clarifying the History of Emotions and Emotional Standards." *American Historical Review* 90, no. 4 (1985): 813–36.

Steininger, Fabian. "Morality, Emotions, and Political Community in the Late Ottoman Empire (1878–1908)." Unpublished PhD diss., der Freien Universitat Berlin, 2017.

Syros, Vasileios. "Galenic Medicine and Social Stability in Early Modern Florence and the Islamic Empires." *Journal of Early Modern History* 17 (2013): 161–213.

Taş, Hülya. "XVII. Yüzyılda Ankara." PhD diss., Ankara Üniversitesi, 2004.

Tekgül, Nil. "Modernite Öncesi Osmanlı Toplumunda Mahremiyet Halkaları." In *Prof. Dr. Özer Ergenç'e Armağan*, edited by Ümit Ekin, 411–33. İstanbul: Bilge Kültür Sanat, 2013.

Tezcan, Baki. "The Definition of Sultanic Legitimacy in the Sixteenth Century Ottoman Empire: The Ahlak-ı Ala'i of Kınalızade Ali Çelebi (1510–1572)." MA diss., Princeton University, 1996.

Tezcan, Baki. "Ethics as a Domain to Discuss the Political: Kınalızade Ali Efendi's *Ahlak-I Alai*." In *IRCICA International Congress on Learning and Education in the Ottoman World (Istanbul, 12–15 April 1999)*, edited by Ali Çaksu, 109–21. Istanbul: IRCICA, 2001.

Tezcan, Baki. *Jadaliyya*. July 20, 2020.

Tok, Özen. "Kadı Sicilleri Işığında Osmanlı Şehrindeki Mahalleden İhraç Kararlarında Mahalle Ahalisinin Rolü (XVII. ve XVIII. Yüzyıllarda Kayseri Örneği)." *Sosyal Bilimler Enstitüsü Dergisi* 18, no. 1 (2005): 155–73.

Trigg, Stephanie. "Introduction: Emotional Histories—Beyond the Personalization of the Past and the Abstraction of Affect Theory." *Exemplaria* 26, no. 1 (2014): 3–15.

Türkal, Nezihe Karaçay. "Silahdar Fındıklılı Mehmed Ağa Zeyl-i Fezleke (1065–22 Ca.1106 /1654–7 Şubat 1695)." PhD diss., Marmara University, 2012.

Unan, Fahri. *İdeal Cemiyet İdeal Devlet İdeal Hükümdar*. Ankara: Lotus Yayınevi, 2004.

Watanabe-O'Kelly, Helen. "Monarchies." In *Early Modern Emotions: An Introduction*, edited by Susan Broomhall, 179–82. London: Routledge, 2017.

Wierzbicka, Anna. *Emotions Across Languages and Cultures: Diversity and Universals*. Cambridge: Cambridge University Press, 1999.

Wiesner-Hanks, Merry. "Overlaps and Intersections in New Scholarship on Empires, Beliefs, and Emotions." *Cromohs (Cyber Review of Modern Historiography)* 20 (2015–16): 1–24.

Wilkins, Charles L. *Forging Urban Solidarities: Ottoman Aleppo 1640–1700*. Leiden: Brill, 2010.

Withers, Charles W. J. "Place and the 'Spatial Turn' in Geography and in History." *Journal of the History of Ideas* 70, no. 4 (2009): 637–58.

Yağcı, Zübeyde Güneş. 2005. "Osmanlı Taşrasında Kadına Yönelik Cinsel Suçlarda Adalet Arama Geleneği." *Kadın 2000* 3, no. 2 (2005): 51–81.

Yaşar, Ahmet. "The Coffeehouses in Early Modern İstanbul: Public Space, Sociability and Surveillance." MA diss., Boğaziçi University, 2003.

Yavuz, Mustafa. "Kütahya Şer'iye Sicilleri 15 Numaralı Defterinin Transkripsiyonu ve Değerlendirilmesi." MA diss., Dumlupınar Üniversitesi, 2009.

Yaycıoğlu, Ali. "Guarding Traditions and Law—Disciplining Bodies and Souls: Tradition, Science and Religion in the Age of Ottoman Reform." *Modern Asian Studies* 52, no. 5 (2018): 1542–603

Yaycıoğlu, Ali, *Stanford News*, August 7, 2020.

Yelçe, Zeynep N. "Royal Wrath: Curbing the Anger of the Sultan." In *Discourses of Anger in the Early Modern Period*, edited by Karl A. E. Enenkel and Anita Traninger, 439–57. Leiden: Brill, 2015.

Yi, Eunjeong. *Guild Dynamics in Seventeenth-Century Istanbul: Fluidity and Leverage*. Leiden: Brill, 2004.

Yildirim, Hacı Osman, Vahdettin Atik, Murat Cebecioğlu, Muhammed Safi, Mustafa Serin, Osman Uslu and Numan Yekeler, eds. *12 Numaralı Mühimme Defteri (978–979/1570–1572)*. Ankara: Devlet Arşivleri Genel Müdürlüğü, 1996.

Yılmaz, Fikret. "XVI. Yüzyıl Osmanlı Toplumunda Mahremiyetin Sınırlarına Dair." *Toplum ve Bilim* 83 (2000): 92–110.

Yılmaz, Fikret. "Zina ve Fuhuş Arasında Kalanlar Fahişe, Subaşıya Karşı." *Toplumsal Tarih* 220 (2012): 22–31.

Yılmaz, Hüseyin. "Osmanlı Tarihçiliğinde Tanzimat Öncesi Siyaset Düşüncesine Yaklaşımlar." *Türkiye Araştırmaları Literatür Dergisi* 1 (2003): 231–98.

Zachs, Fruma and Sharon Halevi. *Gendering Culture in Greater Syria: Intellectuals and Ideology in the Late Ottoman Period*. London: I. B. Tauris, 2015.

Zaharna, R. S. "Understanding Cultural Preferences of Arab Communication Patterns." *Public Relations Review* 21, no. 3 (1995): 241–55.

Zarinebaf-Shahr, Fariba. "Ottoman Women and the Tradition of Seeking Justice in the Eighteenth Century." In *Women in the Ottoman Empire: Middle Eastern Women in the Early Modern Era*, edited by M. C. Zilfi, 253–263. Leiden: Brill, 1997.

Zarinebaf-Shahr, Fariba. "Women and the Public Eye in Eighteenth Century Istanbul." In *Women in the Medieval Islamic World: Power, Patronage and Piety*, edited by G. R. G. Hambly, 301–24. New York: St. Martin's Press, 1998.

Ze'evi, Dror. "Changes in Legal-Sexual Discourses: Sex Crimes in the Ottoman Empire." *Continuity and Change* 16, no. 2 (2001): 219–42.

Ze'evi, Dror. *Producing Desire: Changing Sexual Discourse in the Ottoman Middle East, 1500–1900*. Berkeley: University of California Press, 2006.

Zilfi, Madeline C. "Thoughts on Women and Slavery in the Ottoman Era." In *Beyond the Exotic: Women's Histories in Islamic Societies*, edited by A. E. A. Sonbol, 131–38. Syracuse, NY: Syracuse University Press, 2005.

Zilfi, Madeline C. "We Don't Get Along: Women and the *Hul* Divorce in the Eighteenth Century." In *Women in the Ottoman Empire: Middle Eastern Women in the Early Modern Era*, edited by M. C. Zilfi, 264–96. Leiden: Brill, 1997.

Zilfi, Madeline C. "Women and Society in the Tulpi Era, 1718–1730." In *Women, the Family, and Divorce Laws in Islamic History*, edited by A. E. A. Sonbol, 290–307. Syracuse, NY: Syracuse University Press, 1996.

Zilfi, Madeline C., ed. *Women in the Ottoman Empire: Middle Eastern Women in the Early Modern Era*. Leiden: Brill, 1997.

Index

Abou-El-Haj, Rifa'at 48n13
absence of virtues 34
Abu-Lughod, L. 99
Abu-Manneh, Butrus 135
action, faculty of 31
actions, emotions as 8–9, 24, 31–3, 43, 87–92, 118
Afacan, Şeyma 13
Agmon, Iris 16
Ahlak-i Alai (*The Book of Ethics*) (Kınalızade) 15–16
    center of a circle 35
    dispositions 35–6
    economic thinking and 23n4
    emotions in 33–6
    families, emotionology of 112–17
    in genre of *ahlak* literature 25
    path of love (*mahabbet*) 63–7
    practical wisdom 26–7
    theoretical wisdom 26
    vices 34–5
    virtues 33–4
    wisdom, definition of 26
Ahlak-i Nasiri (Tusi) 25
ahlak literature, genre of
    Ahlak-i Nasiri (Tusi) 25
    Nicomachean Ethics (Aristotle) as influence 25
    non-Muslim ideas in 25n5
    see also Ahlak-i Alai (*The Book of Ethics*) (Kınalızade)
Ahmed, Shahab 24–5
akd-i nikah (legal contracts) 123
Alam, Muzaffar 25n5
Al Jallad, Nader 98
Andrews, Walter G. 12, 13
anger in Ottoman studies 12
animal souls, faculties of 28–9
appetitive faculty 29, 31
    excessive 34
Arabic, contemporary, shame in 98–9
Aristotle 25, 97
ar (shame) *see* shame
autobiographies, absence of emotions in 38–40

Baki, Tezcan 16n46
balance 35, 37
Baldwin, James 81
Barclay, Katie 10, 17, 81
Barkey, Karen 4, 62
Barrett, Lisa Feldman 6, 6n10, 46, 72
Bauer, Karen 49
Bedouin society, shame in 99
Ben-Ami, Ido 13
Bilmen, Ömer Nasuhi 125
Binbaş, İlker Evrim 38
Boddice, Rob 81–2, 82n27
"bonding with the hearts of citizens" 137
The Book of Ethics (*Ahlak-i Alai*) (Kınalızade) 15–16
    center of a circle 35
    dispositions 35–6
    economic thinking and 23n4
    emotions in 33–6
    faculties of the vegetative, animal and human souls 27–33
    families, emotionology of 112–17
    in genre of *ahlak* literature 25
    influences and sources 25–6
    path of love (*mahabbet*) 63–7
    practical wisdom 26–7
    theoretical wisdom 26
    vices 34–5
    virtues 33–4
    wisdom, definition of 26
Broomhall, Susan 10
Burbank, Jane 1
Burçak, Berrak 139
Burckhardt, Jacob 38

Caneque, Alejandro 67n78
caritas (a form of love) 10, 17, 81
cemaat (community) 70–1
    see also communal relations

change, emotions and 7, 7n13, 14, 14n44, 16, 23
Chinese philosophy, shame in 99
circle of justice 64, 64n69
citizens, subjects to 136–7
civilization, emotions and 11
classical view of emotions 5, 72
common sense 28
communal relations
    communal feelings towards members 74
    domains of gratitude 73–8
    expulsion of members 71, 79–80, 83–7
    kendü halinde olmak (being on one's own) 79–82
    morality, emotions and 81–2
    outsiders, treatment of 76–8
    penalties for deviation from social norms 75
    practices, emotions as 87–92
    prostitution, treatment of 81
    protection, understanding of 147–8
    protection by one's community 75
    riza (pleased and satisfied) 73–8
    social norms and 72
    structuralist approach 72
    sub-communities in Ottoman society 70–3
    şükran/şükr (thankfulness and gratitude) 73–8
    sureties, acting as 71 *see also* shame
comparative approach 10–11
compassion
    acts of 147
    demands for 55–6
    as hierarchical 55, 147
    law, changes to 52
    legitimacy of rulers' political actions 55
    "out of compassion for their condition" 51–5
    protection with 46–56, 136
    in the Quran 49
    relationship between ruler and subjects 48
    sultans' decrees 46–56
    synonyms 49
conceptualization of emotions, emotion knowledge as 23
constructed emotions, theory of 6
continence
    excessive 34
    virtue of 33–4
Cooper, Frederick 1
courage, virtue of 33
court records as sources 16–18
courtship 8–9
cultures, meaning of shame in different 97–9
Cyzgan, Christiane 13

Danoff, Robert 12–13
decrees
    communication by 43–6
    politics of emotion and 46–56
    protection with compassion 46–56
diaries. absence of emotions in 38–40
difference, politics of, Muslim/non-Muslim relations and 3–4
dispositions in *Ahlak-i Alai* (*The Book of Ethics*) (Kınalızade) 35–6
divorce (*talak*) 124–9
"doing the do-ables" 32–3
domains of gratitude 70, 73–8
    expulsion from 83–7 *see also* shame
dowries 121

economic thinking in *Ahlak-i Alai* (*The Book of Ethics*) and 23n4
Efendi, Raşid 50–1, 58
Efendi, Sadreddinzade Telhisi Mustafa 39
ego-documents, absence of emotions in 38–40
emic approach (inside perspective) 15
emotional communities 7, 7n13, 18, 69–70, 74
emotional liberty 8
emotional practices *see* practices, emotions as
emotional refuges 8
emotional regimes 8
emotional translations 9, 9n21
emotion knowledge
    defined 18–19
    faculties of the vegetative, animal and human souls 27–33
    medical knowledge and 36–8
    self-narratives, absence of emotions in 38–40
    as theorization and conceptualization of emotions 23
emotionology 7, 7n12, 43

Index

families 112–18
   love 67
emotion-virtues/vices in *Ahlak-i Alai* (*The Book of Ethics*) (Kınalızade) 33–5
emotives 8n14
empires, early modern 1
engagement (*namzedlik*) to be married 119–23, 120n23, 142
equality, protection as 148
equilibrium 35, 37
Ergene, Boğaç 64n69
Ermiş, Fatih 23n4
ethics books as sources 15–16
   see also *The Book of Ethics* (*Ahlak-i Alai*) (Kınalızade)
etic approach (outside perspective) 15, 68
Eustace, Nicole 40
Evrenos, Muhammed b. 39–40
excess of virtues 34–5
experience of emotions 9, 9n20
expulsion of members from neighborhood communities 71, 79–80, 83–7
external senses 28

faculties of the vegetative, animal and human souls 27–33
families
   codes of behavior for husbands/wives 113–17
   divorce (*talak*) 124–9
   dowries 121, 123
   emotionology of 112–18
   engagement (*namzedlik*) to be married 119–23, 120n23, 142
   fetva collections 117–18
   households defined 112
   husbands/wives, relations between 113–17, 146
   hüsn-i zindegani 125–9
   legal contracts (*akd-i nikah*) 123
   musafat 125–7
   nineteenth century changes 142
   nüşuz ve i'raz üzere olmak 128
   protection, understanding of 147
   riza (pleased, satisfied, contented) 123
   vifak/şikak 128–9
fatherland 137
fear in Ottoman studies 12–13
Findley, Carter Vaughn 132, 140–1, 142
Frevert, Ute 14n44

Galenic humoral theory 36–8, 114, 149
Gara, Eleni 4, 5
gaza (Islamic holy war) ideology 59
gender
   expression of shame and 104–5 *see also* families
gender studies, emotions in history and 10
gentle persuasion or gaining hearts (*istimalet*) 61–3, 68
gratitude, domains of 70, 73–8
Greek medical texts 37
Greek philosophy, shame in 99
guild communities
   conduct manuals 72
   as domains of gratitude 73–8
   kendü halinde olmak (being on one's own) 80–1
   practices, emotions as 87–91
   rituals for expressing communal gratitude 89–90
   social norms and 72
   unity and loyalty in 90–1
Gülhane Script 135–6

Hagia Sophia 149–51
Hasan, Seyyid 39
hasham in Bedouin society 99
historical studies, emotions in 5–11
History of Concepts Group (HCG) 9
Households *see* families
hul divorces 124–9
human souls
   faculties of 29–33
   rationality 29–30
humoral theory 36–8, 114
husbands/wives *see* families
hüsn-i zindegani 125–9

Ilgürel, Müctebe 61
illustrative scene 1–3
imagination, faculty of 29
immoderation in virtues 34–5
İnalcık, Halil 61
individualism, path to 38–9
inheritance, daughters' rights to 52
inside perspective 15
intelligence, practical 31, 32
internal senses 28–9
interreligious relations 3–4
intracommunal relations

communal feelings towards members 74
domains of gratitude 73–8
expulsion of members 71, 79–80, 83–7
kendü halinde olmak (being on one's own) 79–82
morality, emotions and 81–2
outsiders, treatment of 76–8
penalties for deviation from social norms 75
practices, emotions as 87–92
prostitution, treatment of 81
protection, understanding of 147–8
protection by one's community 75
riza (pleased and satisfied) 73–8
social norms and 72
structuralist approach 72
sub-communities in Ottoman society 70–3
şükran/şükr (thankfulness and gratitude) 73–8
sureties, acting as 71 see also shame
Islamic judicial court records as sources 16–18
istimalet (gentle persuasion or gaining hearts) 61–3, 68
Ivanova, Svetlana 46

judicial court records as sources 16–18
justice 44–5
circle of justice 64, 64n69
excessive 34
virtue of 34

Kafadar, Cemal 39, 59
Kafi, Hasan 64n69
Kalpaklı, Mehmet 12
kanun 4
Karahasanoğlu, Selim 38, 39
Karateke, Hakan T. 56n37
Katz, Marion Holmes 97
Kayyal, Mary H. 98
kendü halinde olmak (being on one's own) 70, 79–82
Kınalızade Ali Çelebi see *Ahlak-i Alai* (*The Book of Ethics*) (Kınalızade)
"knowing the know-ables" 31, 32–3
knowledge of emotion see emotion knowledge
Koselleck, Reinhart 56, 57
Kovolos, Elias 62–3

legal contracts (*akd-i nikah*) 123
legal records as source 16–18
legal status
factors determining 4–5
Muslim/non-Muslim relations 3–4
legitimacy of rulers
compassion 55
framework for analyzing 56n37
love
caritas (a form of love) 10, 17, 81
in Ottoman studies 12, 13
path of (*mahabbet*) 63–7, 136
romantic love, sexual partnerships and 10
Lowry, Heath 62
loyalty in guilds 90–1
Lutz, Catherine 5n8

mahabbet (path of love) 63–7, 136
marriage(s)
divorce *(talak)* 124–9
dowries 121, 123
engagement (*namzedlik*) to be married 119–23, 120n23, 142
husbands/wives, relations between 113–17
hüsn-i zindegani 125–9
legal contracts (*akd-i nikah*) 123
musafat 125–7
nineteenth century changes 142
nüşuz ve i'raz üzere olmak 128
riza (pleased, satisfied, contented) 123
vifak/şikak 128–9
masculinity, *muru'a* and 105
medical knowledge
changes in nineteenth century 138–40
emotions and 36–8
psychology 139–40
memoirs, absence of emotions in 38–40
men see families
merhamet see compassion
Messner, Angelika C. 23
metaphors
istimalet (gentle persuasion or gaining hearts) 68
te'lif-i kulûb (uniting with the hearts) 58–61, 68
methods for research 14–15
Mexico, colonial, emotions in 67n78

Index

modernization efforts in the nineteenth century 132–6
morality, emotions and 13–14, 81–2
Morea, tax obligations of non-Muslim subjects 61
movement, faculty of 29, 30, 32
multidisciplinary approach, need for 6
muru'a, masculinity and 105
musafat 125–7
Muslim/non-Muslim relations 3–4
    Morea, tax obligations of non-Muslim subjects 61
    nineteenth century 135–6

namzedlik (engagement) to be married 119–23, 120n23
neighborhood communities
    communal feelings towards members 74
    as domains of gratitude 73–8
    expulsion of members 71, 79–80, 83–7
    kendü halinde olmak (being on one's own) 79–82
    morality, emotions and 81–2
    outsiders, treatment of 76–8
    penalties for deviation from social norms 75
    practices, emotions as 87–92
    prostitution, treatment of 81
    protection, understanding of 147–8
    protection by one's community 75
    riza (pleased and satisfied) 73–8
    social norms and 72
    structuralist approach 72
    sub-communities in Ottoman society 70–3
    şükran/şükr (thankfulness and gratitude) 73–8
    sureties, acting as 71 *see also* shame
neuroscience 6, 7–8
Nicomachean Ethics (Aristotle) 25
nineteenth century
    criticism of changes 138
    familial relations 142
    fatherland 137
    Gülhane Script 135–6
    legislation and regulation 137
    medical knowledge, changes in 138–40
    modernization efforts 132–6
    Muslims/non-Muslims 135–6

    protection, shift in meaning of 148
    revabıt-ı kalbiyye-i vatandaşi ("bonding with the hearts of citizens") 137
    societal relations 140–2
    from subjects to citizens 136–7
non-Muslim subjects
    Muslim relations 3–4
    nineteenth century 135–6
    tax obligations of 61
norms
    absence of emotions in self-narratives and 40
    communal relations and 72
    guild communities 72
    penalties for deviation from 75
nüşuz ve i'raz üzere olmak 128

occupational communities
    conduct manuals 72
    as domains of gratitude 73–8
    kendü halinde olmak (being on one's own) 80–1
    practices, emotions as 87–91
    rituals for expressing communal gratitude 89–90
    social norms and 72
    unity and loyalty in 90–1
order in political context 64
Ottoman Empire as early modern empire 1
Ottoman studies, emotions in 11–14
"out of compassion for their condition" 51–5
outside perspective 15, 68
Özizmirli, Görkem 12–13

path of love (*mahabbet*) 63–7, 136
Pentcheva, Bissera 149
perception, faculty of 28–9, 30, 32
performatives, emotions as 24, 31–3
Pernau, Margrit 9, 9n20, 9n21, 46, 56–7
Plamper, Jan 10, 40
politics of difference in Muslim/non-Muslim relations 3–4
politics of emotion
    decrees, communication by 43–6
    istimalet (gentle persuasion or gaining hearts) 61–3, 68
    path of love (*mahabbet*) 63–7
    protection with compassion 46–56
    sultans' decrees 46–56

te'lif-i kulûb (uniting with the hearts) 58–61, 68
practical wisdom 26–7, 31
practices, emotions as 8–9, 24, 31–3, 43, 87–92, 118
presentist view of emotions 5
prostitution, treatment of 81
protection
    with compassion 46–56, 136
    as contested concept/knowledge 47
    emotions and 5
    as equality 148
    experience of by subjects 56–63
    Hagia Sophia 149–51
    law, changes to 52
    by laws of the state 136
    meaning-making underlying 146–7
    reforms during the nineteenth century 132–6
    relationship between ruler and subjects 48
    shift in meaning of 148
    sultans' decrees 46–56
    te'lif-i kulûb (uniting with the hearts) 58–61 see also communal relations; families
psychology 139–40
public shaming 106–9

Quran
    compassion in 49
    heart as prominent theme in 60

Rahman, Abdal 119
Rajamani, Imke 9, 9n20, 9n21
rationality
    action and 32
    contrast of emotion to 5n8
    faculty of 29–31
recollection, faculty of 28–9
Reddy, William 7–8, 8n14, 10
reforms during the nineteenth century 132–6
Reinkowski, Maurus 56n37
religion, interreligious relations 3–4
remembering, faculty of 28
repulsive faculty 29, 31–2
    excessive 34
revabıt-ı kalbiyye-i vatandaşi ("bonding with the hearts of citizens") 137
riza (pleased and satisfied) 73–8, 123

romantic love, sexual partnerships and 10
Rosenwein, Barbara 7, 7n13, 11, 18, 69, 70, 70n3
Russell, James A. 98

Schimmel, Annemarie 73
self-narratives, absence of emotions in 38–40
Şen, A. Tunç 39–40
Şenışı, Pinar 14
senses, external/internal 28–9
sexual partnerships, romantic love and 10
Shahar, Ido 16
shame
    Arabic, contemporary, shame in 98–9
    Bedouin society 99
    Chinese philosophy 99
    community members, shaming of 106–9
    different cultures and 97–9
    expression of in court 96–7
    gender and expression of 104–5
    Greek philosophy 99
    hasham in Bedouin society 99
    in Islamic societies 97
    muru'a, masculinity and 105
    Ottoman sources 100–4
    in Ottoman studies 12–13
    public shaming 106–9
Sheer, Monique 8–9
sicil (court case records) studies 16–17
şikak/vifak 128–9
simulation 6n10
social norms
    absence of emotions in self-narratives and 40
    communal relations and 72
    guild communities 72
    penalties for deviation from 75
souls, vegetative, animal and human, faculties of 27–33
sources for research 15–18
speculation, faculty of 28
state
    protection by laws of the 136
    separation from ruler 48n13
Stearns, Carol Z. 7, 7n12, 43
Stearns, Peter 7, 7n12, 43, 98–9
Steininger, Fabian 13
subjects to citizens 136–7
şükran/şükr (thankfulness and gratitude) 73–8

sultans' decrees
  communication by 43–6
  politics of emotion and 46–56
  protection with compassion 46–56
Syros, Vasileios 37

taife (community) 70–1 *see also* communal relations
talak (divorce) 124–9
Tanzimat era
  "bonding with the hearts of citizens" 137
  criticism of changes 138
  familial relations 142
  fatherland 137
  Gülhane Script 135–6
  legislation and regulation 137
  medical knowledge, changes in 138–40
  modernization efforts 132–6
  Muslims/non-Muslims 135–6
  protection, shift in meaning of 148
  revabıt-ı kalbiyye-i vatandaşi ("bonding with the hearts of citizens") 137
  societal relations 140–2
  from subjects to citizens 136–7
  themes of 134
tax obligations
  of non-Muslim subjects 61
  practices, emotions as 87–8
tax revenues, bestowal of 52–4
tefrik divorces 124
te'lif-i kulûb (uniting with the hearts) 58–61, 68
theoretical wisdom 26, 31
theorization of emotions, emotion knowledge as 23
timar 52–4
translation of emotion-words 98

Tucker, Judith 18n54
Tusi, Nasreddin 25

understanding of emotions, prevailing 40
"uniting with the hearts" (*te'lif-i kulûb*) 58–61
unity in guilds 90–1
universalist view of emotions 5

vegetative souls, faculties of 27–8
vices in *Ahlak-i Alai* (*The Book of Ethics*) (Kınalızade) 34–5
vifak/şikak 128–9
virtues
  absence of 34
  Ahlak-i Alai (*The Book of Ethics*) (Kınalızade) 33–5
  equilibrium and balance 35
  excess of 34–5
  humoral theory and 37–8

willpower 29
"winning the hearts of the subjects" (*te'lif-i kulûb*) 58–61
wisdom
  definition of in *Ahlak-i Alai* (*The Book of Ethics*) 26
  excessive 34
  practical 26–7, 31
  theoretical 26, 31
  virtue of 33
wives/husbands *see* families
women *see* families

Yelçe, Zeynep N. 12

Zachs, Fruma 105, 105n19
Zaifi 39–40
Ze'evi, Dror 16–17, 114
zimmi, legal status of 4

www.ingramcontent.com/pod-product-compliance
Lightning Source LLC
Chambersburg PA
CBHW061837300426
44115CB00013B/2427